Followership

A Theological Understanding of Christian Leadership

Followership

A Theological Understanding of

Christian Leadership

Carl B. Seay

Pocataligo

Pocataligo Books
Danielsville Georgia

Followership: *A Theological Understanding of Christian Leadership*
© 2024 by Carl B. Seay

Pocataligo

Published by Pocataligo Books
Danielsville,Georgia 30633
Email: info@pocataligobooks.com

ISBN: 979-8-9905749-0-8

Unless otherwise attributed, all Scripture quotations are taken from The Holy Bible, English Standard Version (ESV), copyright © 2001 by Crossway, a publishing ministry of Good News Publishers. Used by permission. All rights reserved.

Cover photo:
Sharon Methodist Church
Sharon, Georgia
Photo © 2012 by Carl B. Seay

First published July 2024
Updated February 2025

Please visit our website: *https://pocataligobooks.com*

This book is dedicated to

Yvonne Amana Seay.

Special Thanks

THERE are a several people who deserve my gratitude in helping me make this book possible.

The first person is my wife Yvonne who sacrificed so much of our time together for me to write, edit, and design this book. This book would not be possible without her patience and sacrifice. She also assisted in the final editing of this book.

Pastor Joe Davis was a great encouragement to me in my initial efforts to organize my thoughts into what direction this book should take.

Amanda McMurtrey read the first draft of Chapter 6 and suggested many changes that helped shape that difficult chapter into a much better chapter. Her encouragement and support of my efforts in that complex subject were a big help to me.

The members of the Mad(ison) Writers Group of Danielsville, Georgia have been a great encouragement to me. They have offered many suggestions when I struggled with difficulties in the subject matters. They helped me believe that this book might just be possible when I doubted myself and encouraged me to keep writing. Katherine Cerulean, Eric McMurtrey, and William Timothy Murray especially have helped me with encouragement and suggestions that came from their experiences in writing and publishing their own books. I am certain that this book would have never been finished without their encouragement for me to keep writing and to finish it.

Table of Contents

Introduction

The Story Behind this Book

WHY do we need another book about leadership? There are tens of thousands of them already. Just look on https://amazon.com and search for leadership books. Beyond the many books already available, there are many more leadership books being published everyday.

I dropped out of Bible College many years ago. Several years ago I felt the need to go back to college and finish my degree. I searched for several years for a program that would allow me to finish my degree while still working full-time. Although I had later earned my two-year degree in computer programming, I had never earned my bachelor's degree. Finally, Toccoa Falls College opened up a couple of online programs. I felt drawn to apply and was accepted. There was one minor dilemma. The program was in Ministry Leadership, not a field that I would have contemplated majoring in. I could not believe it at first. I am such an introvert that leadership seemed like the last area I should study. However, I felt as if this was the program that God was leading me to go into. Once I started classes, I quickly rediscovered my love for learning. I could not get enough of learning. I wanted to learn more. After earning my bachelor's degree with honors from Toccoa Falls College, I continued on to earn two Master's degrees in Christian leadership from Liberty Theological Seminary. I also completed about half of the coursework toward obtaining an EdD (Doctor of Education) in Christian Leadership from Liberty.

One of my leadership classes at Toccoa Falls College required me to establish a mentored type of relationship with a pastor or other Christian leader. Although I had been attending a different church, Pastor Joe Davis accepted the challenge of mentoring me in leadership. I quickly grew to love our discussions on leadership and theology. We discovered that we had a shared love for many of the same types of books and we were able to share books back and forth. During one of our discussions, I told him that I did not understand it but that I felt like God was leading me to write a book on leadership. I told him that I did not feel at all qualified to do this but felt as if it was what God wanted me to do. I also told him that I did not know what leadership subject to write about as there are hundreds, if not thousands, of books on Christian leadership. He told me that he had read many books on leadership but none on followership. He suggested that I should consider writing on that subject.

This suggestion became the start of this continuing journey to learn more about followership and what relationship it has with leadership. Through this research, I have discovered that, in many ways, followership is the most important attribute of Christian leadership. Even in the secular leadership, followership should play a more important role than it currently does. In Christian ministry and leadership, there is no leadership at all without followership. If there is a certain amount of leadership without followership, that leadership is not Christian at all. This book will attempt to explain all of this.

Leadership Books

As stated above, there are many thousands of leadership books available. Every leader seems to want to learn how to become a better leader. All of the authors of these books claim to have the best answer on how to become the best leader. One fact that is apparent is that none of these thousands of authors can seem to agree on what makes the best leader. They even argue about if leadership skills are innate (something you are born with) or something that can be learned. I find it awkward that these authors cannot even agree on what the definition of leadership is. Many of these authors have similar definitions but make a few minor changes to make the definition distinctive from other definitions.

To be honest, I am not sure which definition of leadership is the best one either. I like use the simplest definition possible. Some people define a leader simply as someone who has followers. Others define it as someone who leads others in a common goal or project. Christian leadership tends to look much different from secular leadership. We will talk more about that several times in this book.

The purpose of the book is to introduce an idea to the study of leadership that is often overlooked. Since the subject of this book is Christian leadership, the primary source of information will be from the Bible. Several leadership and theological books will be quoted in places, but the emphasis will remain on what the Bible says. Because of this, the Bible is quoted often in this book. Also, please note that all scriptures quoted in the book are from the ESV translation, unless otherwise attributed. This is just a personal choice. Please feel free to open your favorite Bible translation to read the quoted scriptures.

The Purpose of this Book

Let me state from the start that the purpose of this book is not to come across as a know-it-all leadership book telling you what you must do to become a successful Christian leader. The purpose of this book is not to give you a list of steps that you must follow in order to become the best pastor or Christian leader possible. The primary purpose of this book is to assist you in understanding what the distinction is in Christian leadership as opposed to other types of leadership. The idea is to help you realize that Christian leadership is more about followership than it is about leadership. As you read this book I am not asking you to completely forget everything that you have read or learned about leadership. Those things can be useful in leadership but there is something that is even more important. That something is followership. Can we all agree that all those different leadership books list vastly different methods and techniques. How can they all be correct? And which book should we truly follow? Which methods and styles are the best ones for you personally to use? It is time to think of Christian leadership in a different way.

This book does not always follow the traditional ideas about leadership. Instead, it attempts to assist you in forming a theology about Christian leadership according to the Bible. I hope that you will carefully consider what this book says as you contemplate what it means to be a leader as a follower of Christ. As Francis Chan says, "Don't believe something just because you want to, and don't embrace an idea just because you've always believed it. Believe what is biblical. Test all your assumptions against the precious words God gave us in the Bible."

We are not asking you to make this book the basis of your leadership theology. We are asking you use the Bible as your primary source for your theology of leadership. Do not base your theology on what you have always believed. Do not base it on what others have taught you over the years. Do not base it on the tenets of your particular church or denomination. Theology should be based on what the Bible tells us on that subject. Francis Chan goes on to relate, "There are many things I believed and practiced for years, only to change my views after further study of the Bible." Our hope is that you will carefully and prayerfully consider how God would have you develop your theology of Christian leadership according to what the Bible says.

The Differences of Christian Leadership

As mentioned earlier, this book is quite different from most leadership books. It is not a list of things you must do or attributes, skills, and methods that you must have to be a successful Christian leader. It will not ask you to follow certain steps. It will not tell you how to get from Point A to Point B. Most leadership books that attempt to do those things do not work well for everyone. They try to get you to do things their way. They teach that their way is the only way to lead successfully.

The idea behind this book is to introduce you to the concept that Christian leadership is different from other leadership types and is more about followership than it is about leadership skills and models. The hope is that you will better understand this concept and model your leadership style and methods toward following Jesus Christ. As this book will state several times, Christian leadership is different from other leadership. It has different goals and we cannot measure its success by attendance numbers or financial success. Leadership methods and styles are important but we must base these on a leadership theology that is based on Scripture. This is why this book will not give you methods or styles to follow. It will help you develop your own theology of leadership as you learn how to lead in a Christlike manner.

Since all Christians are followers of Jesus Christ, it then follows that Christian leaders must first be followers of Christ. After all, if someone is not a believer in Jesus Christ and a follower of Him, that person may be a leader but they are not a Christian leader. The way that a person follows Christ will greatly affect the success of their leadership. They may be a leader but to be a successful Christian leader, one must first be a believer and follower of Christ. This link between followership and Christian leadership has traditionally been ignored. This link is vital to a Christian leader's success. Let me emphasize here that success in Christian leadership is measured differently than that of secular leadership. The success of a Christian leader is largely linked to how he or she follows Christ.

The thought behind this book is that followership is the major difference in what makes Christian leadership successful. This truth has been largely ignored or overlooked. Fortunately, researchers are conducting more research and study on this subject and more literature about followership is becoming available. Most of this current literature involves the followership abilities and skills of those who follow their leader. Some of this literature ignores the fact that the leader is also a follower. There is a real need for further study and more literature about the need and the importance of followership in Christian leadership. If the Christian leader must succeed at following Christ, then there is a real need to understand the importance of followership and a need to teach followership to future leaders.

As Allen Hamlin, Jr. reminds us in his book, *Embracing Followership: How to Thrive in a Leader-Centric Culture,* "In some sense we are all followers. Whether we have a leadership title, or whether we are self-employed, unemployed, subcontracted, full-time students, homemakers, hobbyists, or pew-warmers, we all have someone who is over us - someone providing direction, accountability, decision-making, and representation. Even CEOs have board members, team captains have coaches, committee chairs report to constituents and general assemblies." So, everyone, no matter what their leadership role or position, is also a follower in some fashion. There is no way around it - we are all followers of someone or some entity.

- 1 -

The Paradox of Christianity

THIS book starts with a subject that seems strange on the surface, but it is an important one. That subject deals with the concept that Christianity is full of paradoxes. On the surface, these paradoxes have nothing at all to do with Christian leadership. However, it is an important subject for followers of Jesus Christ to understand, as it is these paradoxes that make Christian leadership so different. It is even more important for the Christian leader to understand this subject so that he or she recognizes that Christian leadership is different from other leadership. It has different objectives and goals. It must follow different rules from worldly leadership. This chapter will discuss some of these paradoxes. This does not claim to be an inclusive list of paradoxes but those that seem to pertain more closely to Christian leadership.

There are many things that are often misunderstood about Christianity. Most people naturally tend to think of Christianity within their finite way of thinking. They do not understand that God does not see things the same way we do. As it says in Isaiah 55:8, *For my thoughts are not your thoughts, neither are your ways my ways, declares the Lord.* (You will see this verse again in this book). The things of God often do not meet the expectations and logic of mankind. As we read the New Testament we begin seeing many things that Jesus taught are contrary to the way that the world thinks. This situation is the paradox of Christianity. True Christianity has so many paradoxes. If you contemplate Christianity in the light of our human logic and knowledge, you will never understand it at all.

To understand this book's premise, you must first understand just how different Christianity is from what the world expects. God's reasoning and logic is much different from that of the world. Humans are finitely created beings. God is infinite and the Creator. He is eternal. He always has been and will always be. God has no beginning and no ending. We must understand Him as being eternal. Everything that exists was created by Him.

He is all-powerful and all knowing. Therefore, His reasoning and wisdom do not follow that of created and finite mankind.

In contrast to God, all created beings (including mankind) are finite and have limited knowledge and understanding. It is no wonder that the Bible states that the wisdom of God appears as foolishness to mankind. He not only has all knowledge, but He sees everything in the past and the future. Our knowledge and understanding are based on what we have learned and experienced. We must begin to see that an infinite, eternal, all-knowing, and all-powerful God does not, and cannot, fully fit into human understanding and logic. Otherwise, He would not be God. He would just be another human being that is somehow in charge of everything.

The Bible explains that God's wisdom and way of thinking are much different from ours. This is evident when you look at the paradoxes that exist in Christianity. Isaiah 55:8-9 says, *For my thoughts are not your thoughts, neither are your ways my ways, declares the LORD. For as the heavens are higher than the earth, so are my ways higher than your ways and my thoughts than your thoughts.* Paul said it this way in Romans 11:33-34, *Oh, the depth of the riches and wisdom and knowledge of God! How unsearchable are his judgments and how inscrutable his ways! "For who has known the mind of the Lord, or who has been his counselor?"* This Bible verse probably explains why the many paradoxes exist in Christianity.

It is vital to understand this before attempting to understand what God expects of Christian leaders. If we understand that Christianity is a paradox and quite different from our human understanding, it stands to reason that Christian leadership is also quite different from secular leadership and our normal expectations. To understand Christian leadership, we must attempt to look at it from God's viewpoint. Of course, as we all know, that is impossible for us finite humans. We are not God and we can never fully look at things and understand them like God does. However, we can get several hints from the Bible. We just have to recognize that in Christianity, things are much different.

Once you begin to understand just that Christianity is a paradox, it should come as no surprise that Christian leadership is also full of paradoxes. It should come as no surprise that Christian leadership does not follow any type of human logic or format. To be a successful

Christian leader, you must understand these paradoxes. It is possible to be a successful Christian leader while being considered a complete failure according to the world's expectations. The opposite case is true also. It is possible for a Christian leader to appear to being successful to the world while failing to lead in the manner that Christ expects from us.

Please note that many of these paradoxes pertain to all believers, not just Christian leaders, as stated before. To be a Christian leader, a person, by definition, must first be a follower of Jesus Christ. Therefore, every one of these paradoxes applies to the Christian leader as a believer in Jesus Christ.

Must Lose Your Life to Live

One of the strangest paradox scriptures in the New Testament is found in John 12:20-26. It clearly states that if a man wishes to live, he must lose his life: *Now among those who went up to worship at the feast were some Greeks. So these came to Philip, who was from Bethsaida in Galilee, and asked him, "Sir, we wish to see Jesus." Philip went and told Andrew; Andrew and Philip went and told Jesus. And Jesus answered them, "The hour has come for the Son of Man to be glorified. Truly, truly, I say to you, unless a grain of wheat falls into the earth and dies, it remains alone; but if it dies, it bears much fruit. Whoever loves his life loses it, and whoever hates his life in this world will keep it for eternal life. If anyone serves me, he must follow me; and where I am, there will my servant be also. If anyone serves me, the Father will honor him.*

That is a wild statement! To the world, this paradox makes no sense at all. To gain life, one must lose his or her life. Also please note that to follow Jesus involves becoming His servant. That means that to be a Christian leader, one first must also be a servant of Jesus Christ. This subject will be discussed in greater detail in Chapter 9.

First - Last

Jesus introduced several paradoxes in His ministry. There was one idea that He taught the people made no sense to them at all. It was contrary to everything that they had observed and been taught in their lives. Jesus told the people that he who would be first must be last and that the last will be first. He introduced this paradox in a parable.

Matthew 20:1-16 gives us this parable: *"For the kingdom of heaven is like a master of a house who went out early in the morning to hire laborers for his vineyard. After agreeing with the laborers for a denarius a day, he sent them into his vineyard. And going out about the third hour he saw others standing idle in the marketplace, and to them he said, 'You go into the vineyard too, and whatever is right I will give you.' So they went. Going out again about the sixth hour and the ninth hour, he did the same. And about the eleventh hour he went out and found others standing. And he said to them, 'Why do you stand here idle all day?' They said to him, 'Because no one has hired us.' He said to them, 'You go into the vineyard too.' And when evening came, the owner of the vineyard said to his foreman, 'Call the laborers and pay them their wages, beginning with the last, up to the first.' And when those hired about the eleventh hour came, each of them received a denarius. Now when those hired first came, they thought they would receive more, but each of them also received a denarius. And on receiving it they grumbled at the master of the house, saying, 'These last worked only one hour, and you have made them equal to us who have borne the burden of the day and the scorching heat.' But he replied to one of them, 'Friend, I am doing you no wrong. Did you not agree with me for a denarius? Take what belongs to you and go. I choose to give to this last worker as I give to you. Am I not allowed to do what I choose with what belongs to me? Or do you begrudge my generosity?' So the last will be first, and the first last."*

Mark relates the story where the disciples began arguing who among them were the greatest in the group as they traveled with Jesus. You can imagine that each one of them thought highly of themselves. They each thought that they were the best and should be second in command after Jesus. Mark 9:33-35, *And they came to Capernaum. And when he was in the house he asked them, "What were you discussing on the way?" But they kept silent, for on the way they had argued with one another about who was the greatest. And he sat down and called the twelve. And he said to them, "If anyone would be first, he must be last of all and servant of all."* Not only must the first be last, but he or she must also be servant to all.

The Servant Leader

Several times in the New Testament, Jesus calls Himself a servant. He also emphasizes that fact that leaders must be servants. We just read Mark 9:33-35 where Jesus tells His disciples that they must be servants and that the first must be last. Mark 10:42-45 (also in Matthew 20):

And Jesus called them to him and said to them, "You know that those who are considered rulers of the Gentiles lord it over them, and their great ones exercise authority over them. But it shall not be so among you. But whoeverever would be great among you must be your servant, and whoever would be first among you must be slave of all. For even the Son of Man came not to be served but to serve, and to give his life as a ransom for many."

Here Jesus is plainly stating that Christian leadership is to be much different from leadership in the world. The Christian leader is foremost to be a servant. He or she is not in the leadership position to lord over those following them. The idea of a leader lording over their followers is the way of the world, not the way of those leaders who are followers of Christ. Jesus makes it clear that they are in the leadership position to serve those to whom they are leading. This is quite a different concept from other leadership thoughts. He makes it clear that even Jesus came to serve, not to be served. As a follower of Christ, should we not also be servant leaders?

If we return to Matthew 20 again, we can find another instance in which Jesus expects His leaders to be servants. In Matthew 20:20-28 we find the story of a mother who wants her two sons, who are disciples of Jesus, to be elevated into positions of honor and leadership.

Then the mother of the sons of Zebedee came up to him with her sons, and kneeling before him she asked him for something. And he said to her, "What do you want?" She said to him, "Say that these two sons of mine are to sit, one at your right hand and one at your left, in your kingdom." Jesus answered, "You do not know what you are asking. Are you able to drink the cup that I am to drink?" They said to him, "We are able." He said to them, "You will drink my cup, but to sit at my right hand and at my left is not mine to grant, but it is for those for whom it has been prepared by my Father." And when the ten heard it, they were indignant at the two brothers. But Jesus called them to him and said, "You know that the rulers of the Gentiles lord it over them, and their great ones exercise authority over them. It shall not be so among you. But whoever would be great among you must be your servant, and whoever would be first among you must be your slave, even as the Son of Man came not to be served but to serve, and to give his life as a ransom for many." Here again is the proclamation that the first must be last and that the leader is a servant.

Prostitutes and Tax Collectors

When we read about the ministry of Jesus in the New Testament, we begin noticing that He had a different way of doing things. His own brothers and sisters thought that He had lost His mind. The Pharisees and the Sadducees thought that He was demon possessed. Besides the fact that He refused to obey their rules and interpretations of the Law, He dared to interact and socialize with sinners. How would we feel if our pastors, deacons, elders, and other church leaders started hanging out with prostitutes, drug addicts, drunks, and other sinners in our community? Most of our churches would probably quickly fire their pastors if they started doing these things, but this is exactly what the New Testament said that Jesus did. The Pharisees and other religious leaders gave Him a lot of grief over that. This book is not telling you that, as a Christian leader, you must do this, but that maybe we need to reevaluate some of the preconceived ideas that we have about ministry. Today's church says that the pastor (and members) must avoid sinners and worldly people. Jesus hung out with them and even sat down to eat with them.

We are going to toss out a strange thought here. Sometimes we act like God was created for our own pleasure, providence, entitlement, and enjoyment. The paradox here is that instead of that, we were created to worship, follow, and serve Him. As followers of Jesus Christ, we are to follow in His footsteps, not doing what is wise in our finite and limited minds.

The Foolishness of God or the Wisdom of God

This is a strange concept that is hard to wrap our minds around - the foolishness of God! You would never consider anything about God to be foolish, even if it was something that you were unable to fully understand. There is much about God that we all struggle to understand fully. There are many things that we must end up accepting just because he is God and we are not. He has infinite knowledge and wisdom while our wisdom and knowledge are limited. We are incapable of fully understanding some things about God. We would never call anything about God foolishness, even if it appears to be foolish to us. However, the Apostle Paul uses that exact phrase.

1 Corinthians 1:25-31: *For the foolishness of God is wiser than men, and the weakness of God is stronger than men. For consider your calling, brothers; not many of you were wise according to worldly standards, not many were powerful, not many were of noble birth. But God chose what is foolish in the world to shame the wise; God chose what is weak in the world to shame the strong; God chose what is low and despised in the world, even things that are not, to bring to nothing things that are so that no human being might boast in the presence of God. And because of him, you are in Christ Jesus, who became to us wisdom from God, righteousness and sanctification and redemption, so that, as it is written, "Let the one who boasts, boast in the Lord."*

For the foolishness of God is wiser than man and His weakness is stronger than man. Paul is not talking directly about leadership. He is talking about salvation through Jesus Christ and the preaching the gospel. Paul is not saying that God is foolish or weak but that the gospel message seems foolish to the world. He is introducing a concept here that flows through much of what God does. He is trying to explain that God's knowledge and wisdom are so much beyond man's understanding and wisdom. Mankind is incapable of even understanding God's wisdom and knowledge. We cannot procure and comprehend the knowledge and wisdom of God. Actually, this thought is not original to Paul. It comes from the Old Testament. Isaiah 55:8-9: *For my thoughts are not your thoughts, neither are your ways my ways, declares the Lord. For as the heavens are higher than the earth, so are my ways higher than your ways and my thoughts than your thoughts.*

Even in his weakest moment, God's strength and wisdom far surpass that of man. We are unable to even comprehend the depth and width of God's understanding and wisdom.

Weak - Strong

The world expects strength, wisdom, ability, and knowledge from its leaders. As we will see in the section of this chapter, we will see that God's ideas on weakness and strength look much different from that of the world's philosophy. Paul emphasizes his own lack of wisdom and strength. He has to depend on Christ's wisdom and strength. He reiterates several times that he has no room to brag. What accomplishments that he has achieved, are only through the wisdom and strength of Christ. Contrary to what the world believes about leadership, Christian leaders must rely on the wisdom and strength of Christ. Since success only comes through the work of the Holy Spirit working through us, the leader does not earn the glory or distinction for any of their successes. It is only thorough Christ that we can achieved any success.

2 Corinthians 12:9-10, *But he said to me, "My grace is sufficient for you, for my power is made perfect in weakness." Therefore I will boast all the more gladly of my weaknesses, so that the power of Christ may rest upon me. For the sake of Christ, then, I am content with weaknesses, insults, hardships, persecutions, and calamities. For when I am weak, then I am strong.* Christ's grace is sufficient for you and me. His strength is what we depend on in our weakness. Christ can use us best of all when we are weak and we rely on His strength and wisdom. Success does not come through our own wisdom, knowledge, and strength. It comes only through Christ working within us. The last sentence in those verses is quite a paradox. When I am weak, only then am I strong. I recognize my weakness and dependence on Christ.

1 Corinthians 1:25-31, *For the foolishness of God is wiser than men, and the weakness of God is stronger than men. For consider your calling, brothers: not many of you were wise according to worldly standards, not many were powerful, not many were of noble birth. But God chose what is foolish in the world to shame the wise; God chose what is weak in the world to shame the strong; God chose what is low and despised in the world, even things that are not, to bring to nothing things that are, so that no human being might boast in the presence of God. And because of him you are in Christ Jesus, who became to us wisdom from God, righteousness and sanctification and redemption, so that, as it is written, "Let*

the one who boasts, boast in the Lord." God chose the foolish, the weak, the low, and the despised so that no one can boast and brag. We have to give Christ all of the glory and honor for every success.

2 Corinthians 11:30, *If I must boast, I will boast of the things that show my weakness.* Paul boasts in his weakness and his need for Christ. Without Christ, we are nothing and we have nothing within ourselves to brag about. If we have anything to brag about it is that we can brag about our weaknesses and our great need for Christ.

The Trinity

The theology of the Trinity is another paradox. It defies all natural logic. God is the one and only God. He is one but at the same time, He is three in one. In all human logic, this paradox does not make sense. It is no wonder that many people have trouble comprehending the theology of the Trinity.

The purpose in introducing the subject of the Trinity is not to argue the theology of the Trinity or to discuss the Oneness versus the Trinity debate. The point is that God is different from any other being. All other beings besides God were created by Him. God Himself was not created. He always was and always will be. We cannot consider God using human terms and logic. He is who and what He is. He is not who and what we think He is.

When we discuss Christian leadership, we have to understand that God is different and He expects there to be a difference in His followers. This includes those He has chosen to be leaders. He desires us to look and act differently that the leaders of the world. We must think differently and lead differently. This difference is directly linked to followership. In other words, the difference in Christian Leadership is the way we follow Christ.

Love Your Enemy

At about the age of 30, Jesus began His teaching ministry. He immediately began teaching a message that sounded strange to the Jews of His time. He was teaching things that were opposite of everything they had been taught by the rabbis and Temple leaders. Probably His most famous teaching is found in the Sermon on the Mount. In this sermon, Jesus became famous for teaching things that were contrary to what the Rabbis, scribes, Pharisees, and Sadducees had been teaching the people for many years. The people were astonished at what they heard Jesus say. They were not sure what to think.

Matthew 5:43 - 48: *You have heard that it was said, You shall love your neighbor and hate your enemy. But I say unto you, Love your enemies and pray for those who persecute you, so that you may be sons of your Father who is in heaven. For he makes his sun rise on the evil and the good., and sends rain on the just and on the unjust. For if you love those who love you, what reward do you have? Do not even the tax collectors do the same? And if you greet only your brothers, what more are you doing than others? Do not even the Gentiles do the same? You therefore must be perfect, as your heavenly Father is perfect.*

Or as Luke tells it in Luke 6:27-31, *"But I say to you who hear, Love your enemies, do good to those who hate you, bless those who curse you, pray for those who abuse you. To one who strikes you on the cheek, offer the other also, and from one who takes away your cloak do not withhold your tunic either. Give to everyone who begs from you, and from one who takes away your goods do not demand them back. And as you wish that others would do to you, do so to them.* This gives a whole new meaning to the idea of loving one's enemy. It goes way beyond that.

Luke goes further and relates that Jesus expected a little more from us than merely loving our neighbor. Jesus tells us that are not even supposed to judge or condemn others. Luke 6:37, *"Judge not, and you will not be judged; condemn not, and you will not be condemned; forgive, and you will be forgiven."* Many Christians seem to have a problem following this command from Jesus.

One the best examples of loving one's enemy happened in Pennsylvania in 2006. A man entered an Amish school and killed five young Amish girls before taking his own life. The Amish community did the unbelievable thing. The Amish community and the families involved immediately forgave the murderer. They even reached out to the murderer's wife in love and forgiveness for what her husband did. They took up a collection of money and gave it to her to help her out in her trying time. The Amish people not only said that they loved their enemies but they also proved it in their actions. The love and forgiveness the Amish showed to the murderer and to his wife amazed the news media and people all over the world.

Preston Sprinkle relates this story in his book *Charis*. He states that Amish forgiveness mirrors the forgiving love that Christ bestowed from the cross. He says, "Performing random acts of kindness doesn't change the world. Doing nice things for nice people doesn't change the world. Returning a wallet to the one who left it at the restaurant is a kind gesture, but it won't change the world. Jesus wants to change the world. Only unconditional, stubborn love toward your enemy produces ripple effects strong enough to change the world." As Paul reminds us in Romans 5:13 that we were the enemies of God but Jesus loved anyway, *"For if while we were enemies we were reconciled to God by the death of his Son, much more, now that we are reconciled, shall we be saved by his life."*

The Paradoxes of the Sermon on the Mount

The last section of this chapter is about the Sermon on the Mount. The previous section briefly mentioned this sermon. The Sermon on the Mount (also known as the Beatitudes) found in Matthew 5-6 is probably the best-known sermon by Jesus. We have all heard many sermons preached on little snippets from this sermon. If you pay attention, this sermon has many paradoxes in it. These paradoxes are important for believers. In this sermon, they were not directed toward leadership. However, Christian leaders are first believers in Christ. We will only mention a few of the many paradoxes in this sermon here. We will discuss the Sermon on the Mount further in Chapter 11.

The message of Jesus's sermon must have amazed and confused the people listening to Him. Everything He taught was contrary to everything the Pharisees, the scribes, and the rabbis had taught them. The teachings in his sermon were different from everything they had previously been taught all of their lives. They had been taught that the rich, the Sadducees, and the Pharisees were the ones who had been most blessed by God. Now Jesus was teaching something quite different from what they had heard all of their lives.

Jesus was teaching such things as:

* Blessed are the poor in Spirit.
* Blessed are those who mourn.

* Blessed are the meek.

* Blessed are those who hunger and thirst after righteousness.

* Blessed are the merciful.

* Blessed are the pure in heart.

* Blessed are the peacemakers.

* Blessed are the persecuted.

That is quite a list!

Even today, we often do not get this message right. We usually praise and bless the rich, the government officials, the athletes, the famous singers, and the movie stars. Even in the church world, we tend to honor and praise the television evangelists, the star musicians, and the pastors of the megachurches. We honor and praise those who are winners according to the world's standards, not God's standards. We often ignore those (the underdogs and the nobodies) whom Jesus said are blessed.

The point here is to point out that Christian leadership is different similar to being a follower of Jesus Christ is different. Christian leadership is completely different than other leadership. It has different goals and expectations. It is time that Christian leadership stops measuring itself by the world's standard leadership expectations and measurements. Christian leadership success cannot be measured by neither (attendance) numbers or financial success. Those things may be nice to have but God expects something different from us. After all, Jesus never told us that we are to pastor a megachurch with thousands of members. He told us that we are to make disciples.

An example of this is found in James 1:27, *Religion that is pure and undefiled before God the Father is this: to visit orphans and widows in their affliction and to keep oneself unstained from the world.* Another example is when Jesus told the disciples that Christian leaders are not to lord over those following them. They are to serve them instead. This is a paradox that the world cannot understand. If Christianity is full of paradoxes, then Christian leadership also contains many paradoxes.

Conclusion

Christianity is full of paradoxes. The same is true for Christian leadership. The Christian leader must understand that Christian leadership is different from other leadership and determine what those differences are. Christian leaders cannot measure their success through metrics. Numbers and finances do not tell the whole story. The Christian leader will discover the true status of their success of their leadership and ministry when they stand before the Judge.

- 2 -

What is Leadership and What is Different about Christian Leadership

AS referred to before in the Introduction to this book, none of the leadership teachers and writers can agree on an exact definition of leadership. And we are not sure that there will ever be a definition that everyone can agree on. Otherwise, the many attempts to define leadership over the last sixty or more years would have been successful. We will not attempt to succeed in creating a good definition where others have failed. Leadership is one of those things that are difficult to define but most people seem to recognize it when they see it. We need to change our way of thinking about Christian leadership. It is not exactly what we previously thought it was.

Christian leadership is a calling, not a choice. The Blackabys say it simply, "People do not choose to become spiritual leaders. Spiritual leadership flows out of a person's vibrant, intimate relationship with God. You cannot become a spiritual leader if you are not meeting God in profound life-changing ways." The role of a Christian leader is to develop an intimate relationship with God and then to lead others to develop that same type of relationship with God. Geiger and Peck state, "We are leading people to properly reflect the nature of God and to join us in leading others to do the same thing.".

The first thing a Christian leader must remember is that they are called to this role by God. Christian leadership is different from secular leadership. As mentioned above, Christian leadership has different goals and methods. John Bowling puts it this way, "The ways of business, military, or governmental leadership should not necessarily be the leadership ways of the Christian leader. Secular methods of management need not always be the model for men and women whose hearts have been impacted by the grace of God." Bowling states that it is the grace of God working in the life of leaders that makes everything different. He calls this the grace-full leadership. "If an individual is to be a grace-full leader, God must be rightly placed at the center of his or her life, work, and relationships. The grace of God at work in those dimensions produces a leadership difference of style but of spirit." The role of a Christian leader then is to be full of the grace of God and the Holy Spirit. This will be evidenced by the production of the Fruit of the Spirit in his or her life.

For the last fifty years or more, leadership has become a major subject in the academic world as people began realizing that good leadership was important. These researchers and scholars began understanding that there were good leaders as well as bad leaders. Studies were necessary to determine what made a good leader good and what skills and attributes contributed to good leadership. After all of these years of studies and research, the scholars, authors, teachers, and researchers still are not able to agree on a good definition of exactly what leadership is. As Barbara Kellerman says, "We know there is no widely accepted definition of leadership." They cannot even come to an accord on exactly what skills, characteristics, and responsibilities are necessary for successful leadership.

This also holds true for Christian leadership. We know that Christian leadership is different in many ways from non-Christian leadership. In some ways, Christian leadership is similar to other leadership but is quite different in other ways. Christian leadership often uses some of the same styles, methods, theories, and abilities as other leadership. However, it goes way beyond those things. Besides the fact that the Christian leader uses some of the same leadership styles and methods, he or she is also a follower. They, by the nature of being a Christian, are followers of Jesus Christ. As we will see, this difference makes a major difference in Christian leadership.

Jesus plainly told His disciples that they were called to lead differently than the leaders of the world led. Mark 10:42-45 (Matthew 20 also): *And Jesus called them to him and said to them, "You know that those who are considered rulers of the Gentiles lord it over them, and their great ones exercise authority over them. But it shall not be so among you. But whoever would be great among you must be your servant, and whoever would be first among you must be slave of all. For even the Son of Man came not to be served but to serve, and to give his life as a ransom for many."*

Arthur Boers states, "But for Christians, the priority is followership. Some people define leadership simply as having followers. Yet, from the Christian perspective, since we are followers, it can faithfully and truthfully be said that only Jesus is the leader" As the Apostle Paul says, *And he put all things under his feet and gave him as head over all things to the church, which is his body, the fullness of him who fills all in all.* Ephesians 1:22-23. A Christian leader may use all of the leadership skills and methods available to the world, but if he or she fails in following Jesus Christ (the Leader and head of the church and the body of Christ), he or she fails at Christian leadership.

One thing that confuses many people about leadership is that they link leadership to a position or assigned role. Many roles or positions indeed have leadership duties and roles as an important part of those positions. This is especially true for supervisory or management positions. The same is also true within Christian Leadership. We usually think of Christian leadership as only occurring in certain positions. Examples of these are pastors, deacons, elders, Sunday School teachers, or leaders of non-profit religious organizations.

Most leadership scholars agree that true leadership does not only occur within assigned positions or roles. Leadership can and often does, occur outside those roles. This is true in any type of leadership, whether secular in nature or Christian leadership. Leadership occurs whenever someone, no matter what their position or role, steps forward and leads others in some way. The lowest follower may, at some time, step forward and lead a team or group of people in some project or role. It may be in a minor situation or major. These temporary leaders may be leading just one other person, or they may be leading many people. At that point, they are leading (with or without a corresponding job title). This is true even if that person does not want the responsibility or does not get paid extra for it. Often the person leading does not even recognize that they are leading. These people just see a need and step forward to make sure the need is met.

Everyone in the world is a follower and in some ways, they are also a leader (at least at times). They may never have an assigned leadership position or get paid for that leadership. They may, or may not, earn a title of leadership. Nowhere is this thought more obvious than in ministry and

Christian service. Christian leadership is all about loving others and serving them.

As stated previously, Christian leadership is not about power or influence. The first characteristic of a Christian leader is that he or she is a follower of Jesus Christ. A theology of leadership must include furthering the kingdom of God as its primary goal. Russell Huizing explains, "Its primary elements should include a Scripture-based, God-governed, Christ-centric reflection on the use of the gifts that the Holy Spirit has empowered all believers with to accomplish His mission in and for the world." Huizing admits that developing a theology of leadership is not an easy task. "Still, this is not a simple process precisely because Scripture is not written or designed to be a leadership textbook." Geiger and Peck put it this way, "The primary purpose for our leadership mandate is to make known the glory of God by leading others to flourish in God's design. It's that simple."

Boers says it this way, "Christian leadership as I understand it, is always closely related to ministry. All Christian leadership should concern itself primarily with whether or not it directs attention to God and God's kingdom." According to Jimmy Clinton, Paul's purpose in Galatians 5 is to point out the characteristics of a Christian leader. "His goal is a Spirit-filled leader through whom the living Christ ministers, utilizing the leader's spiritual gifts. The fruit of the Spirit is the mark of the mature Christian. The gifts of the Spirit are a mark of a leader being led by God."

The world does not need a theory of Christian leadership. It needs a biblical-based theology of leadership. There is a big difference between these two things. Stephen Smith states, "A false god to success has been built in our lifetime." He also states, "We can prostitute our very souls in our attempt to be successful. We can sell out, cave in, and go morally bankrupt chasing the god of success." Leadership is not about numbers or production. It is about the kingdom of God and doing God's will. Boers stated, "Jesus never explicitly said that we are to be leaders but commanded us all – specifically in contrast to the leaders and rulers of his age – to be servants." The emphasis needs to change from leadership to followership. Following Christ and living in the Spirit will produce the Fruit of the Spirit.

Ann Gibson puts it this way, "Finally, Wilton Brunch reminds us that whether or not we consider ourselves to be leaders, we are followers. To follow is a noble calling, and requires each follower to reach that noble status through understanding and application of the virtues in his or her life. These virtues include...those identified as the fruit of the Spirit by the Apostle Paul." To repeat, Jesus never told anyone to become a leader. He told people to follow Him and to be servants.

The Role of a Leader

Leadership, generally, is about leading followers through certain tasks or achieving shared goals. This is also true in Christian or ministry leadership. Simultaneously, the Christian leader is also a joint follower of Christ along with those followers that he is leading. He or she is a brother or sister to those they lead as a fellow member in the church and in the body of Christ. This means that Christian leadership is not only being a follower of Christ but also leading other followers of Christ.

As stated several times previously, Christian leadership has different goals from secular leadership. Christian leadership is not just about leading a team or organization in achieving a common goal. Christian leadership, like Christianity itself, is about following Jesus Christ together in community. The pastoral leader is not only a leader but also a joint member of the Global Church of Christ. The Christian leader, to be successful, must succeed in being a follower. There is no other way to measure success in Christian leadership. Allen Hamlin says it this way, "In some sense, we are all followers. Whether we have a leadership title, or whether we are self-employed, unemployed, subcontracted, fill-time students, homemakers, hobbyists, or pew-warmers, we all have someone who is over us." This means that everyone is a follower including those who are a pastor, a board member, a Sunday School teacher, or an usher. Followers are not only those who sit in the pew while having no other leadership roles in the church.

We obtain the character of Christ and display the Fruit of the Spirit in our lives through spiritual development and growth – the transforming us into the image of Christ. Aubrey Malohurs says this about transformation, "Transformation is the work of the Holy Spirit in the lives of Christians that changes and conforms them to Christ's image. It occurs when Christians present themselves as living sacrifices to God." Malphurs reminds the reader that Paul states that the believer can be transformed only through the renewing of their mind. Paul says this is done through the believer presenting his body as a living sacrifice. Romans 12:1-2, *I appeal to you therefore, brothers, by the mercies of God, to present your bodies as a living sacrifice, holy and acceptable to God, which is your spiritual worship. Do not be conformed to this world, but be transformed by the renewal of your mind, that by testing you may discern what is the will of God, what is good and acceptable and perfect.* This transformation will renew the believer's mind. Malphurs says, "Only as the Holy Spirit refreshes and revitalizes his spirit will he be able to lead and influence the church in its transformation to Christlikeness."

The leader offers his or her body as a living sacrifice by crucifying one's self or one's flesh. Craig Blomberg states, "Once again…Paul declares the flesh to have been crucified, but he immediately goes on to command his readers not to commit the acts of the flesh but to walk by the Spirit." He is talking about Galatians 5:24, *And those who belong to Christ Jesus have crucified the flesh with its passions and desires.* These actions are not a set of rules or laws to be obeyed or discarded. Blomberg continues, "But the overriding impression one gets from Paul's discussion in [Galatians] 5:13 – 6:10 is that Christian ethics, reflecting life in the Spirit, flow from the heart and a love relationship with God and others much more than from a specific list of do's and don'ts." This process will not be easy or pain-free. John Stott puts it this way. "Secondly, our rejection of the old nature will be painful. Crucifixion was a form of execution attended with intense pain."

This process involves an intentional development process on the part of the leader. Stott continues, "But it is a mistake to suppose that our whole duty lies in passive submission to the Spirit's control as if all we had to do was to surrender to His leading. On the contrary, we are ourselves to walk, actively and purposely, in the right way. And the Holy Spirit is the path we walk in, as well as the guide who shows us the way." It is important to remember that this character development is more than doing the right things in the right way. Smith adds, "To walk in the way is more than managing sins or bad habits. To walk in the way is to walk toward transformation – toward change at the DNA level of our souls." It is important to note here that the transformation does not come through any actions we take. Transformation only occurs through the work of the Holy Spirit within us as we allow Him to make changes in our lives.

Leadership Setting

ALL Christian leadership should be involved in some way in helping other followers find Christ and leading them in walking in the Spirit. However, Christian leadership does not only include those who are in active ministry. Having a theology of leadership that includes the involvement of the Fruit of the Spirit is even more important for the pastor or other minister. As a spiritual leader to other followers, it is important that the minister not only have the head knowledge of the gospel but that he or she is living and walking in the Spirit. The Christian leader must have their relationship with Christ correct before they can help lead others in their relationship with Him. Ruth Barton states, "But one of the things I know for sure is that those who are looking to us for spiritual sustenance need us to first and foremost be spiritual seekers ourselves."

The Christian leader faces many challenges from both inside and outside the church. Sometimes, the most challenging situations for the leader may come from within the church itself. The church leader needs a close and intimate relationship with Jesus. He or she needs the power of the Holy Spirit within them and thereby have the Fruit of the Spirit active in their life in order to be able to overcome these challenges. Barton goes on, "The only way to begin facing these challenges is to keep seeking tenaciously after God through spiritual disciplines that keep us grounded in the presence of God at the center of our being."

This is not to say that that the spiritual disciplines have any type of magical or mystical power in them. The spiritual disciplines can help keep the leader grounded in Christ, ever drawing closer to Him. This is what Paul called taking up one's cross, denying self, crucifying flesh, and renewing one's mind. In doing this, the leader is opening himself or herself to the Spirit's leading. The Fruit of the Spirit will then be operational in the life of this leader. The effective Christian leader will also minimize the emphasis on numbers, attendance, finances, and meeting goals. He or she will concentrate on following the leading of the Holy Spirit and allowing the Fruit of the

Spirit to operate in his or her life. These things are much more important than numbers. Success in Christian leadership has to be redefined to meet the expectations of Christ.

Boers has three thoughts about Christian leadership that leaders should take into consideration. "First, true motivation, change, transformation, and action (whether by individuals or groups) is accomplished by the Holy Spirit whose movements cannot be tracked or predicted. Second, we are not called to have followers but to be followers of Jesus Christ. Third, getting things done is rarely a biblical priority; we are encouraged rather to cooperate in God's purposes and rely on God for fruitful results." He goes on to add, "Leaders are spiritual orienteers; they are also on the journey and also need constant orientation and reorientation. They, too, require the compass and map of scriptures, accountability, community, formation, and worship."

Jesus Christ is the perfect example of what a Christian leader looks like, The goal of a Christian leader is to become like Christ and lead like Him. Jesus Christ had the Fruit of the Spirit active in His life in every area. The Christian leader must have those same Fruit of the Spirit active in his or her life. Christopher Wright states, "We could say that the nine-fold fruit of the Spirit in Galatians 5:22-23 is a beautiful picture of Jesus." The Christian leader has different goals than the secular leader. His or her goal is to draw ever closer to Christ and to produce the Fruit of the Spirit while helping others do the same. Obeying the following of the Spirit is more important than any other task or program.

Kyle Strobel had this to say, "Ascending in Christ is having Christ as the center of our life and existence. It is communing with him in such a manner that we come to be like him, taking on the way of life he lived. Ascending in Christ is becoming one with the human nature Christ sanctified in his life, death, resurrection, and ascension to the Father." This ascension in Christ is accomplished through the spiritual disciplines. These disciplines are not mystical actions within themselves. Practicing the spiritual disciplines places the leader in an ever closer relationship with Christ. The leader sacrifices his time and himself to Christ. He or she then allows the Holy Spirit to do the work within him or her that the Spirit wishes to do. In this manner, the Christian leader can be effective and doing the work that the Holy Spirit wishes him or her to do. Strobel adds, "The goal of spiritual discipline is often explained as a transformation of character."

In his book, Wright quotes a prayer that he says John Stott prayed every day. It seems applicable here. "Heavenly Father, I pray that this day I may live in your presence and please you more and more. Lord Jesus, I pray that this day I may take up my cross and follow you. Holy Spirit, I pray that this day you will fill me with yourself and cause your fruit to ripen in my life; love, joy, peace, patience, kindness, goodness, faithfulness, gentleness, and self-control." This is a good daily prayer for every Christian leader.

Leading With Love

As we have said previously Christian leadership looks different and has different goals from non-Christian leadership. We may then ask the question as to what the difference is between these types of leadership. One of the biggest differences between the two is that the Christian leader, as a follower of Christ, will lead in love. Love is the major distinction between them. This is not to say that non-Christian leaders cannot lead in love, but it does seem to be unusual. The followers of Christ are commanded to love one another. Not only are they to love their fellow believers, but they are also to love their neighbor and their enemy. In Matthew 22:39, Jesus says that believers are to love their neighbor as themselves. Jesus even went a step beyond that and stated, *"You have heard that it was said, 'You should love your neighbor and hate your enemy.' But I say unto you, Love your enemies and pray for them who persecute you."* Matthew 5:43-44. The non-Christian leader is often not required or encouraged to love others, including their followers. He or she does not have to lead in love. In contrast, the Christian leader must lead in love.

The biggest contrast between Christian leadership and secular leadership is love. A secular leader can and should lead in love although they are not usually required to do so. He or she should love their followers and ensure that they have the tools they need. He or she should also care about the follower's needs and situations. However, he or she is not required to lead in love. Their employment and goals depend on producing the desired results and profits. Their contract or mandate may not depend on the followers being happy, satisfied, well compensated, or their needs being provided.

Jesus mandated that His followers love others. This is even truer for Christian ministers and leaders. Jesus even declared that His followers must love their enemies. The followers of Christ are not allowed to only love their relatives and friends. They are not allowed to solely love those who love them back. They are required to even love those who mistreat and abuse them. The Christian must love those who persecute and kill the Christians. Matthew 5:43-47, *"You have heard that it was said, 'You shall love your neighbor and hate your enemy.' But I say to you, Love your enemies and pray for those who persecute you, so that you may be sons of your Father who is in heaven. For he makes his sun rise on the evil and on the good, and sends rain on the just and on the unjust. For if you love those who love you, what reward do you have? Do not even the tax collectors do the same? And if you greet only your brothers, what more are you doing than others? Do not even the Gentiles do the same?* In other words, the Christians must do what is impossible for them to so within their own power. This type of love can only be achieved by those who have been forgiven by Christ and have His love dwelling within.

The Apostle Paul understood that Christians were to love others: *If I speak in the tongues of men and angels, but have not love, I am a noisy gong or a clanging cymbal. And if I have prophetic powers, and understand all mysteries and all knowledge, and if I have all faith, so as to remove mountains, but have not love, I am nothing. If I give away all I have, and if I deliver up my body to be burned, but have not love, I gain nothing.* (1 Corinthians 13:1-3). One wonders if possibly, Paul could have added another sentence with the idea that one can lead others well, but if he or she does not lead with love, his or her leadership is meaningless. Successful Christian leadership must involve love, otherwise, there is nothing Christian (Christlike) about it. We will take this one step further. Christianity without love is not Christian at all. As the Apostle John states, *God is love, and whoever abides in love abides in God, and God abides in him.* (1 John 4:16).

The Christian leader must show love in his or her leadership. To do otherwise is not Christian leadership at all. Jonathan Edwards says it this way, "Hence, it is no wonder that Christianity so strangely requires us to love our enemies, even the worst of enemies, as in Matthew 5:44. For love is the very temper and spirit of a Christian: it is the sum of Christianity. "We will discuss the subject of love in leadership in greater detail in Chapter 8.

Servant Leadership

Over the last fifty or sixty years, many leadership experts have come to understand true leadership done in love involves servant leadership. This definitely sounds like a contradiction but bear with us here. Paul called the apostles and ministers of the Gospel to be servants. 1 Corinthians 4:1-2: *This is how one should regard us, as servants of Christ and stewards of the mysteries of God. Moreover, it is required of stewards that they be found faithful.*

Servant leadership first became widely known in 1970 through an essay by Robert K. Greenleaf. In it, he states: "The servant-leader is servant first...It begins with the natural feeling that one wants to serve, to serve first. Then conscious choice brings one to aspire to lead. That person is sharply different from one who is leader first, perhaps because of the need to assuage an unusual power drive or to acquire material possessions...The leader-first and the servant-first are two extreme types. Between them there are shadings and blends that are part of the infinite variety of human nature. The difference manifests itself in the care taken by the servant-first to make sure that other people's highest priority needs are being served. The best test, and the most difficult to administer, is: "Do those served grow as persons? Do they, while being served, become healthier, wiser, freer, more autonomous, more likely themselves to become servants? And, what is the effect on the least privileged in society? Will they benefit or at least not be further deprived?"

After Greenleaf proposed this theory of leadership, many Christian leaders soon realized that Servant Leadership was a good description of the leadership style of Jesus Christ. Jesus taught and exemplified the idea of a leader being first of all a servant. The leader is not in charge in order to lord over the followers but in order to serve them. Let us be honest here, if there ever was a leader that had every right to lord over and boss over everyone else, it was Jesus. After all, he was the Son of God. God has the right to rule any way that He wants to. He is the Creator of everything. If He created all of us, He has the right to tell us what we are to do and how we are to lead in any way He wants to. Instead of lording over us, the Jesus of the Bible chose to lead by being a servant. The Son of God came to earth to lead us through serving us. While He led His followers, He also served them at the same time.

- 3 -

The Fruit of the Spirit

But the fruit of the Spirit is love, joy, peace, patience, kindness, goodness, faithfulness, gentleness, self-control; against such things there is no law.
Galatians 5:22-23 (ESV)

THIS idea may well sound strange to some people. In some ways, this chapter may be the most difficult subject to understand in the way that it pertains to leadership. At the same time, it may well be one of the most important ones. As we state several times, Christian leadership is heavily involved in and depends on the leader being a follower of Christ. A major part of being a follower of Jesus Christ involves the Holy Spirit dwelling within us. If the Holy Spirit dwells within us and we are living and walking in the Spirit, then the Fruit of the Spirit will be evident in our lives. This Fruit of the Spirit is in the stead of the fruit of the flesh that we all previously displayed in our lives. It then stands to reason that we who are Christian leaders, through following Christ, will have the Fruit of the Spirit evident in our lives. If this is true, the Fruit of the Spirit plays an important part in whether or not a Christian leader is successful.

The New Testament does not directly mention the Fruit of the Spirit many times but this is a vital subject in Christian leadership. The followers of Jesus Christ who do not have the Fruit of the Spirit active in their lives are missing so much. We might even say that they are probably not following Christ well at all. This is not meant to be a judgment, but a believer who is actively following Christ must have the Fruit of the Spirit active in his or her life. The Fruit of the Spirit is proof that the Holy Spirit is dwelling within you and is active in your life. What does the Fruit of the Spirit have to do with Christian leadership?

As previously mentioned, there are hundreds, if not thousands, of differing definitions of leadership. Many of these involve such words as influence, command, power, control, and other similar words. Christian leadership is different and thereby needs a different definition. Many

Christian leadership definitions often use such terms as serving, servant leadership, furthering the Kingdom of God, and the leader being under the influence of the Holy Spirit. Those would be accurate in helping define what Christian leadership is. Sukumarakurup Krisnakumar states, "Leadership is not simply about power and authority – it is also about emotional connections, authenticity, and spiritual values." Martin Hanna uses this definition, "Leadership is a dynamic relational process in which people, under the influence of the Holy Spirit, partner to achieve a common goal...which is...serving others by leading and leading others by serving." Hanna also states, "The Bible also makes explicit that servant-leadership is connected with Christ-centered, Spirit-empowered consecration-obedience."

These definitions are valid but do not fully define Christian leadership. A Christian must have the Fruit of the Spirit active in his or her life to be an effective follower of Christ. The New Testament teaches that a believer must show forth love to one's neighbor, brother, and even one's enemy. This love manifests itself through the Fruit of the Spirit and is itself a vital ingredient of the Fruit of the Spirit. It is imperative for the Christian leader to have this Fruit of the Spirit active in their life to in order to be an effective Christian leader. However, the Christian leader can only have this Fruit through living and walking in the Spirit, thereby allowing the Fruit of the Spirit to be active within his or her life. This chapter will show that an effective Christian leader must have the Fruit of the Spirit active in his or her life in order to be successful. This fruit will be produced through the active and intentional efforts of the leader in living in and walking in the Spirit. A leader who does not display the Fruit of the Spirit may be a leader of sorts but is not a successful Christian leader. This person will not be successful in leading the same way that Jesus Christ did. They most likely will not be creating disciples of Jesus Christ or adding to the Kingdom of God.

In the last few years, several secular leadership experts have begun to recognize the importance in the role of spiritual leadership within leadership. Although these experts may or may not be Christian they still recognize the importance that spiritual matters in effective leadership. Louis Fry says it this way, "With the dawn of the twenty-first century, there was an emerging and exponentially accelerating force for global societal and organizational change. From this realization has come a call for more holistic leadership that integrates the four fundamental arenas that define the essence of human existence – the body (physical), mind (logical/rational thought), heart (emotions, feelings), and spirit." More organizations are recognizing and trying to incorporate the spiritual into their organizations. Fry continues, "There is an emerging and accelerating call for spirituality in the workplace. Companies…are extolling lessons usually doted out in churches."

Christians look toward Jesus Christ as being the perfect leader. They normally point out that He was a servant leader. Jesus was not only a servant leader, but He also taught and mentored His disciples to be servant leaders. He not only taught them that they were to be servant leaders, but He also showed them how to be servant leaders. Many leadership experts also point out that the Christian leader must be a shepherd leader. Jesus was a shepherd leader and He used the shepherd leadership analogy in many of His teachings. Jesus even called Himself the good shepherd. John 10:11, *I am the good shepherd. The good shepherd lays down his life for the sheep.* And John 10:14, *I am the good shepherd. I know my own and my own know me.* The Christian leader must be both a servant leader and a shepherd leader.

Most people leave out the all-important message of the necessity of the Christian leader displaying the Fruit of the Spirit. The message of Jesus was full of contrasts (paradoxes). These include the thoughts that the person who wishes to first, must be last, and that the person who wants to lead, must also follow. The Christian leader is foremost a follower. This is the foundational truth about Christian leadership. He or she must first be a follower of Jesus Christ. This seeming contrast is the major difference in Christian leadership. The leader must not only believe in Jesus, but he or she must also follow Jesus daily and to allow the Holy Spirit to live within and direct them. The Christian leader must take up his or her cross and die to himself or herself daily. As Paul says it, the Christian leader must live and walk daily in the Spirit. A successful Christian leader cannot have a lukewarm relationship with Jesus Christ. He or she must intentionally develop a daily relationship with Christ that involves walking in the Spirit and denying oneself. It is by intentionally drawing ever close to Christ that the leader will have all of the Fruit of the Spirit active within his or her life. It is only through the leader's intentional and disciplined use of the spiritual disciplines that they can develop their spiritual formation. Please understand that this is not advocating that the Fruit of the Spirit is accessible through any effort or labor on our part. The Fruit of the Spirit is only evident in those who allow the Spirit to dwell within them and allow the Holy Spirit to do the work that He wants to do in us. We are incapable of doing it ourselves any more than we can earn our salvation.

Any leader who does not have the Fruit of the Spirit active in his or her life cannot be a servant leader like Jesus Christ was. It is impossible to be a true servant leader without the Fruit of the Spirit being active in the leader's life. These two cannot have one without the other. This book will show that the Fruit of the Spirit comes only through an intentional act of living and walking daily in the Spirit. The Apostle Paul also called living and walking in the Spirit as dying to oneself daily. This is not an easy process and is not one to achieve without pain and sacrifice. It involves the Christian leader taking up his or her cross daily. It involves dying to oneself daily and living in the Spirit instead of living for self.

Most Christians know and understand that the Fruit of the Spirit describes the attributes of someone who is a follower of Jesus Christ and who is living in the Spirit. The Fruit of the Spirit is in contrast to the fruit of the flesh. The fruit of the flesh is what is evident in the life of someone who is living for self and only pleasing their own selfish desires. This is in opposition to the attributes that are evident in the life of someone who is following Christ, living daily in the Spirit, and trying to please God.

We can find these phrases (the Fruit of the Spirit and the fruit of flesh) in Ephesians 5. In Galatians 5, the apostle Paul gives us several hints on how to have the Fruit of the Spirit in our lives. He encourages us to be imitators of God and to walk in love. He then continues on to suggest some things to avoid in our lives and other things that we should be practicing. It is through doing these things and avoiding others, we too can have the Fruit of the Spirit evident in our lives. As a side note, the Fruit of the Spirit is a great subject for further study for believers. It is worth taking time to study and ensure that we have the Fruit of the Spirit in our lives whether we are a leader or not. The Fruit of the Spirit is directly related to followership. If we follow Christ as we should, this will allow the Fruit of the Spirit to be operational in our lives.

All of this is all well and good, but what exactly does the Fruit of the Spirit have to do with Christian leadership? This is a great question and it is one that we have never heard anyone ask before. If the Fruit of the Spirit is a vital ingredient in Christian leadership, then why has it been ignored by other Christian leadership authors for so long? The answer to that question is unknown but we suspect that the omission was probably not intentional. Most Christian leadership teachers and authors have concentrated on the same skills and attributes that secular leadership teachers and authors have concentrated on. They have concentrated on the traits, personality types, and skills that most people believe make someone a great leader. There is nothing wrong with that in one way. Leadership is better with certain skills and abilities. However, most of these authors disagree on which ones of these skills and abilities are important. They also disagree on if these attributes and skills are innate or have to be learned. In the process of arguing leadership methods and skills, the link to the Fruit of the Spirit was just overlooked.

The first lesson that we must learn as a Christian or ministry leader is that while Christian leadership may share many skills and aspects with secular leadership, it is very different. As stated earlier, Christian leadership has different goals. The ultimate goal of every believer and Christian leader should be the Great Commission in Matthew 28:18-19 to make disciples. *Go therefore and make disciples of all nations, baptizing them in the name of the Father and of the Son and the Holy Spirit, teaching them to observe all that I have commanded you.* One can argue that this ultimate goal is what makes Christian leadership goals and methods so different from secular leadership.

The Fruit of the Spirit is an important attribute to have in Christian leadership. A Christian leader who does not have the Fruit of the Spirit active in his or her life may be a type of leader, but they cannot truly be a Christian leader. This is one important place where Christian leadership is so entwined with followership. The Fruit of the Spirit is only active in the lives of those believers who follow Christ. This Fruit of the Spirit is not necessarily active in those who say that they believe in Christ. It is only in the lives of those who are actively following Christ. How is this following Christ accomplished? Paul teaches that the believer must live and walk daily in the Spirit!

Although the Bible only mentions the Fruit of the Spirit once, the idea of the Fruit of the Spirit is present in places throughout it. Starting back with the Old Testament leaders, the Bible lists what they did right and what they did wrong when they strayed from obeying God. When the leaders did the right things and obeyed God, the Fruit of the Spirit was obvious in their lives. The Fruit of the Spirit can be linked to several Old Testament scriptures. The metaphor of fruit being produced by the Spirit is obvious. Isaiah 53:15-17, *Until the Spirit is poured upon us from on high, and the wilderness becomes a fruitful field, and the fruitful field is deemed a forest. Then justice will dwell in the wilderness, and righteousness abides in the fruitful field. And the effect of righteousness will be peace, and the result of righteousness, quietness, and trust forever.* Here Isaiah is foretelling of the coming of the Holy Spirit and the fruit that the Holy Spirit will produce in the lives of the faithful.

The prophet Joel also prophesied about the future outpouring of the Holy Spirit. *And it shall come to pass afterward, that I will pour out my Spirit on all flesh; your sons and your daughters shall prophesy, your old men shall dream dreams, and your young men shall see visions. Even on the male and female servants in those days I will pour out my Spirit.* Joel 2:28-29.

Even David referenced the fruit of living righteously in Psalm 1:1-3, *Blessed is the man who walks not in the counsel of the wicked, nor stands in the way of sinners, nor sits in the seat of scoffers; but his delight is in the law of the Lord, and on his law he meditates day and night. He is like a tree planted by streams of water that yields its fruit in its season, and its leaf does not wither. In all that he does, he prospers.* We can clearly see from these scriptures that even in the Old Testament the Holy Spirit produced fruit. Not only does the Holy Spirit empower the believer, but He also produces fruit in those who live in the Spirit and allow Him to work in their lives.

Jesus also displayed and taught the Fruit of the Spirit without using that phrase. G. Walter Hansen states, "Jesus also taught that the genuineness of his followers would be demonstrated by good fruit from their lives, and he promised that the presence of the Spirit and communication with him would produce the fruit of love and obedience." Jesus often used the metaphor of fruit in His messages. He taught that every person would be known by their fruit – either good fruit or bad fruit. *You will recognize them by their fruits. Are grapes gathered from thornbushes, or figs from thistles? So, every healthy tree bears good fruit, but the diseased tree bears bad fruit. A healthy tree cannot bear bad fruit, nor can a diseased tree bear good fruit. Every tree that does not bear good fruit is cut down and thrown into the fire. Thus you will recognize them by their fruits."* Matthew 7:16-20. The good fruit is the fruit of the Spirit produced by the believer who is living and walking daily in the Spirit. The bad fruit here is what the Apostle Paul called the works of the flesh.

We can find one of the strongest metaphors about fruit that is found in John 15. Here Jesus states that He is the true vine and that the believers are the branches that produce fruit. *I am the true vine, and my Father is the vinedresser. Every branch in me that does not bear fruit he takes away, and every branch that does bear fruit he prunes, that it may bear more fruit. Already you are clean because of the word that I have spoken to you. Abide in me, and I in you. As the branch cannot bear fruit by itself unless it abides in the vine, neither can you, unless you abide in me. I am the vine; you are the branches. Whoever abides in me and I in him, he it is that bears much fruit, for apart from me you can do nothing. If anyone does not abide in me he is thrown away like a branch and withers; and the branches are gathered, thrown into the fire, and burned.* John 15:1-6, For the leader to produce the good fruit, in other words the Fruit of the Spirit, he or she must not only have Christ dwelling within him or her, but they must also dwell in Christ. The way they do this is to live and walk daily in the Spirit. If they do this, they will produce the Fruit of the Spirit. This is what Jesus expects from His followers.

In Ephesians 5, Paul warns the Ephesian believers to avoid the darkness that they used to live in. He encouraged them to walk in the Spirit and thereby to produce the Fruit of the Spirit. *For at one time you were darkness, but now you are light in the Lord. Walk as children of light (for the fruit of light is found in all that is good and right and true), and try to discern what is pleasing to the Lord.* Ephesians 5:8-10.

When a leader lives and walks in the Spirit daily, he or she is becoming the image of Christ. The image of Christ, that the believer is striving for, is the production of the Fruit of the Spirit in his or her life. Just as Jesus had the Fruit of the Spirit operational in His life, the leader needs to also be producing the Fruit of the Spirit. F.F. Bruce puts it this way, "The Spirit pours the love of God into the hearts of believers and brings them increasingly into conformity with the character of Christ...And we all, with unveiled face, beholding the glory of the Lord, are being changed into his image from one degree of glory to another, for this comes from the Lord who is the Spirit." What does the image of Christ look like? Bruce answers, "What this image amounts to in practical experience is spelled out in the ninefold fruit of the Spirit in Galatians 5:22." If the Christian leader has the goal of being the image of Christ, which should be the goal of every follower of Christ, then the Christian leader must produce the Fruit of the Spirit in his or her life to be a successful Christian leader.

Love

We could write whole books about love, especially about the way that the New Testament teaches us to love others. There have been many books written about biblical love available to us. The subject of love will be discussed in greater detail in Chapter 8.

The love that Jesus taught His followers to practice is much different from love as the world sees it. Jesus taught His followers that they were to love their neighbor as themselves. They were expected to put their brothers and sisters in Christ before themselves. And then He asked them to do the impossible. Jesus actually expected His followers to even love their enemies.

We cannot state it strongly enough that love is a vital component of Christian leadership. Is it any wonder that the world looks down on the church when its members constantly fight and argue, and some churches even split over minor (and many times stupid) issues? All of us need to work on this issue because most of followers of Christ are still working to get this biblical love thing down right. If we are not able to love our fellow members in the Body of Christ, how can we attract the world to Christ by showing Christ's love to the lost? If others cannot see the love of Christ in us toward others then they cannot see any godly love operational in our lives. Love is something that is generally lacking in leadership. Unfortunately, this is even true in Christian leadership. Many Christian leaders do not understand the importance of love in leadership.

The underlying foundation of the Fruit of the Spirit is love. The first fruit is love and all of the other fruit flow out from that love. G. Walter

Hansen says this about love, "All the other moral qualities in the list define and flow from love." Love is central to the gospel message. Love starts with the Father's love for us and is displayed in the birth, death, and resurrection of His only Son Jesus Christ. The primary message that Jesus Christ taught centered around love. He showed His love for mankind through His death. Thomas Schreiner adds, "The first fruit listed is love, and this is scarcely surprising since love is the mark of new life in Christ according to Paul."

The Christian leader should be taking his or her theology of Christian leadership straight from the Bible. This leadership theology can be taken primarily from the teachings and the example of Jesus Christ. Paul and Peter also teach much about what is expected from the godly leader in their writings. There are many examples of leaders in the Bible in both testaments. Not all of these leaders are good examples for us to follow. Boer says, "Positive leader terminology is scant in the scriptures. Few officeholders are regarded favorably. Official rulers usually look out for interests contrary to God's purposes; their characters are deficient." The Bible is faithful to point out the good and bad in each leader. Scripture often shows what the results are when the leader fails to walk close to and obey God. As Paul says in Galatians 5, these leaders produce the work of the flesh instead of producing the Fruit of the Spirit.

Forgiveness

There is another related, but often overlooked, aspect of love. That aspect of love is forgiveness. Paul did not directly include forgiveness as one of the Fruit of the Spirit. However, the other listed characteristics of the Fruit of the Spirit must incorporate forgiveness also. While forgiveness is an important part of love, this does not mean that you can never discipline, correct, or even fire a problem employee when it becomes necessary. However, even then, forgiveness should be an important part of the process and those things should always be done in love. Just as Christ forgives us for our sins, we must also forgive others for theirs.

Remember what Jesus said in Matthew 6:14-15 just after teaching the people the Lord's Prayer. *For if you forgive others their trespasses, your heavenly Father will also forgive you, but if you do not forgive others their trespasses, neither will your Father forgive your trespasses.* Jesus states this in plain language. If we expect to be forgiven for our sins and failures, we must be willing to forgive others for theirs.

We are going to see these next two verses later in this chapter but in them, Paul mentions the importance of forgiveness. Colossians 3:12-13, *Put on then, as God's chosen ones, holy and beloved, compassionate hearts, kindness, humility, meekness, and patience, bearing with one another and, if one has a complaint against another, forgiving each other; as the Lord has forgiven you, so you also must forgive.* If God has forgiven you for your sins, you must also forgive others for any offense against you. We know that forgiveness is not always the easiest thing to do. Sometimes it almost seems impossible to forgive others for what they have done to us.

Now here comes a tough one. Not only are we to forgive others, but we must be willing to forgive them multiple times. Matthew 18:21-22 tells how Peter asked Jesus how many times must he forgive his brother for offending him. His answer was, *Then Peter came up and said to him, "Lord, how often will my brother sin against me and I forgive him? As many as seven times?" Jesus said to him, "I do not say to you seven times, but seventy-seven times."* There is no rule with a set number of times that we must forgive others. After forgiving someone seventy-seven times, we are not given the choice of telling them that we are not going to forgive them any more. Jesus states a new concept that we must always forgive others, just as He always forgives us. After all, we have been forgiven by God for many more than seventy-seven sins. God never fails to forgive us, no matter how many times we sin. We must be the same way with others. Peter thought he was showing just how loving and forgiving he could be. He was willing to forgive his brother seven times in one day. We must be willing and able to forgive them in love as many times as they need forgiveness.

And Jesus reiterated this message in Mark 11:25-26, *And when you stand praying, forgive, if you have anything against anyone, so that your Father also who is in heaven may forgive you your trespasses."* The ESV does not include Mark 11:26 as it is not included in the oldest manuscripts found. But here it is in the KJV, *But if ye do not forgive, neither will your Father which is in heaven forgive your trespasses.*

Joy

The subject of joy in the New Testament makes for a good word study. Joy is mentioned often in the story about the birth of Christ. Over and over, there was great joy in the news of the birth of the Messiah. Jesus also relates joy in suffering trials and tribulations. There is much joy in having the indwelling of the Holy Spirit and living in the Spirit daily even when undergoing trials and tribulations.

A good example of this is when Jesus told the disciples that they would see much adversity and suffering for His name's sake. He told them that when this occurred, they were to rejoice. Luke 6:22-23, *"Blessed are you when people hate you and when the exclude you and revile you and spurn your name as evil, on account of the Son of Man! Rejoice in that day, and leap for joy, for so their fathers did to the prophets."* Even in times of suffering, we are to have joy in our souls. In Acts 13:51-52, Paul and Barnabas face persecution and trouble from the local Jews. What did they do when that happened? *But they shook off the dust from their feet against them and went to Iconium. And the disciples were filled with joy and the Holy Spirit.* They continued on their way and they were filled with both joy and the Holy Spirit!

Peace

The third attribute listed as one of the Fruit of the Spirit is peace. Peace has to be important to Christian leadership then. The importance of peace is noted many times in the New Testament. It is often mentioned as a part of our relationship to God and to Jesus Christ. Besides being called one of the Fruit of the Spirit, peace is also linked with being filled with the Spirit and walking in the Spirit. Without the indwelling of the Holy Spirit, there is no peace in our lives. Even in times of trials, tribulations, pain, and suffering, the Holy Spirit can bring peace within our souls.

The presence of joy starts even before Christ is born. Luke 1 relates the story of Zechariah, the father of John the Baptist. An angel appears to him to tell him that he and his wife are going to have a son who will proclaim the message about the coming Messiah. Zechariah is then filled with the Holy Spirit and begins to prophesy. The end of that prophecy states in Luke 1:79, *"To give light to those who sit in darkness and the shadow of death, and to guide our feet into the way of peace."* Next, we see in Luke 2:14 where the angel appeared to the startled shepherds out in the field with their sheep in order to announce the birth of the Messiah. After the proclamation of His birth, a heavenly host appears and praises God with, *"Glory to God in the highest, and on earth peace among those with whom he is pleased."* Jesus was bringing the way of peace to the earth.

Before His ascension, Jesus promised to send the Holy Spirit to His disciples. He also promised them peace. He knew that they were going to endure many tribulations and trials so He sent them the Holy Spirit (the Helper and the Comforter) to provided them peace they needed. John 14:25-27, *"These things I have spoken to you while I am still with you. But the Helper, the Holy Spirit, whom the Father will send in my name, he will teach you all things and bring to your remembrance all that I have said to you. Peace I leave with you; my peace I give to you. Not as the world gives do I give to you. Let not your hearts be troubled, neither let them be afraid.*

When Peter was talking to Cornelius, he called the gospel the good news of peace. Acts 10:36, *As for the word that he sent to Israel, preaching the good news of peace through Jesus Christ (he is Lord of all).* In Ephesians 2:14-18, Paul states that Jesus Christ is our peace. *For he is our peace, who has made us both one and has broken down in his flesh the dividing wall of hostility by abolishing the law of commandments expressed in ordinances, that he might create in himself one new man in place of the two, so making peace, and might reconcile us both to God in one body through the cross, thereby killing the hostility. And he came and preached peace to you who were far off and peace to those who were near. For through him, we both have access in one Spirit to the Father.*

Paul teaches about walking and living in the spirit in several of his epistles, especially Romans. You are encouraged to reread Romans 8 while studying this section. It deals with the subject of peace through the work of the Holy Spirit in better detail. Romans 8:5-6 says *For those who live according to the flesh set their minds on the things of the flesh, but those who live according to the Spirit set their minds on the things of the Spirit. For to set the mind on the flesh is death, but to set the mind on the Spirit is life and peace.* Paul contrasts walking and living in the flesh with living and walking in the Spirit. Living in the flesh leads to death while living, while walking in the Spirit leads to life and peace. In Romans 15:13, he states, *May the God of hope fill you with all joy and peace in believing, so that by the power of the Holy Spirit you may abound in hope.*

James links peace to godly wisdom. Surely every Christian leader desires to have godly wisdom in his or her life. James 3:13-18, *Who is wise and understanding among you? By his good conduct let him show his works in the meekness of wisdom. But if you have bitter jealousy and selfish ambition in your hearts, do not boast and be false to the truth. This is not the wisdom that comes down from above but is earthly, unspiritual, and demonic. For where jealousy and selfish ambition exist, there will be disorder and every vile practice. But the wisdom from above is first pure, then peaceable, gentle, open to reason, full of mercy and good fruits, impartial and sincere. And a harvest of righteousness is sown in peace by those who make peace.* Notice what James stated about leaders having jealousy and selfish ambitions. Leaders who display those attributes will find disorder instead of peace.

Paul states that the kingdom of God is one of peace. Romans 14:17-19, *For the kingdom of God, is not a matter of eating and drinking but of righteousness and peace and joy in the Holy Spirit. Whoever thus serves Christ is acceptable to God and approved by men. So then let us pursue what makes for peace and for mutual upbuilding.* In Romans 15:33, Paul calls God a God of peace, *May the God of peace be with you all. Amen.* And he concludes 2 Corinthians by calling God the God of love and peace. 2 Corinthians 13:11, *Finally, brothers, rejoice. Aim for restoration, comfort one another, agree with one another, live in peace; and the God of love and peace will be with you.* And lastly, our sanctification comes from the God of peace. 1 Thessalonians 5:23, *Now may the God of peace himself sanctify you completely, and may your whole spirit and soul and body be kept blameless at the coming of our Lord Jesus Christ.*

These verses are just a few of the many in the New Testament that speak about peace. Time and space preclude exploring every verse about peace in the New Testament, but there is another usage of peace in the New Testament. When you read and study the epistles in the New Testament you will begin noticing that most of the epistle writers had a basic formula for greeting those they were writing to. These writers greet the recipients of the letters and wish them grace and peace. The exact wording of the greeting may vary somewhat and sometimes the authors add the words mercy or love to the greeting. Ephesians 1:1-2 is an example, *Paul, an apostle of Christ Jesus by the will of God, To the saints who are in Ephesus, and are faithful in Christ Jesus: Grace to you and peace from God our Father and the Lord Jesus Christ.* Paul mentions both grace and peace here. Peace is a vital attribute in our lives as followers of Christ and as Christian leaders.

This short section on peace will close with three verses written to the church at Ephesus. They sum up what Paul teaches us about peace and the Fruit of the Spirit. It is a powerful message that is needed by the Christian leaders of today. *Ephesians 4:1-3, I therefore, a prisoner for the Lord, urge you to walk in a manner worthy of the calling to which you have been called, with all humility and gentleness, with patience, bearing with one another in love, eager to maintain the unity of the Spirit in the bond of peace.*

Patience (Steadfastness)

You might think that this next subject is a strange thought. That is the idea that patience has anything at all to do with leadership, or even worse, that steadfastness has anything to do with leadership. At first glance, patience does not appear to have anything to do with leadership. Patience does have a lot to do with following Jesus Christ. As we have seen previously, Christian leadership has everything to do with following Christ. Although Jesus usually practiced much patience, He is not recorded as pushing patience at all. Many of the New Testament epistles mention patience a lot.

Patience is a direct result of love. Love and patience are intertwined together. If you really think about it, you will recognize that love, patience, and forgiveness are all interlinked. If you truly love someone, you will be patient with them. It is impossible have love without patience. If you start losing your patience with someone, maybe you should look at your love, or rather your lack of it, toward them. You might need to recognize the root of the problem and make an adjustment in yourself. Recognize that a lack of patience may indicate a problem or lack of loving others. A lack of patience is not because of what the other person is doing or saying, but rather in the way you are reacting to what they are doing or saying. This is not to deny that certain people have the ability to drive you crazy. Some people seem to thrive on being difficult and argumentative. They may even have major emotional, mental, or anger issues. Also drug or alcohol usage may influence how people act or react with you. The direct problem, though, is not how they treat you, but rather in how you respond to them. Becoming angry back at them, argumentative, or impatient shows a lack of love and patience in you. We humans are not capable of loving other people who act out and talk to us in this manner in and of ourselves. It takes the love of Christ acting within us.

As mentioned above, Jesus says little about patience. He does mention enduring with patience in the last days in Luke 21:19. Also in Luke 8:15 at the end of the parable about seed falling on good soil or bad soil, He states, *As for that in the good soil, they are those who, hearing the word, hold it fast in an honest and good heart, and bear fruit with patience.* In other words, those who have received the Gospel message and responded as if they were good soil, should then bear fruit with patience.

Paul talks in several places about having patience. Romans 2:6-7, *He will render to each one according to his works: to those who by patience in well-doing seek for glory and honor and immortality, he will give eternal life; but for those who are self-seeking and do not obey the truth, but obey unrighteousness, there will be wrath and fury.* Once again, Paul teaches patience in 1 Thessalonians 5:14 to all believers. *And we urge you, brothers, admonish the idle, encourage the fainthearted, help the weak, be patient with them all.* One thing to note is that he teaches that we are to be patient with those who may be the most troublesome in the church.

The ones who cause you the most grief and trouble are the ones that he says to be most patient with.

In 1 Timothy 3, Paul lists the qualifications of being a bishop or overseer. The KJV uses the word patient whereas the ESV uses the word gentle. In verses 1-3, he says, *The saying is trustworthy: If anyone aspires to the office of overseer, he desires a noble task. Therefore an overseer must be above reproach, the husband of one wife, sober-minded, self-controlled, respectable, hospitable, able to teach, not a drunkard, not violent but gentle, not quarrelsome, not a lover of money.*

2 Timothy 2:24, *And the Lord's servant must not be quarrelsome but kind to everyone, able to teach, patiently enduring evil.* 1 Timothy 6:11, *But as for you, O man of God, flee these things. Pursue righteousness, godliness, faith, love, steadfastness, gentleness.* The translators here used the word steadfastness while the KJV used the word patience.

James has a different slant on patience in James 1:4, *And let steadfastness have its full effect, that you may be perfect and complete, lacking in nothing.* Here again, the word steadfastness is used in place of patience. Even in tribulation and in waiting for the coming of the Lord, James urges us to be patient. James 5:7-8 says, *Be patient, therefore, brothers, until the coming of the Lord. See how the farmer waits for the precious fruit of the earth, being patient about it, until it receives the early and the late rains. You also, be patient. Establish your hearts, for the coming of the Lord is at hand.* Patience helps bring about perfection. According to James, it also helps you to be complete and lacking in nothing.

Peter's outlook on patience is one of the most unusual ones. Please note that the word steadfastness is used again here in this translation (ESV). He links virtue, knowledge, self-control, patience, godliness, brotherly affection, and love. All of these things are tied together for the believer. 2 Peter 1:5-9, *For this reason, make every effort to supplement your faith with virtue, and virtue with knowledge, and knowledge with self-control, and self-control with steadfastness, and steadfastness with godliness, and godliness with brotherly affection, and brotherly affection with love. For if these qualities are yours and are increasing, they keep you from being ineffective or unfruitful in the knowledge of our Lord Jesus*

Christ. For whoever lacks these qualities is so nearsighted that he is blind, having forgotten that he was cleansed from his former sins.

The Christian leader is to supplement his or her faith with virtue. Then they are to supplement their virtue with knowledge. They are to then supplement their knowledge with self-control. Next they are to supplement their self-control with patience, and then on to godliness. They will then supplement their godliness with brotherly affection. They will next supplement their brotherly affection with love for others. These qualities assist the believer (and leader) in being effective and fruitful. Patience is a must for the believer and particularly for the Christian leader.

Perhaps the most important verse about patience is Galatians 5:22-23, where is included as one of the Fruit of the Spirit. *But the fruit of the Spirit is love, joy, peace, patience, kindness, goodness, faithfulness, gentleness, self-control; against such things there is no law.* Also, as mentioned in the previous section about peace, Ephesians 4:1-3. *I therefore, a prisoner for the Lord, urge you to walk in a manner worthy of the calling to which you have been called, with all humility and gentleness, with patience, bearing with one another in love, eager to maintain the unity of the Spirit in the bond of peace.*

Patience is not an easy skill to learn. In fact, it is difficult to develop this characteristic in our lives. Patience goes against our very nature. Patience is the enemy to ego and selfishness. It can only come through the work of the Holy Spirit within us. There are no easy steps on how to train you to become patient. There is no class that you can take to learn patience. It is truly the fruit of the work that the Holy Spirit does within you.

Kindness

Kindness is often overlooked as a characteristic of leadership. Much of Christian leadership has little to do with leadership in the world. Kindness should always be an aspect of Christian leadership. To start off the subject of kindness we include a small portion from the Love Chapter. 1 Corinthians 13:4-5a, *Love is patient and kind; love does not envy or boast; it is not arrogant or rude.*

Next we include one of the Bible verses that many Christian parents insist that their children memorize at a young age. Ephesians 4:32, *Be kind to one another, tenderhearted, forgiving one another, as God in Christ forgave you.* The reason why parents had their children learn this verse was so that the parents would not have to deal with their children squabbling and fighting like children are often apt to do. Parents often joined this verse along with the verse that tells children to obey their parents as ones for their children to memorize.

Colossians 3:12-13, *Put on then, as God's chosen ones, holy and beloved, compassionate hearts, kindness, humility, meekness, and patience, bearing with one another and, if one has a complaint against another, forgiving each other; as the Lord has forgiven you, so you also must forgive.* Paul's choice of words is interesting here. He says that we are to put on these characteristics (the Fruit of the Spirit) just as we would don a robe. These things are the Fruit that we display in our lives through the power of the Holy Spirit within us. Paul desires that we wear these Fruit like we would a robe

One theme keeps appearing throughout all of these verses. That is the concept that all of the Fruit of the Spirit are linked together. You cannot have one without the others. Patience, love, compassion, kindness, meekness, and humility are woven together through the power of the Holy Spirit working within you. All of these fruit work together in your life.

Goodness

What does Paul mean by goodness here? Strong's Concordance defines goodness as a virtue or beneficence. Goodness is a fruit of the Spirit that is a consequence of being filled with the Holy Spirit and living in the Holy Spirit.

Paul is not talking about goodness as being about following a set of rules or laws. He is speaking about an attitude of goodness and doing good for others in love. Goodness only comes through the work of the Holy Spirit within us and God's love within us causing us to love our neighbor as ourselves.

Perhaps a better idea of what Paul is talking about can be found in Romans 12:9-13, *Let love be genuine. Abhor what is evil; hold fast to what is good. Love one another with brotherly affection. Outdo one another in showing honor. Do not be slothful in zeal, be fervent in spirit, serve the Lord. Rejoice in hope, be patient in tribulation, be constant in prayer. Contribute to the needs of the saints and seek to show hospitality.* Goodness is tightly entwined with the idea of loving your neighbor as yourselves. One might even say that goodness is an outcome from loving your neighbor as yourselves.

Faithfulness

Faithfulness is the word used in the ESV. The KJV translation uses the word faith. The word faithfulness does not appear in the KJV translation of the New Testament. So, whichever translation you choose to use, the wording here seems to indicate that Paul is talking about having faith. Christianity is based on faith, as we all know. In Galatians 5, faith (or faithfulness) is one of the Fruit of the Spirit. Our salvation only comes through faith in Christ. That faith is a work of the Holy Spirit within us.

Gentleness

Why did Paul sneak gentleness into this list? Jesus lived in a rough and violent time. There was little gentleness in existence in that culture. The Romans ruled Israel and did so with an iron fist in many ways. The Roman Army was not invited to take over Israel but they invaded the country in order to take control of it as Rome desired to rule the world. Those times were anything but gentle. Life at that time was not easy at all. Gentleness was not something that the people at that time were used to.

The Romans ruled Israel from many miles away. This was a rough land and bandits were common on the roads between the towns. The Roman Army ruled the nation of Israel and Roman judgment was swift and often cruel. Remember how Jesus was treated at His trial? The soldiers spat on and mocked Him. He was slapped, beaten, and whipped. He was crucified on a cruel cross between two thieves. The crimes He was accused of by the Pharisees and Sadducees were crimes against the Hebrew religion. His supposed crimes had nothing to do with Roman law at all. In order to appease the Jews, the Roman leaders agreed to condemn Him to death anyway. He was led away by the soldiers to be crucified.

In contrast to this violent world, Paul mentions the gentleness of Jesus several times in His writings. He mentions the meekness and gentleness of Christ. 2 Corinthians 10:1, *I, Paul, myself entreat you, by the meekness and gentleness of Christ—I who am humble when face to face with you, but bold toward you when I am away!* When writing to both Timothy and Titus about being Christian leaders and ministers, he reminds them that they are to be gentle. 2 Timothy 2:24-25 says, *And the Lord's servant must not be quarrelsome but kind to everyone, able to teach, patiently enduring evil, correcting his opponents with gentleness. God may perhaps grant them repentance leading to a knowledge of the truth.* Titus 3:1-2, *Remind them to be submissive to rulers and authorities, to be obedient, to be ready for every good work, to speak evil of no one, to avoid quarreling, to be gentle, and to show perfect courtesy toward all people.*

The point here is that there was nothing gentle at all about that culture and life. Life was hard and full of many different types of danger. Yet, Paul is telling the believers and leaders that they must practice gentleness. Unfortunately, gentleness is often a missing ingredient in some churches today. Gentleness is a characteristic of following Christ. Gentleness is an outcome from loving your neighbor as yourselves. It is sad that the Fruit of the Spirit is ignored by many believers and their leaders.

Self-Control

Self-control is not a subject discussed much in the New Testament. The KJV called it temperance. Here in Galatians it is listed as one of the Fruit of the Spirit. As it is one of the Fruit of the Spirit, it has to be important for the believer to practice self-control. We tend to think of self-control as being something that we control. And, to a certain extent, it is an action that we willfully attempt to practice. Paul proclaims that it is one of the Fruit of the Spirit. This makes you wonder just how much self-control we can have without the working of the Holy Spirit within our lives. Any self-control that we had active in our lives without the work of the Holy Spirit would be severely lacking.

The apostle Peter gives us a hint about self-control in 2 Peter 1:3-11, *His divine power has granted to us all things that pertain to life and godliness, through the knowledge of him who called us to his glory and excellence, by which he has granted to us his precious and great promises, so that through them you may become partakers of the divine nature, having escaped from the corruption that is in the world because of sinful desire. For this very reason, make every effort to supplement your faith with virtue, and virtue with knowledge, and knowledge with self-control, and self-control with steadfastness, and steadfastness with godliness, and godliness with brotherly affection, and brotherly affection with love. For if these qualities are yours and are increasing, they keep you from being ineffective or unfruitful in the knowledge of our Lord Jesus Christ. For whoever lacks these qualities is so nearsighted that he is blind, having forgotten that he was cleansed from his former sins. Therefore, brothers, be all the more diligent to confirm your calling and election, for if you practice these qualities you will never fall. For in this way, there will be richly provided for you an entrance into the eternal kingdom of our Lord and Savior Jesus Christ.*

We all need to allow the Holy Spirit to work on self-control in our lives. Our selfish and sinful natures tend to get in the way of doing this though. As Paul states, if we practice these qualities we will never fail.

Conclusion

This chapter is not intended to be a comprehensive discussion about the Fruit of the Spirit. Having the Fruit of the Spirit evident in the life of the believer (and leader) is important. This is also a subject that is often overlooked in today's world. If we are following Jesus Christ and have His Spirit dwelling within us, the Fruit of the Spirit should be obvious in our lives. If it is not apparent in our lives, we need to reevaluate ourselves to determine if we are truly walking and living in the Spirit. A Christian leader, in order to be successful, must have the Fruit of the

Spirit active in his or her life. Those who do not display these qualities in their lives are doomed to be a failure as a Christian leader.

- 4 -

The Failures

(The Failures Who Became Leaders)

THIS chapter goes in a little different direction from the subjects that we have been discussing. It is a subject that at first seems to have little or maybe even nothing at all to do with our discussion about followership. This subject does not help you directly develop a theology of Christian leadership. It is however, an important subject to understand as you study Christian leadership. This subject will help you understand that God selects leaders in a much different way than man does.

This subject is about God using people who were failures in some way. You may well ask what does failure have to do with successful leadership. We tend to think of successful leadership to be directly linked to success and winning. We even tend to choose leaders who were successful athletes who played on winning teams. We like the winners, while we do not like losers or failures near as much. We seem to believe that winning games in sports, playing or singing music, or acting in movies qualifies people to be successful leaders. Sometimes there seems to be some truth to that thought. Many great athletes do go on to be good business leaders, ministers, or politicians. The lessons that they learned in sports may help them develop good leadership skills and attributes.

The truth is that in God's eyes, there is no link between winning games on the football field and successful Christian leadership. God often takes the loser and the failure and empowers them to become successful Christian leaders. They become successful because they depend on Christ and the power of the Holy Spirit instead of relying on their own strength, knowledge, and wisdom. Many times God uses the weak and the failures to further His work.

In studying Christian leadership, many people suggest that we look to the Bible first in our studies. That makes sense since Christian leadership is supposed to be based on what the Bible says. Although the Bible is not a leadership manual, we are to use it as if it was. As we read through the Bible, we are reminded that the Bible is full of leaders, both successful and failed ones. It is suggested that we apply many of the characteristics of successful leaders in the Bible and avoid those of the failures. If you truly study the leaders in the Bible, though, you will notice that every single leader in the Bible that God used, other than Christ, was flawed in some way. Even the most successful leaders in the Bible had their faults and failures. In other words, they were imperfect humans just as we are. Some of them started as failures and became successful leaders. God chose them despite their previous failures and empowered them to become successful leaders. How did we get the idea that Christian leaders had to be perfect in every way? Does the leader have to be faultless and never fail? Did we forget that they are human and subject to temptations and failures like the rest of us? Why do we think that leaders all have to have these great leadership qualities and not have any of the bad habits or weaknesses that we all possess?

If you pay careful attention you will notice that God often uses the weak and the flawed person to lead, not the strongest or greatest. God empowers these imperfect people to do His work. These leaders become great leaders only through the power of the Holy Spirit working within their lives. As an example, consider the disciples. They were simple and imperfect men who were filled with the Holy Spirit and led the early church through its beginnings and spread the Gospel throughout the known world.

This chapter discusses several people from the Bible who by all appearances did not deserve to be leaders. They did not have the right qualifications or attributes to be good leaders. They were not winners on the sports field or anywhere else. However, God chose them to be leaders even with all their disqualifications. God specifically chose these failures who then became successful leaders. These people who were failures definitely did not qualify or deserve to be Christian leaders or ministers. If these people were to apply for the position of pastor or leader in our churches today, we would resoundingly vote against them. They did not meet our standards or expectations for leadership. Then we will go into our Sunday School class and study what great leaders these same people (whom we would reject) were.

If we were studying Christian leadership in college, we would be studying these leaders' leadership styles and qualities and what made them successful Christian leaders. At the same time, we would never vote for a pastor or leader that resembles these previous failures who became great leaders in the Bible. This makes you stop and wonder if we look at the qualifications for our leaders in the wrong way. Are we looking for the wrong qualities and personalities in leaders? These failures that God chose to be leaders became some of the greatest leaders in the Bible.

What do failures have to do with leadership? When you read the Bible with an eye out for leadership, you will notice another paradox that exists with God. Many times in the Bible God chooses a person who does not fit the image of what we would normally consider for leadership. Who wants a failure to be chosen as our leader? This does not sound like someone whom we would willingly invite to lead us. These stories show us that God does not choose His leaders the same way that the world does. He does not go looking for the perfect person with the perfect background, education, and record. God selects the man or woman that He can empower with the Holy Spirit to become the leader that He wants them to be.

Some of these people may be uneducated. They may be a murderer or adulterer. They may be a liar and a thief. They may even be a slave. They may be major failures in every way imaginable. But as they follow Christ, He empowers them with wisdom, knowledge, and the ability to lead in spite of their weaknesses and failures. God's idea about leadership is completely different from man's idea. Man's thoughts center around such things as power, knowledge, and strength. God's ideas about leadership center around following God and success through the empowerment, leadership, and wisdom that comes from the Holy Spirit that dwells within the believer. Remember what Isaiah said about God in Isaiah 55:8-9, *For my thoughts are not your thoughts, neither are your ways my ways, declares the LORD. For as the heavens are higher than the earth, so are my ways higher than your ways and my thoughts than your thoughts.*

There are two primary reasons for writing this chapter. The first reason is that God often takes the loser, or the failure, and turns him or her into a mighty leader for God. These leaders do not have the right qualities or clean past that we would normally look for in a Christian leader. They may not even look like what we think a leader should look like. They may not have the right skin color or speak with the right accent. These leaders have to depend on God for their authority, their power, their guidance, and their abilities. This shows that true Christian leadership is only available through God empowering us. Contrary to what the world thinks, leadership has little to no dependence on natural attributes and abilities. God can take the worst loser and make him or her into a mighty leader. God looks at and considers the heart, not the outward man. He selects a follower of Christ to be the leader.

The second reason for writing this chapter is meant to be a reminder to the believer. Your past mistakes and failures do not make you. According to man, these things may disqualify you, but they do not disqualify you with God. A careful study of the leaders in the Bible will show this to be true. According to our current standards for pastors and leaders, the apostle Paul would never qualify. Peter with all his lapses and missteps would never be allowed in the pulpit. God has vastly different standards than we do. Remember that while your past mistakes and failures do not define you, they do help you develop into the person that you are right now. If you did not have those past uncomfortable experiences in your life, you would not have developed into the person you currently are with God's help. You would not have learned to be more loving and forgiving of others in their mistakes and failures. In other words, you would not be quite as close to being Christlike as you probably are now. It should go without saying that this does not give you a reason to purposely go out and sin just so that you can gain these experiences.

Leslie Weatherhead has this to say about Jesus and how He often chooses to use the failures in leadership. "That is another strange thing about Jesus. He has the power to see below the surface into the inner depths of the heart. He sees the seeds of the lovely flowers where others see only the ugly brown soil that hides them. It is not so true to say that He loves the unlovable as to say that in every one He sees something loveable." Remember the story of when God sent the prophet Samuel to choose the next king of Israel who would replace King Saul. Samuel kept seeing the big, strong brothers of David and thinking that they had to be who God wanted to be the next king. God had other ideas though. God did not choose the man who looked the part. He did not select the biggest and strongest man for the job. In 1 Samuel 16:7, God told Samuel, *But the LORD said to Samuel, "Do not look on his appearance or on the height of his stature, because I have rejected him. For the LORD sees not as man sees: man looks on the outward appearance, but the LORD looks on the heart."* No matter what we see in the potential leader, God looks into their heart and knows better than we do.

Abraham

We are going to look at Abraham first. Abraham was one of the early great leaders in the Old Testament. He was originally named Abram until God changed his name. Abraham was not a bad person and at first, he does not seem to be a great failure. After all, God chose him to became the father of a great nation. He is lauded in the Bible for his great faith several times. He held on to the promises of God even when it appeared that those promises were impossible. He just did not meet all the qualifications to be a good leader in some ways.

The first thing to notice is that Abraham was a simple shepherd. Like many shepherds in Old Testament times, he was a nomad without a home to call his own. Shepherds often had to travel from place to place searching for fresh water to drink and plenty of grass for their sheep to eat. What seems strange to us is that he was married to his half-sister. God had not given Moses the Law yet so marrying your half-sister was not illegal. It is interesting to note that while God blessed Abraham and Sarah, He later outlawed marrying one's sister. Abraham led his wife and servants from place to place seeking food and water for his sheep, family, and servants. Since he had no land to call his own, he constantly traveled around seeking to provide for his family and flock. When he and the family got into dangerous situations, he was quick to lie to protect his own life. Twice he lied to others about Sarah just being his sister. It is true that she was his half-sister but she was also his wife. He did not seem to worry about these foreign kings taking Sarah into their fold to be their concubine or wife as long as the lie saved his own life. As John Shelby Spong puts it, "Adultery was said to be evil, but both Abraham and Isaac tried to pass their wives off as their sisters, even though this meant having them sexually used by Abimelich, the king of Gerar." Even when he was caught in his lie, Abraham appears to be unapologetic. He just packs up his stuff and moved on to the next location. It seems that Abraham had been a failure to his family. He was quick to protect himself, but he placed his wife in great danger. Some might even say he was a loser for mistreating his wife that way. In these two incidents, he was a great failure as a husband.

Occasionally, Abraham did not display strong leadership skills. When God seems slow to fulfill His promise to make Abraham the father of a great nation, Sarah is getting desperate since her childbearing years are long gone. She knows that it is impossible for her to bear any children. Abraham listens to Sarah's request that he have a child for them through Sarah's servant, Hagar. Abraham and Sarah decided that they would help God out in fulfilling His promise to them. They decided that God needed help since He was taking so long to fulfill His promise to Abraham. They decided that the resulting child would then be the start of the great nation that God had promised them.

Instead of leading Sarah to be patient for God to fulfill His promise in His own time and way, Abraham made Hagar pregnant. They did not understand that God was well able to fulfill His promise to them in His own way and in His own timing. Because of this failure, this son, Ishmael was born into a family situation of jealousy and great strife. Because of this situation that caused much conflict there came many centuries of enmity and strife that still continues today. Once again, Abraham had proven himself to be a failure. Although this birth came about through Sarah's request, Sarah asks Abraham to send Hagar and Ishmael away.

Despite all his failures and disqualifications, God chose Abraham to be a great leader and the father of His chosen people. As often happens, God chooses an apparent failure to become a great leader. God uses people to succeed in spite of their failures and weaknesses. Abraham was 90 years old. Sarah was way past the age of bearing children. Without God's intervention, he could not become the leader and the father of a great nation that God promised to establish through him. Abraham had not established himself in the land that God had promised him and he had no children to get this great nation established. Even worse, it was humanly impossible for him and his wife to have children.

They had tried to bypass God's plans and help God out by doing things their own way. They were too old to even be considering raising children even if it was possible to give birth to them. God specializes in making the impossible a reality.

Why did God choose Abraham? He had nothing going for him that would indicate that he was the best candidate for the position. He was a failure in many ways. He was way past his prime in age to be placed in the position that God was putting him into. God chose him despite all this. Remember, God's ways and His wisdom do not resemble mankind's ways and wisdom in any shape or fashion. The Bible does give us one great attribute of Abraham that God appreciated. Abraham had great faith. He did not seem to have anything else going for him. In so many ways, he was a failure and a loser. Up to this point, he had no children and there was no way for him and Sarah to give birth to any. From the human perspective, he was a failure but God chose him anyway. And God brought about the miracles needed to place this failure as a leader and father to a great nation. Despite his failures, Abraham had great faith in God and His promises and he followed God.

Moses

In some ways, Moses was one of the least likely to be chosen by God as a leader for His chosen people. He was born during the time that the Israelites were slaves in Egypt. Pharaoh became worried about the Israelite population becoming too large and strong. If that happened, they might form an army and rebel against the Egyptians to gain their freedom. The Egyptians depended heavily on the slave labor by the Israelites. To assure that the Israelites remained in slavery, Pharaoh insisted that all of the male Israelite babies must be put to death by the midwives. The female babies were allowed to live in order to become slaves. This would insure that the Israelites did not get too strong and revolt against the Egyptians. Moses was saved from being put to death by his mother's midwife. After being placed into a basket in the river by his mother he was found by Pharaoh's daughter who was bathing. She pulled him out of the water and adopted him into her family. His adoption meant that he was brought up as royalty. He was served the best food and had the best education available. He also had royal servants to wait on him hand and foot. Although he was an Israelite, he was considered an Egyptian prince.

Moses is one of the favorite leaders in the Bible. His whole life is an impossible story. He should not have survived his birth since the midwives were under strict orders to immediately kill all of the Israelite male babies when they were born. The midwife placed herself in great danger of prison or death by ignoring that order from Pharaoh. Moses' mother knew she could not keep him because a crying baby would soon be heard and reported to the authorities. He would then be put to death when he was found to be Israeli male child.

We all know the story of Moses' birth and how his mother weaved a basket, put Moses in it, and placed the basket into the Nile River. Pharaoh's daughter found Moses and adopted him to be her own. Of course, she needed an Israelite wet nurse to nurse him and raise him so Moses' own mother was soon taking care of her son that was supposed to be killed. After he was weaned, Moses was placed in Pharaoh's daughter's home and grew up as her son. The baby that was supposed to die is now living a life of luxury, power, and riches. He had the best of everything as a member of the royal family. He realized that there was something different about himself. He knew that he was an Israelite by birth and adopted into the royal family.

The Israelites were slaves in Egypt and like many slaves in history, the masters treated the slaves terribly. One day after he was grown, Moses went out for a stroll and saw an Egyptian man striking an Israelite. Moses intervened in the situation, and in the process, he killed the Egyptian man. He then buried the Egyptian man in the sand and thought that would be the end of it. The next day Moses was out walking again and came across two Israelites arguing. He intervened again and tried to stop their argument. The men snapped back at him and asked him if he was going to kill one of them like he did the Egyptian the day before. Moses realized that his secret was now out and that he would soon have to answer to the authorities for committing murder and covering it up. If it had been an Israelite that he killed there would have probably been no repercussions. However, this was an Egyptian man that he had killed. There was only one thing left for Moses to do and that was to flee Egypt. He packed his bags and left Egypt as quickly as he could. He fled to the wilderness where he could hide out from the Egyptian authorities.

Once he was in the Wilderness, his royalty, money, privilege, and education were worthless. He quickly went from being a rich prince in Egypt with everything he could ever want into becoming a fugitive who was hiding out from the Egyptian authorities in the Wilderness. He once had everything going for him but now he was a complete failure. He went from being a rich man to a poor man. He could no longer depend on his adopted family for support. He had to find a way to support himself so he became a common shepherd for Jethro. He had no money, land, flocks, or possessions to call his own. For forty long years he wandered around the wilderness looking for enough water and grass to feed the flocks. He was once destined to become an Egyptian leader, but now he was protecting and leading the flocks of sheep that belonged to someone else. Going from royalty to a hired shepherd was a great failure for Moses. He had been destined to be a leader in Egypt and now the only thing he was leading was some sheep.

We all know the story of how God appeared to Moses in the form of a burning bush. Please note that God was now speaking directly to this failure (a murderer and a felon on the run). How many of us would be willing to have a face-to-face conversation with a murderer on the run from the authorities like Moses was? How many of us would be willing to choose that convict on the run to become the spiritual and political leader of a great nation? At this time, he had been roaming the Wilderness for forty years leading a herd of sheep. God took time to come down and talk directly to him. God told Moses that he, Moses, was to lead God's chosen people, the Israelites, out of slavery in Egypt and into freedom in the land that God had promised Abraham.

Moses began to argue with God. He knew that he was not qualified to be a leader but instead was a loser and a failure. For forty years he had been leading sheep around in the wilderness. Moses was no longer used to being around many people. He liked it that way. He did not want the Egyptians to find him and kill him for murdering the Egyptian who had been arguing with an Israelite forty years before this. He was used to talking to sheep, not thousands of people. How does leading many sheep train and prepare you to lead hundreds of thousands of people. Now God wanted him to lead these people out of bondage and into freedom. He knew that the people would never listen or follow him. After all, they had already rejected him. They probably were not sure whose side he was on. He was an Israelite but had been raised as an Egyptian. Who knew where his loyalty truly lay? They had not even seen him in forty years.

To top off all those reasons why Moses did not qualify to be a leader, he told God that he stuttered. Can you imagine that? God wanted this proven loser who stuttered to lead God's chosen people out of slavery and into their own promised land. How was he to lead this great number of people? To make things even worse, how was he going to be able to talk to Pharaoh in order to negotiate the release of these slaves to freedom? How would people follow someone who stutters? Would Pharaoh listen to a murderer who stutters? Would you choose a murderer who stutters to lead your church, state, or nation? This is another proof that God's ways are not ours and that He empowers those who He chooses to be leaders no matter what their past failures, education, and abilities are.

All of the reasons that Moses gave God on why he could not be the leader that God chose him to be were valid ones. He was not qualified at all. God knew all this before He chose Moses to lead the people out of Egypt. God chose him (the murderer, fugitive from justice, and failure) in spite of these valid excuses. As we know, Moses did obey God to go on and became the great leader of the Israelites. He led them out of slavery and to the border of the land that God promised Abraham. This journey took forty years to undertake. Moses was 80 years old when God chose him to lead the Israelites. Surely, Moses was looking to slowing down and retiring rather than taking on so great a responsibility. Despite being such a failure, Moses became known as the greatest leader in the Old Testament. During this time of leading the Israelites to the Promised Land, God spoke to Moses personally many times. Even in the face of great adversity and with his many shortcomings, Moses continued to follow God and became the great leader that God chose him to be.

Even in Moses' successful leadership in leading the Israelites out of Egypt, Moses employed great deception and theft in his success. John Shelby Spong explains, "Bearing false witness was prohibited by the Ten

Commandments, but that is exactly what Moses did in his conversations with Pharaoh. His request was for temporary leave for the people of Israel so that they might hold a religious feast in the wilderness. Later Moses promised that it would be for only three days. Obviously, neither Moses or Pharaoh believed this." It must be noted that at the time of the Exodus, the Ten Commandments and the Torah had not been given. Spong continues, "The Torah said, 'do not steal' but at Moses' command, the Exodus from Egypt was accomplished after the Israelites had robbed the Egyptians of their jewelry, silver, gold, and clothing." It is a strange thought that much of this stolen gold was melted down to make the golden calf idol that Aaron made while Moses was on the mountaintop receiving the Law from God.

Jacob

One of the most unusual stories in the Old Testament is the story of Isaac's twin sons, Esau and Jacob. Esau was the older son and thereby destined to inherit their father's wealth. Esau was a large hairy man who was a hunter. He appears to be what some would call a man's man. He was big and rough and he loved to hunt. In today's world, he would be considered a good old country boy. In contrast, Jacob was a momma's boy. He was smaller and not nearly as hairy. He kept the sheep and stayed close to his mother (Rebecca). Jacob would do whatever his mother told him to do. Esau was their father's favorite while Jacob was their mother's favorite. Because of their big differences, the two boys did not seem to get along well at all.

With Rebecca's encouragement and leadership, Jacob deceived his father into believing that he was Esau in order to obtain the family blessing and birthright from Isaac. Traditionally the oldest son, Esau should have received the blessing and inheritance. Because of the deceit of Rebecca and Jacob, Isaac thought he was giving them to Esau. Once the deception was discovered, Esau demanded that Isaac reissue the blessing and birthright to him, as it was his lawful right. Isaac was disappointed about the deception, but pointed out that once the blessing was issued, it was a done deal and could not be taken back from Jacob.

The blessing and the birthright had been stolen from its rightful heir through dishonesty.

As can be expected, Esau went into a murderous rage and Jacob had to flee from his home in order to escape Esau's wrath. Esau had vowed to kill Jacob for stealing his blessing and inheritance. In order to save Jacob's life, Rebecca sent him to her brother Laban's house to work and to find a wife from Laban's household. There the deceiver will become the deceived.

At Laban's Jacob goes to work tending the flocks for his uncle. Since he had to flee for his life, he has not received what inheritance he is wrongfully due. He falls in love with Laban's younger daughter, Rachel. However, he has no assets for a dowry so Laban agrees to let him work seven years to earn the right to marry Rachel. Jacob loved Rachel greatly so he willingly worked seven hard years to win the right to marry her. After the seven years are up, the marriage takes place. After the wedding, Jacob realizes that he had been deceived by Laban and that he is now married to Rachel's older sister Leah. Laban will only allow Jacob to marry Rachel if he agrees to work seven more years for Laban. He does work the seven extra years and eventually he gets to marry Rachel after completing a total of fourteen long years of labor.

Jacob was a failure in so many ways. This is especially true in his relationships. He deceived his father to receive the blessing due to his brother. He cheated his brother out of his blessing and inheritance. He worked seven long years to marry Rachel, only to find himself deceived and married to Leah. He was married to a woman that he did not want to be married to. He then had to work seven more long and miserable years before he obtained permission to marry Rachel, the one he truly loved and desired. Finally, he had the wife that he loved and wanted. Unfortunately, his family relationships did not get better.

At first, Leah gave Jacob many sons but Rachel remained barren. This caused jealousy and strife between the two wives. Eventually, Jacob's two wives and two concubines gave him 13 sons and one daughter. Finally, Jacob was blessed with a family. However, Jacob still remained a failure in his relationships.

Rachel finally became pregnant and gave birth to Joseph. Since Rachel was the one wife who Jacob truly loved, Joseph soon became

Jacob's favorite son. This caused much hatred and contention between Joseph's brothers and himself. Since it had been obvious that Joseph was the favorite son, his brothers were jealous. They wanted to kill Joseph, but instead, they sold him into slavery. They went back and told Jacob that a wild animal had killed Joseph. Jacob grieved greatly for his son who he thought was dead.

Despite all of the deception and contentious family relationships, God chose Jacob to become a great leader and the start of the great chosen people of God that God had promised Abraham. Jacob overcame his devious ways and he learned to follow God and became a great leader.

King David

Why is King David in this list of failures? King David is considered by many Jews to be the greatest king and leader in Israelite history. The only other Israelite king that had greater success than David was his son Solomon because of his wealth and wisdom. God chose David to become the king of Israel when it became evident that Saul was not being the king that God desired him to be.

A short side note is the story of how King Saul lost God's favor. The Israelite people were demanding God to allow them to have a king just like all of the other nations around them had. The people had rejected the invisible God as their king. They wanted a powerful and visible king in order to display to the other nations that they too had a king. Finally, God relented and gave them the king that they demanded from Him. God sent Samuel to anoint Saul to be the new king of Israel. It helped that Saul looked like a king was supposed to look. He even originally acted like a king is supposed to act. The Israelites were happy with their new king. They were now like the other nations around them. However, King Saul became jealous of David after he killed Goliath and delivered them from the Philistines. Saul was beset with wide mood swings and fits of depression, jealousy, and anger. Saul, who looked and originally acted like a king, quickly became a great failure. He is a leader who fits the image of a decent leader at first and then becomes a failure. This was different from those leaders that God chose who looked like a failure and God turned them into great leaders.

King Saul became jealous of David. David had become popular with the population after he killed Goliath and delivered the Israelite army from that dangerous situation. When King Saul had failed to take care of Goliath, David stepped in and took care of the situation. The people who had once praised King Saul now sang praises about David. David was now the people's hero in place of King Saul. Even worse, Saul's son Jonathan had become best friends with David. Saul had dreamed of Jonathan succeeding him in reigning as king. But King Saul knew that God had rejected Saul as king and had chosen David to be the next king instead of Jonathan. Samuel had already anointed David to become the next king. King Saul's jealousy and hatred caused him to go into a rage and attempt to kill David multiple times.

David, who had been anointed to be the next king escaped and was now on the run and hiding out from King Saul and his army. The selected and anointed heir to the kingdom was now sleeping in caves and hiding from King Saul and his army. Jonathan was forced to sneak out of the palace to meet his best friend David. David was a failure at this point through no fault of his own. It did not look like it would ever be possible for David to become the king. Even staying alive seemed to be impossible with the king's army searching for him everywhere. The shepherd boy was on the run from the king just as another shepherd, Moses, had been on the run from the Egyptian pharaoh. Despite the odds being against him ever reigning as king, David eventually became the second king of Israel.

David had many successes as king. He became known as Israel's greatest king. His army had many successes in battles. Even after becoming the king, King David showed his humanity and had major failures. Usually with royalty there comes a lot of pomp and fancy rituals. The king is expected to wear purple robes and wear a crown with many jewels in it while sitting on a golden throne. Royalty is supposed to act like royalty, with decorum, not act like the common folks. Once David got so excited while worshiping God that he took off his clothes and danced before the altar. The king's wife was not pleased at all. She loved the trappings and benefits of being royalty and expected her husband to act like royalty is supposed to act.

King David's greatest failure came with his affair with Bathsheba. He observed her bathing on the roof of her house nearby. David was smitten with her great beauty. He called for her to be brought to him and then he seduced her. Who could say no to the king? So King David had an affair with her. We all know the story that, as a result of the affair, Bathsheba becomes pregnant with David's baby. Now King David had a major problem. His sin was about to be discovered. Bathsheba's husband was in the army and he was away at the war. There is no way that he could be the father of Bathsheba's baby. Instead of admitting to his failure, he decided to cover it up. Since Bathsheba's husband was off fighting in the war, David had the general put Uriah in the middle of the heaviest fighting. David then had the general withdraw the rest of the troops from where Uriah was at so that he would be killed by the enemy. Since Bathsheba was now a widow, King David was now free to marry her and be the father to her baby. David paid heavily for this failure.

The once successful king was now an adulterer and a murderer. The previously successful leader had become a failure. He had yielded to temptation and paid the consequences in the long run. Although he remained king, he had to deal with many problems from his rebellious children. Despite his failures, the Bible states that David had a heart after God's heart. Even with his failures, King David was aware of his many weaknesses and failures. He was sorrowful and repented of his sins. It makes one wonder how an imperfect man like King David could be a man after God's heart and used in God's work?

Even from the start David seemed to be an unlikely choice to become the king. Before David became the king, Saul was the king. God had selected him after the people of Israel had repeatedly demanded from God a king. They wanted to be like the nations around them who were ruled by a king. King Saul was a failure in many ways. He was beset by deep depression and anger. He tried to kill David several times. It became obvious that Saul needed to be replaced by a new king. Samuel came to King Saul and gave him a message from God. 1 Samuel 13:14-15, *And Samuel said to Saul, "You have done foolishly. You have not kept the command of the Lord your God, with which he commanded you. For then the Lord would have established your kingdom over Israel forever. But now your kingdom shall not continue. The Lord has sought out a man after his own heart, and the Lord has commanded him to be prince over his people, because you have not kept what the Lord commanded you."* What a blow to King Saul's ego that must have been for God to have sent the prophet with such a strong message to the sitting king. He now knows that he is to be replaced by someone who is a man after God's own heart.

Centuries later, Paul refers to this incident in a sermon he is preaching in the synagogue. Again the emphasis is on the fact that King David, while being an imperfect person, was a man after God's heart. Acts 13:21-22, *Then they asked for a king, and God gave them Saul the son of Kish, a man of the tribe of Benjamin, for forty years. And when he had removed him, he raised up David to be their king, of whom he testified and said, 'I have found in David the son of Jesse a man after my heart, who will do all my will.'*

We humans tend to consider what we can see and observe in choosing our leaders. God does things quite differently. God looks in the person's heart. He does see the imperfections and the failures in that person but He also sees what is truly in their hearts. Remember the story of when Samuel went to see Jesse. God had told Samuel that one of Jesse's sons was to be the next king in replacement of King Saul. As Samuel met each son, he thought to himself that surely this is the one. He saw the strength and the good looks of each son. These sons all met Samuel's idea of a good leader. God had other thoughts though. 1 Samuel 16:6-7, *When they came, he looked on Eliab and thought, "Surely the Lords anointed is before him." But the LORD said to Samuel, "Do not look on his appearance or on the height of his stature, because I have rejected him. For the Lord sees not as man sees: man looks on the outward appearance, but the Lord looks on the heart."* Often God chooses the person to lead that no one else would choose because He sees what is in the heart. Too often, we tend to choose leaders like Samuel wanted to do - on their appearance and strengths.

Joseph of the Old Testament

Joseph sticks out in the Old Testament as someone who became a leader despite the unbelievable odds against him. These obstacles were not due to his own faults or actions. In some ways, he is one of the most fun leaders to write about. Here we have a young lad whose own brothers were so jealous of him that they seriously considered killing him. Fortunately, one of the brothers was able to talk the rest of the brothers out of killing him. Instead of killing him, they sold him into slavery to some traveling traders. Somehow, God was able to take this lowly slave and turn him into the second most powerful man in Egypt after Pharaoh. And because of this, this one-time slave was able to be instrumental in rescuing the Israelites during a time of a great drought. By all rights, he should not have been chosen to be a leader in the first place. People just do not move from being a slave to becoming the second most powerful person in the country. In many ways, he became one of the greatest leaders in the history of the Israelites.

Although we have been mostly discussing people who became godly leaders after being failures in many ways, Joseph is a different story from the rest of them. His failures were mostly not the result of any wrong-doing that he did, but were rather from evil done to him because of the jealousy of his brothers. Without God's intervention, these failures should have been enough to prevent him from becoming any type of leader. While we now consider Joseph to have been a great leader in the history of the Israelites, he originally did not appear to be a likely candidate for good leadership. John Shelby Spong says this about Joseph, "Joseph was an arrogant and spoiled favorite son upon whom his father heaped lavish gifts and special favor,"

Joseph was the twelfth son in the family. His parents were Jacob and Rachel. When the story begins, he was the youngest son in the family. At that time, he was Jacob's favorite son. His older brothers became very jealous of him due to Joseph being the favorite son. To make things even worse, Joseph had several dreams that indicated that he would rule over his brothers. Needless to say, this did not sit well with his brothers at all. Young Joseph seems to be a bit naive. He could not understand why his brothers hated him so much or why his dreams upset the brothers so badly. If he had understood this better, he would probably have kept his dreams to himself.

The older brothers were in charge of tending the sheep for the family. They had traveled to a distant land in order to find better grass and water for the sheep. Jacob became concerned about them as they had been gone for quite a while. So Jacob sent Joseph out on a mission to find his brothers and to check on them to make sure they were okay. Eventually, Joseph was able to find where his brothers had gone and traveled to where they were with the sheep.

The jealous brothers saw him coming from a distance. Several brothers abhorred him enough that they wanted to kill him. They were jealous of the extra attention Jacob gave to Joseph. They decided to kill him and tell their father that a wild animal had attacked and killed him. They decided that they were going to kill a goat and splatter its blood on Joseph's beloved multi-colored coat that Jacob had given him. They would then take the coat to Jacob in order to convince him that Joseph had been killed by a wild animal. Fortunately, cooler heads were able to prevail. Reuben (the oldest brother) suggested that instead of killing him, they would just throw him into a cistern. He had thought that he would come back later without his other brothers and rescue Joseph.

After tossing Joseph into the cistern, the brothers saw a camel caravan traveling through on its way to Egypt. They agreed to sell Joseph to the traders so that they could sell him into slavery. The brothers thought that their problems were all taken care of then. Their father's favorite son was out of their hair and he could no longer taunt them with his wild dreams about being over them. After selling him to the caravan, the brothers took Joseph's coat and ripped it and covered it with a goat's blood. They took the ripped coat and returned it to Jacob claiming that Joseph must have been killed by a wild animal in the wilderness. Jacob was heartbroken that his favorite son Joseph was now presumed dead. Joseph was at that time the only child of Jacob and his favorite wife. What no one could foresee was that God has a plan in the middle of trouble and trials. God had a purpose in this troublesome story and would provide a way to turn it into something different than anyone expected.

Joseph had to be aware that he was now in major trouble. He was sold in bondage and now owned by the slave traders. We know the story of how the traders traveled to Egypt and sold Joseph to Potiphar, who was the captain of the guard for Pharaoh. Joseph did exactly the opposite of what most people would have done in that situation. He went from being the favored and pampered son to a lowly slave. Instead of moping around and acting like a spoiled brat, Joseph decided to make the best of his situation. He might be a lowly slave but he would work hard to become a good slave. He proved himself to be dependable and completely trustworthy. Because of this, he eventually became Potiphar's personal servant and he later was placed in charge of Potiphar's whole household.

Even though Joseph had worked his way up to a higher level than a slave could even imagine, more trouble was about to appear in his future. For some reason, Potiphar's wife desired Joseph and she decided that she had to have him so she tried to seduce him. With his integrity, Joseph refused her efforts. He knew that he could not do that to Potiphar. Potiphar's wife was so furious with his refusal that she tore her gown and screamed for help. She then accused Joseph of attempting to rape her. Now Joseph was in big trouble again despite his claims of innocence. He was thrown into jail. A death sentence would almost certainly be the next step. There was no way out for the innocent man. He was sure that he was doomed to die a horrible and painful death.

We all know the story about Joseph interpreting the dreams of several other prisoners. This eventually led to his release from jail. This release only occurred after Pharaoh had a strange dream that greatly worried him. Pharaoh believed in dreams and was concerned about the meaning of this dream. None of his advisors and consultants could tell him what the dream meant. Joseph was able to interpret the dream and this pleased Pharaoh. Pharaoh had him released from prison and restored him to freedom. He was now elevated to the second in command of all of Egypt under Pharaoh. This was quite a jump from a lowly prisoner who was looking at getting the death penalty. The impossible had occurred again. God was working behind the scenes to place Joseph in the position that He wanted him in.

The story continues about how Joseph's leadership provided food for the Egyptians and the Israelites during a horrible seven-year drought and saved them from certain starvation. While other nations around them were starving to death, these two countries were able to survive with plenty of food that they had stored up under Joseph's leadership. The Israelites were saved from starvation through these strange incidents that led Joseph from being a failure to becoming a great leader.

The Apostle Paul

Paul's story is a little different from the rest of these stories. In the eyes of man and the religious leaders (the Pharisees) of that day, he had become a great success. The Pharisees loved Saul (his original name) for his zeal and energy toward stamping out this new sect of the followers of Jesus Christ. They loved his knowledge of and his devotion to the Law. Although he originally believed that he was doing great work for God, he came to realize that all of his successes were harming God's work and people. Paul became one of the greatest leaders mentioned in the New Testament. Most, if not all, of you, will remember the story of his conversion. Paul is included here for one reason. Even though he originally was mostly considered a success, that supposed success was a major failure spiritually.

Saul (Paul's original name) was quite a religious success. He was a well-educated Pharisee. He ardently followed every one of their rules. He thought that he was the ultimate Pharisee. As a Pharisee, he hated Jesus Christ and all of His followers. Saul decided that he was going to do everything he could to help wipe out this 'heretical' cult of Christians. He obtained permission from the High Priest to arrest any believers that he found and bind them and take them to Jerusalem for trial. He was extremely successful in this and was able to arrest many Christians and take them to Jerusalem to be imprisoned or put to death. Many early believers lost their lives because of Saul's efforts.

By the Pharisee's standards Paul was originally a success. However, this success was a failure at the same time although he did not realize it. Saul showed so many great leadership skills while succeeding in all of the wrong things. His successes were in his efforts against God. He truly believed that he was doing all of these things for God but he later learned that he was so wrong. He was actually fighting against God and His will.

An example of successful leadership that is a failure might be the leader of a gang. This gang has gone around robbing many banks and stores. They have stolen millions of dollars. They have been in several shootouts with the police. They may have even killed a couple of people who resisted them in their robberies. Now this gang leader has been successful. His gang has been successful in stealing millions of dollars. He has somehow been able to keep the gang together and keep these violent criminals in line and working together for their common goals. In that one sense he could be considered a very successful leader. He has shown great leadership skills and methods that work well for that gang. This successful leader is at the same time a failure legally and morally.

This same idea is true for Saul/Paul. The High Priest considered him to be a great leader. The High Priest probably heaped great praise on Saul/Paul. However, that leadership was misguided and misdirected. Just like the hypothetical gang leader we mentioned, Saul/Paul in his early life cannot be considered to be a success. He was a failure and did much harm to the early church.

Peter the Apostle

Peter was another failure who God changed to make him a great leader in the early church. Peter, like the other disciples, was a Galilean. The Pharisees and others seem to consider Galileans to be like the modern-day rednecks. They were considered unlearned, uncouth, unclean nobodies who talked with a funny accent. Who was this redneck to dare to try to preach to a seminary-trained Pharisee and leader of the Jewish religion? After all, in their eyes, no one on that day was more righteous, knowledgeable, and perfect than a Pharisee.

We know that Peter was a simple fisherman. As you know, generally speaking, fishermen are not known for being the best-educated people around. They have hard, smelly, and dirty jobs. They are using their hands and muscles. They do not need to be highly educated. Simple math skills along with maybe some reading and writing, was enough for them to do their jobs. A fisherman, while smart in his or her way, could afford to be simple and unsophisticated. Peter's concerns were about finding and hauling in the fish. His Galilean ways come through in many different ways. He was quick to anger. He often spoke without thinking. He was rough around the edges like most fishermen. He probably smelled like fish. He spoke roughly and acted rough. Peter was no great intellectual by any stretch of the imagination. As it was recorded in the New Testament, he often spoke without thinking things through first. He was quick in responding with his initial thoughts. Those thoughts and words often got him in trouble with Jesus

What happened to this uncouth man who was quick to state his mind even if it was often the wrong thing to say? Despite his failings, Peter loved Jesus Christ and was devoted to Him, even after His death. Peter was among the others in prayer in the Upper Room on the Day of Pentecost. Like a mighty wind, the Holy Spirit blew into the room and filled each of them with the Holy Spirit. Immediately, Peter and the others were filled with power and began to speak in other tongues. We know the story of how the people outside the room heard the great noise and wondered what was happening. Then the unexpected happened. The awkward and unsophisticated Peter stood up and began preaching with great power and knowledge. He spoke with wisdom. Peter had been completely changed by the power of the Holy Spirit. After that, Peter became one of the greatest leaders of the Early Church. He went about preaching and doing many miracles. He became a powerful evangelist and one of the most influential leaders of the early church. We have no record of Peter ever speaking out of turn again after the Day of Pentecost. He had completely changed.

The Rednecks of the Bible

Wait a minute! You are probably saying, "Rednecks did not exist in the Bible times!" And you would be correct in a way. Consider that maybe rednecks are mentioned in the New Testaments without using the word *redneck*. Who exactly are these rednecks? The answer is Peter and the other disciples. These were the twelve men chosen by Jesus to become His closest followers and the first leaders of the early church. Each of these men was individually chosen by Christ and He personally told them to follow Him.

One might ask why Jesus chose these particular twelve men to be His followers and the leaders of the Early Church. It might be worth briefly looking at this question. The twelve men He chose were nothing special on the surface. These were the last men that you would choose to be Christian leaders, pastors, missionaries, or evangelists. They had never been to a Bible college or seminary. These men were not considered to be intellectuals by any stretch of the imagination. They were not even considered to be qualified to be the religious leaders of their time. They were looked at by the Pharisees and Sadducees to be unlearned and uncouth. Their Galilean accent gave them away. They even dressed differently from the rest of the population. They would have laughed if someone told them that they would soon be leaders in the greatest revival that the world has ever seen and become the first leaders of the church. These men were early version rednecks. A number of them were rough fishermen. They worked with their hands, not their minds.

Remember the story of the Upper Room on the Day of Pentecost after Jesus returned to heaven. The disciples along with other believers were gathered together in the Upper Room as Christ had instructed them to do. The room was suddenly filled with a mighty wind and the believers were filled with the Holy Spirit and began speaking in tongues and worshipping God. The noise filled the room and then filled the streets around the house. The streets were filled with devout Jewish people from all over the world. They were startled to hear these believers speaking in their native languages. Acts 2:7 says, *"And they were amazed and wondered, saying, "Are not all these who are speaking Galileans?"*

These Galileans, like modern-day rednecks, were known for their strange accents and clothing style. Consider that this occurred during a time when it was common to speak and understand several languages. Aramaic was the language of the common Jewish people. The Greek influence had been great during this time so many people spoke Greek. Hebrew was the language of the Torah (Old Testament) of the Jewish religion. Israel was ruled at this time by the Romans who spoke Latin. So speaking multiple languages was common to allow communication to take place between people from different cultures. The people in the street could not believe that common Galileans (the rednecks) were smart enough and educated enough to speak and understand multiple languages. They were considered to be unintelligent, uneducated, and uncouth individuals. They were low-class people who were not considered to be worthy of any consideration by the other Jews. Some people even considered them to be as low-class as the Samaritans, who were considered to be half-breeds and heretics. The Galileans were considered to be lower-class, uneducated people with lower intelligence much like today's rednecks are thought of.

Jesus chose these twelve men who were considered to be unimportant nobodies to be the first leaders of His church. Not only that, they were the primary ones who were instrumental in the spreading of the Gospel message throughout the known world. These same early rednecks were also responsible for writing parts of the New Testament.

Peter and the other disciples were not initially successful leaders. They fumbled their way through everything they did while traveling with Jesus. They tended to do the wrong things and say the wrong words. It was only after they were filled with the Holy Spirit in the Upper Room that they were filled with wisdom and power and became the leaders and missionaries that Christ expected them to become. At times they displayed their arrogance, ignorance, and anger.

The point here is that the successful leaders of the early church were not successful at all when they were operating within their own power, knowledge, and wisdom. It was only after they were filled with the Holy Spirit and His power that they were successful. Also note that while speaking in tongues was an important part of being filled with the Holy Spirit, it was not the speaking in tongues that made them successful. The speaking in tongues drew the crowd in the streets that first day of the church, but it was the power and leading of the Spirit within them that made them successful. By the same token, Christian leaders today cannot be truly successful in their own power, knowledge, education, or wisdom. They can only truly become successful in leading through the power, knowledge, and wisdom of the Holy Spirit within them! The disciples went from being lowly rednecks (Galileans) to powerful and successful leaders of the Early Church. They were the first administrators, pastors, missionaries, and evangelists of the church.

John (the Apostle)

The apostle John is considered separately from the other apostles. We do not know much about John's youth or his failures. We do know that Jesus chose him to be one of the twelve. We know that John's mother went to Jesus and asked him to select John and his brother to sit on Jesus' sides - one on the right and one on the left. They thought that Jesus, as the Messiah, was going to throw out the Romans and establish His kingdom on earth shortly. She wanted to make sure that her two sons were going to be ruling the kingdom on earth from the sides of Jesus' throne. We can forgive her not fully understanding the nature of Jesus's purpose and for wanting to make sure her sons were recognized and honored for their efforts. John and his brother did not dare to approach Jesus directly to request this. They sent their mother to ask Jesus. After all, John was called the disciple that Jesus loved, so surely he would be chosen to rule alongside Jesus.

From this failure, John went on to become a major leader in the Early Church. He wrote one of the four gospels about Jesus. He wrote three epistles that are included in the New Testament. He also wrote the book of Revelation. He went from being the weak disciple that Jesus loves to being the powerful Apostle of Love who wrote five books of the New Testament.

Conclusion

It is obvious from studying these and other leaders in the Bible that God does not always select the best looking, smartest, strongest, wisest, or best educated to be His leaders. He often took the most improbable and seemingly worst choices to lead. He wanted leaders who followed Him and depended on Him for their wisdom, knowledge, and strength. God often took the failures and made them into the greatest leaders on earth. The purpose of this chapter is not to condemn these leaders in their failures or to play down their importance. The point is that God can and often does use sinful, weak, simple, uneducated failures to do His work. God forgives them of their failures and empowers them with the Holy Spirit to be the leaders that He wants them to be. It is as if God wishes the leaders to recognize and acknowledge that everything they accomplish is strictly through the work of the Holy Spirit in their lives, not through their own power, intelligence, power, and strength.

As Preston Sprinkle says about the Old Testament leaders, "Most of the characters in the Old Testament are not good examples to follow. Abraham was a liar, Jacob was a cheater, Moses was a tongue-tied murderer, Esther broke more commandments than she kept and never ever mentioned God, and Samson was a self-centered, vengeful porn star enslaved to lust and bloodshed." Not only does this show that God often chooses failures and losers, but that it is Jesus who we need to be following. Sprinkle goes on to state, "The Bible is filled with social outcasts, slaves, prostitutes, and thugs - all of whose lives are delightfully wrecked by a gracious Creator who enjoys wrecking undelightful people. God isn't just able to use messed-up sinners to accomplish His plan. He actually prefers to. 'God chose what is low and despised in the world...so that no human being might boast in the presence of God' (1 Cor 1:28-29)." Who knows? God even might wish to use imperfect you and me.

Sprinkle also has this to say this about the leaders in the New Testament, "God aggressively and delightfully values and uses thugs and misfits to build His glorious kingdom: abrasive, thick-headed people like Peter, hotheaded racists like James and John, violent brawlers and extortionists like Simon and Matthew, and mentally deranged bag ladies like Mary Magdalene. He doesn't give them a bowl of soup and shuffle them out of the church. He gives them responsibility - the hallmark of genuine value - and trusts in the God who uses the weak to shame the strong." Those failures and losers became the great leaders of the early church and were also successful in spreading the gospel message around the known world.

- 5 -

Humility

THIS book discusses many important but difficult subjects relating to Christian leadership. Many people may consider humility to be the most difficult attribute (of being a follower of Christ) to achieve. Humility is something that does not come naturally to human beings. It is contrary to our innate pride and ego. Humility is difficult to achieve for many leaders. It is hard to be humble when you are successful in your ministry. This is even more pronounced when other people, including your overseers, brag about your successes. You may even be considered a success by other Christian leaders and ministers. You may entertain requests to share your ministry methods and knowledge on leadership to others. Jesus made it plain that pride, arrogance, and ego are detrimental to successful Christian leadership. That sounds like a contradiction to some people, but being a follower of Jesus Christ involves humility, not pride. To many people, pride is a natural outcome from success.

Humility is one of the most difficult subjects to write about. For the first thing, if you know a lot about the subject and are writing a book about humility to teach others, it is difficult to not come across as being arrogant and a know-it-all. Arrogance has nothing at all to do with humility. How do you write with authority on a subject as an expert and not sound like a know-it-all? If you are not an expert on the subject, why are you even writing about it? Who are you to try to teach others about humility? This makes it a hard subject to discuss while remaining humble.

This author does not claim to be an expert on humility. The purpose of this chapter is to introduce the subject and to allow us all to work on obtaining biblical humility while forsaking pride. This is such a difficult subject to discuss in some ways. How do you come across as an expert on humility? The answer is that you cannot. It is impossible to do so. Once you make that claim, it comes across as being prideful. If you claim to know everything there is to know about humility, then you are no longer humble. The second thought is that if you are truly the most humble person in the world then you have reason to be proud about being so humble. At that point, you are proud of your humility and you are no longer truly humble. Your pride and humility are always in a battle with each other. Can we stand on the rooftop and shout, "I'm humble and proud of it?"

Leaders are unwittingly caught up by pride and arrogance way too often. Pride is a natural outcome of being the leader and being the one in charge of others. Humans tend to be naturally egotistical and prideful. The leader has often been chosen to lead others because of their hard work, education, and great leadership skills. He or she has often been highly trained and educated in the latest leadership methods. It is considered something to be proud of to be chosen over one's peers to lead others. It would be natural to have some pride in thinking that you are better than the others. All of the followers are looking to the leader for answers and guidance.

There is a major spiritual problem with this. Arrogance is never pretty in the first place. Arrogance in leadership leads to some pretty horrible behavior and usually leads to a contentious and uncomfortable environment. This environment can lead to much strife and a high employee (or church member) turnover rate. This causes both an uncomfortable workplace and also costs money due to the constant hiring and training of employees. Nobody wants to work or worship in this type of hostile environment.

What exactly is humility? We probably think of it as the opposite of pride. That is not a horrible way to describe humility but Andrew Murray describes it in a better way. "Humility, the place of entire dependence upon God, is from the very nature of things the first duty and the highest virtue of His creatures. And so pride - the loss of humility - is the root of every sin and evil." Murray relates humility to the holiness of God. This is an unusual take on the subject of holiness. Many churches have used man made rules to be their standard for holiness. Just as God called us to be holy, He called us to be humble in the same way that Jesus Christ was humble. Murray states that this call to humility has largely been overlooked by the church through the centuries because the church has not understood the nature and importance of humility. He goes on to say that the believer must confess and deplore pride as it is satanic.

Christian leaders are to follow Christ. There should not be any question about that. Christian leaders should model their lives and leadership after Christ. Christian leaders must study His life and leadership as it is portrayed in the New Testament. The New Testament was not written as a leadership book. At the same time, it has a lot to say about leadership. Jesus does have some things to say about leadership in His teachings.

Jesus Christ was both God and man. If there was ever a man on earth that had every reason to be proud of him self, it was Jesus. He was both God and man. He was the most unique person to ever live on earth. He was the Creator, but He lowered Himself to become a man (the created). As God, He had the ability and power to call down 10,000 angels to do His bidding. He had power over sickness, death, and even the weather. He did many miracles such as healing the sick and raising the dead. There has never been anyone else like Him. So if anyone in the world ever had the right to be proud, it was Jesus. Instead of being prideful, Jesus always displayed humility.

The word humble does not appear in the Bible at all. If we study what the Bible tells us about Jesus, we can see that He never displayed pride or arrogance. In contrast, he always displayed love and humility. He also taught humility to His disciples. This is especially true even in His leadership style. He could have demanded that His disciples bow down and worship Him as the Son of God. He could have demanded that they obey His every wish and command. Even though He was the Son of God, He did not insist on being treated as the Son of God. He wished to be treated as the Son of Man. He taught and displayed humility even though He was due all worship and praise as the Son of God.

One question that you may ask is, "How do we move away from sinful pride and into the holiness of humility?" There are no three or four step instructions available on how to do this. We must first recognize that pride is sinful and that Christ calls us to be humble. Murray relates two major truths about this subject. The first one is, "External teaching and personal effort are powerless to conquer pride or create the meek and lowly heart in a person." The second truth is "That it is only by the indwelling of Christ in His divine humility that we can become truly humble." Did you catch that? We do not have the power or ability within ourselves to move from pride to humility. We cannot make that change in ourselves any more than we can earn our salvation. It is only through the power of the Holy Spirit dwelling within us that we can do this. It is only through dying to one's self daily and walking and living in the Spirit that true humility is possible at all. As Galatians 5:25-26 says, *"If we live by the Spirit, let us also keep in step with the Spirit. Let us not become conceited, provoking one another, envying one another."*

Jesus taught us much about humility in the Beatitudes. The way of serving and worshiping that Jesus taught us was in great contrast to the way the Pharisees and the religious people of that day. Pride was a major part of the religion practiced by the Sadducees and the Pharisees. Their false religion involved following man-made rules in order to please God. In their thinking, you could be proud of just how closely you followed these rules. Humility and love had nothing to do with their way of living or worshipping God. Jesus wants us to worship in love and humility. He makes it clear that all of our rewards and recognition will be in heaven not here on earth.

Matthew 6:1-6, *"Beware of practicing your righteousness before other people to be seen by them, for then you will have no reward from your Father who is in heaven. "Thus, when you give to the needy, sound no trumpet before you, as the hypocrites do in the synagogues and the streets, that they may be praised by others. Truly, I say to you, they have received their reward. But when you give to the needy, do not let your left hand know what your right hand is doing, so that your giving may be in secret. And your Father who sees in secret will reward you. "And when you pray, you must not be like the hypocrites. For they love to stand and pray in the synagogues and at the street corners, so that they may be seen by others. Truly, I say to you, they have received their reward. But when you pray, go into your room and shut the door and pray to your Father who is in secret. And your Father who sees in secret will reward you.*

Matthew 18:1-4: *At that time the disciples came to Jesus, saying, "Who is the greatest in the kingdom of heaven?" And calling to him a child, he put him in the midst of them and said, "Truly, I say to you, unless you turn and become like children, you will never enter the kingdom of heaven. Whoever humbles himself like this child is the greatest in the kingdom of heaven. "Whoever receives one such child in my name receives me, but whoever causes one of these little ones who believe in me to sin, it would be better for him to have a great millstone fastened around his neck and to be drowned in the depth of the sea.*

We have all heard these verses read in Sunday School and church to in order to show us how much Jesus loves the little children. Jesus does loves and care for the children. He mentions great punishment awaits those who cause little ones to sin. We use these verses to show that the church is to love the little children and to reach out to them. Reaching out to children must indeed be a major goal of the church.

The purpose in using these verses here is to point out a different understanding. Read verse three by itself next. It says, *"and said, "Truly, I say to you, unless you turn and become like children, you will never enter the kingdom of heaven."* That is an amazing thought! If we wish to enter the Kingdom of Heaven, we must become like children. We have all heard it preached many times that this is talking about the simple faith of a child. Just as a child has simple faith in his or her parents, we must have that same simple faith in our heavenly Father. This simple truth is important. Believing in Jesus is not a complicated process. It involves simple childlike faith.

Simple faith is an important aspect of these verses. We have been overlooking another truth in these verses though. As many times as we have read these verses, how many times have we overlooked what verse four says? *"Whoever humbles himself like this child is the greatest in the kingdom of heaven."* Did you catch it this time? We are not only to love and reach out to the children and have the simple faith of a child, but we are to also have the humility of a little child.

As adults, we have learned many lessons and experienced many things. We are aware of what we have learned through schooling and many different experiences. We adults tend to gain some pride and arrogance because we know some things that others may not know and have experienced things that others have not. However, Jesus plainly said that we must have the humility of a small child. Think of a small child that trusts the adults around them to love them, to provide them with the things they need in life, to teach them what they need to know, and to guide them through making good decisions in life.

How we can leave our pride and ego behind and in the process obtain the humility of a small child? Jesus said that is what we must do though. Here a few suggestions that may help us get from here to there. Of course, this process must be accompanied by much prayer and relying on the Holy Spirit working within us.

We have to understand that all of our knowledge, training, and experience is worth nothing in comparison to the wisdom and teaching of Jesus Christ. Remember what Paul said in 1 Corinthians 1:25, *"For the foolishness of God is wiser than men, and the weaknesses of God is stronger than men.* When we come to understand this truth then we will recognize that we must not and cannot rely on our own knowledge, experience, and training. We must rely on the wisdom of God to guide us in leading others. It is only then that we can begin to lose some of our pride and ego and thereby gain some of the humility that Christ asks from us. When we rely solely on our own wisdom, it is like we are trying to say that we are smarter and wiser than God. At the same time, it is important not to throw out all of our knowledge and experiences. We must learn how to use those things joined with the wisdom of God to lead correctly.

Rabbi or Servant

Matthew 23:8-12, *Then Jesus said to the crowds and his disciples, "The scribes and the Pharisees sit on Moses' seat, so do and observe whatever they tell you, but not the works they do. For they preach but do not practice. They tie up heavy burdens, hard to bear, and lay them on people's shoulders, but they are not willing to move them with their fingers. They do all their deeds to be seen by others. For they make their phylacteries broad and their fringes long, and they love the place of honor at feasts and the best seats in the synagogues and greetings in the marketplaces and being called rabbi by others. But you are not to be called rabbi, for you have one teacher, and you are all brothers. And call no man your father on earth, for you have one Father, who is in heaven. Neither be called instructors, for you have one instructor, the Christ. The greatest among you shall be your servant. Whoever exalts himself will be humbled, and whoever humbles himself will be exalted.*

This Scripture is directed toward the disciples (the then future leaders of the Early Church). Jesus makes sure that they understand that pride and arrogance have no place among Christian leaders. Fancy titles, honors, and recognitions are not to be desired or sought after. In today's world it is common for leaders to demand and expect honor and praise just as the Pharisees and scribes did. This is even true in the church world today. All honor is to be given to God, not His servants.

Jealousy and Self-Ambition

James 3:13-18. These verses are included here without any commentary. The word humility is not used in these verses but the hope is that you carefully read and think about these verses.

Who is wise and understanding among you? By his good conduct let him show his works in the meekness of wisdom. But if you have bitter jealousy and selfish ambition in your hearts, do not boast and be false to the truth. This is not the wisdom that comes down from above but is earthly, unspiritual, and demonic. For where jealousy and selfish ambition exist, there will be disorder and every vile practice. But the wisdom from above is first pure, then peaceable, gentle, open to reason, full of mercy and good fruits, impartial and sincere. And a harvest of righteousness is sown in peace by those who make peace.

Humble Yourself

James 4:6, 10, *But he gives more grace. Therefore it says, "God opposes the proud but gives grace to the humble...Humble yourselves before the Lord, and he will exalt you".* These are two short and simple verses in James. God opposes the proud but gives grace to the humble. We have to learn how to humble ourselves before God. We must recognize that all of our strength, knowledge, abilities, and wisdom come only from Him. We do not accomplish anything through our own strength and wisdom.

Simon Peter is probably the one disciple that we see the greatest change happen in after the Upper Room. He starts out being a fumbling and at times arrogant disciple. He changes into a great leader and minister of the Gospel. He agrees with James says above as he writes to the church leaders in 1 Peter 5:1-7:

So I exhort the elders among you, as a fellow elder and a witness of the sufferings of Christ, as well as a partaker in the glory that is going to be revealed: shepherd the flock of God that is among you, exercising oversight, not under compulsion, but willingly, as God would have you; not for shameful gain, but eagerly; not domineering over those in your charge, but being examples to the flock. And when the chief Shepherd appears, you will receive the unfading crown of glory. Likewise, you who are younger, be subject to the elders. Clothe yourselves, all of you, with humility toward one another, for "God opposes the proud but gives grace to the humble." Humble yourselves, therefore, under the mighty hand of God so that at the proper time he may exalt you, casting all your anxieties on him, because he cares for you.

Peter fully understood that Christian leadership is a completely different experience from leadership in the world. There is little resemblance between the two. Peter states that we are not only to be humble but that we are to clothe ourselves in humility. Once again we are reminded that God opposes the proud but gives grace to the humble. We are required to humble ourselves under the hand of God. His key words in describing Christian leadership are shepherding, not domineering, being an example, and clothing oneself in humility. God gives grace to and will reward the humble.

In 1 Peter 4:7-11, Peter does not directly mention humility but he is clearly talking about humility. What he is saying for us to do is impossible without love and true humility. *The end of all things is at hand; therefore be self-controlled and sober-minded for the sake of your prayers. Above all, keep loving one another earnestly, since love covers a multitude of sins. Show hospitality to one another without grumbling. As each has received a gift, use it to serve one another, as good stewards of God's varied grace: whoever speaks, as one who speaks oracles of God; whoever serves, as one who serves by the strength that God supplies—so that in everything God may be glorified through Jesus Christ. To him belong glory and dominion forever and ever. Amen.*

Walk in a Worthy Manner

Ephesians 4:1-3, *I therefore, a prisoner for the Lord, urge you to walk in a manner worthy of the calling to which you have been called, with all humility and gentleness, with patience, bearing with one another in love, eager to maintain the unity of the Spirit in the bond of peace.*

Paul is talking to all believers here, not just the leaders. He is not beating about the bush here. He is speaking plainly about a need for all believers. It is important to note that Paul said that we are to walk worth to our calling. This is what is expected of us as followers of Christ. We are to walk in humility. Then we are to walk in gentleness and patience. When you think about it, humility, gentleness, and patience are intertwined and each of those three things depends on the others. This reminds us of walking with the Fruit of the Spirit evident in our lives, doesn't it? It sure does not sound much like the world's idea of leadership. So, let us say it again, Christian leaders are to walk in humility, gentleness, and patience. Paul states that these things are necessary for us to be worthy of our calling.

Unity, Love, and Humility

Philippians 2:1-11, *So if there is any encouragement in Christ, any comfort from love, any participation in the Spirit, any affection and sympathy, complete my joy by being of the same mind, having the same love, being in full accord and of one mind. Do nothing from selfish ambition or conceit, but in humility count others more significant than yourselves. Let each of you look not only to his own interests but also to the interests of others. Have this mind among yourselves, which is yours in Christ Jesus, who, though he was in the form of God, did not count equality with God a thing to be grasped, but emptied himself, by taking the form of a servant, being born in the likeness of men. And being found in human form, he humbled himself by becoming obedient to the point of death, even death on a cross. Therefore God has highly exalted him and bestowed on him the name that is above every name, so that at the name of Jesus every knee should bow, in heaven and on earth and under the earth, and every tongue confess that Jesus Christ is Lord, to the glory of God the Father.*

There plenty of scriptures in the Bible that speak of humility, but these verses talking about the humility of Jesus Christ may be some of the strongest for emphasizing the importance of humility. Here the author hints at walking in the Spirit. He emphasizes the importance of humility in how we treat others. Most importantly, he reminds us of the humility of Jesus - how He was God but took the form of a servant by being born in the likeness of a man. As followers of Jesus Christ, a believer, must abandon all selfish ambition and conceit and walk in love and humility. This is not an option. It is mandatory as a follower of Christ.

Gentle and Lowly in Heart

Matthew 11:25-30, *At that time Jesus declared, "I thank you, Father, Lord of heaven and earth, that you have hidden these things from the wise and understanding and revealed them to little children; yes, Father, for such was your gracious will. All things have been handed over to me by my Father, and no one knows the Son except the Father, and no one knows the Father except the Son and anyone to whom the Son chooses to reveal him. Come to me, all who labor and are heavy laden, and I will give you rest. Take my yoke upon you, and learn from me, for I am gentle and lowly in heart, and you will find rest for your souls. For my yoke is easy, and my burden is light."* Jesus proclaims that He is gentle and lowly in heart. Although He is the Son of God, He still arrives on earth in human form and comes as a gentle person who is lowly in heart. That is the perfect definition of humility that the Son of God lowers Himself to take on the flesh of humanity.

Pride

Mark 7:21-23, *"For from within, out of the heart of man, come evil thoughts, sexual immorality, theft, murder, adultery, coveting, wickedness, deceit, sensuality, envy, slander, pride, foolishness. All these evil things come from within, and they defile a person."* Here Jesus is talking about the evil that comes out of the heart of mankind. He was explaining to His disciples that sin does not enter man through any forbidden foods they may eat. Rather, sin comes from the evil heart of man. He is not explicitly asking them to be humble but pride is one of the sins that He lists as coming from the heart of man. Pride is listed right there along with murder, adultery, lying, and the other evils that defile man. Who would have thought that pride was on an equal standing with murder and theft? The follower of Jesus Christ must avoid pride. We must display humility just as He did.

Humbleness

Colossians 3:12-13, *Put on then, as God's chosen ones, holy and beloved, compassionate hearts, kindness, humility, meekness, and patience, bearing with one another and, if one has a complaint against another, forgiving each other; as the Lord has forgiven you, so you also must forgive.*

These two short verses are powerful ones. We often overlook them in reading the Bible. Throughout the Bible, both in the Old Testament and in the New Testament, we are called to be holy. Too often the church has linked holiness to man-made rules, traditions, and cultural expectations. Here though, Paul seems to be linking holiness to compassionate hearts, humility, meekness, and patience. Then he goes on to link holiness to bearing with each other in trying times and forgiving one another. To do this takes real love and humility. Maybe it is time to link Christian leadership with holiness through love and humility. This verse also seems to make clear that forgiveness is heavily linked to humility. As Murray reminds us, "Manifestations of temper and touchiness and irritation, feelings of bitterness and estrangement, have their roots in nothing but pride."

John the Baptist

Luke 7:28, *I tell you, among those born of women none is greater than John. Yet the one who is least in the kingdom of God is greater than he."* As Jesus was teaching the crowds, He mentioned John the Baptist. What He says is quite interesting and humbling at the same time. Although Jesus considered John the Baptist to be the greatest man, at the same time, John was less than the least of those in the Kingdom of God. This truth holds for each of us also. No matter how great we are or how successful we are, or what leadership or ministry role we have, we are still the least in the kingdom. Whatever success we have had is solely due to Christ and the power of the Holy Spirit within us - not because of anything great that we have done in our strength and power. That is quite humbling to consider.

Exalting Yourself

In Luke 14, Jesus went to dine at the home of one of the leaders of the Pharisees one Sabbath. Jesus notices that the invited people were all attempting to sit at the seats of honor. They did not want to be sitting in the lesser seats. They wanted everyone there to see and understand just how important they were.

In *Luke 14:7-11 He gives them an example that we are to follow. Now he told a parable to those who were invited, when he noticed how they chose the places of honor, saying to them, "When you are invited by someone to a wedding feast, do not sit down in a place of honor, lest someone more distinguished than you be invited by him, and he who invited you both will come and say to you, 'Give your place to this person,' and then you will begin with shame to take the lowest place. But when you are invited, go and sit in the lowest place, so that when your host comes he may say to you, 'Friend, move up higher.' Then you will be honored in the presence of all who sit at table with you. For everyone who exalts himself will be humbled, and he who humbles himself will be exalted."* The key verse here is Luke 14:11, *For everyone who exalts himself will be humbled, and he who humbles himself will be exalted.* This all goes back to what Jesus previously said about the first will be last and the last will be first. Humility should be apparent in every area of the leader's life, ministry, and leadership.

The people were not catching on to this idea of humility that Jesus was asking for in the previous parable. Humility was a strange idea to them. In Luke 18, He gave them another parable about humility. Luke 18:9-14, *He also told this parable to some who trusted in themselves that they were righteous, and treated others with contempt: "Two men went up into the temple to pray, one a Pharisee and the other a tax collector. The Pharisee, standing by himself, prayed thus: 'God, I thank you that I am not like other men, extortioners, unjust, adulterers, or even like this tax collector. I fast twice a week; I give tithes of all that I get.' But the tax collector, standing far off, would not even lift up his eyes to heaven, but beat his breast, saying, 'God, be merciful to me, a sinner!' I tell you, this man went down to his house justified, rather than the other. For everyone who exalts himself will be humbled, but the one who humbles himself will be exalted."* Remember that the Pharisees were considered to be the most righteous and holiest at that time. Their lack of humility and compassion showed their true worth in God's eyes.

Jesus stated in Matthew 18 that we are to humble ourselves as little children. Twice more in Luke, Jesus reminds us that we are to humble ourselves. He warns us of the danger of exalting ourselves. Our natural inclination is to be full of pride and to make our actions and words to be exalting toward our selves. We all tend to want to make ourselves look good and receive accolades and honors from others. We need to remember that ego is not a pretty thing to behold in followers or leaders. Any good or holiness inside us is not due to any action that we have taken. It is definitely not because we are more holy than anyone else. Any good in us is strictly through the work of the Holy Spirit within us.

In Luke 17, Jesus gives us a strange parable. In it, He reminds us that we are servants. As servants, we are not to find pride in doing what we are supposed to do. We are lowly (unworthy) servants and are just doing what is our duty. Luke 17:7-10, *"Will any one of you who has a servant plowing or keeping sheep say to him when he has come in from the field, 'Come at once and recline at table'? Will he not rather say to him, 'Prepare supper for me, and dress properly, and serve me while I eat and drink, and afterward you will eat and drink'? Does he thank the servant because he did what was commanded? So you also, when you have done all that you were commanded, say, 'We are unworthy servants; we have only done what was our duty.'"*

1 John 2

John is often called the apostle of love for a good reason. His writings are full of proclamations about the involvement of love in following Christ. He tells us that love is a natural outcome of being a follower of Jesus. Just as Christ loves us, we are to love one another. In three short verses in 1

John 2, he briefly covers the love of the world, the desires of the flesh, and pride. These three items are detrimental to the believer. John says that these things do not come from God and should be avoided. 1 John 2:15-17, *Do not love the world or the things in the world. If anyone loves the world, the love of the Father is not in him. For all that is in the world-- the desires of the flesh and the desires of the eyes and pride in possessions-- is not from the Father but is from the world. And the world is passing away along with its desires, but whoever does the will of God abides forever.*

Various Verses on Pride

Luke 1:51-52, *He has shown strength with his arm; he has scattered the proud in the thoughts of their hearts; he has brought down the mighty from their thrones and exalted those of humble estate;*
1 Timothy 6:11. *But as for you, O man of God, flee these things. Pursue righteousness, godliness, faith, love, steadfastness, gentleness.*
2 Timothy 3:1-5, *But understand this, that in the last days there will come times of difficulty. For people will be lovers of self, lovers of money, proud, arrogant, abusive, disobedient to their parents, ungrateful, unholy, heartless, unappeasable, slanderous, without self-control, brutal, not loving good, treacherous, reckless, swollen with conceit, lovers of pleasure rather than lovers of God, having the appearance of godliness, but denying its power. Avoid such people.*
James 4:1-6, *What causes quarrels and what causes fights among you? Is it not this, that your passions are at war within you? You desire and do not have, so you murder. You covet and cannot obtain, so you fight and quarrel. You do not have, because you do not ask. You ask and do not receive, because you ask wrongly, to spend it on your passions. You adulterous people! Do you not know that friendship with the world is enmity with God? Therefore whoever wishes to be a friend of the world makes himself an enemy of God. Or do you suppose it is to no purpose that the Scripture says, "He yearns jealously over the spirit that he has made to dwell in us"? But he gives more grace. Therefore it says, "God opposes the proud but gives grace to the humble."*
1 Peter 5:5b - 7, *Clothe yourselves, all of you, with humility toward one another, for "God opposes the proud but gives grace to the humble.*

"Humble yourselves, therefore, under the mighty hand of God so that at the proper time he may exalt you, casting all your anxieties on him, because he cares for you.
Ephesians 4:1-3, *I therefore, a prisoner for the Lord, urge you to walk in a manner worthy of the calling to which you have been called, with all humility and gentleness, with patience, bearing with one another in love, eager to maintain the unity of the Spirit in the bond of peace.*

Conclusion

As we can see from these many Bible verses that humility is one of the key characteristics of a true follower of Christ. This is even more important for the Christian leader. Jesus Christ is our example for what humility looks like. Two characteristics of Jesus that are so different from what our human nature expects are love and humility. He loves us so much that He humbled Himself as the Son of God to become the Son of Man. Very simply, we are to also display love and humility just as He did. We are not in any position of leadership because of our greatness or abilities. We are only in these positions through the grace of God. We do not become good leaders because of any inner knowledge or power. It is only through the grace of God as we are empowered by the Holy Spirit.

There is no magic formula to change yourself from a life of pride and ego into one of humility. There are no listed steps to follow in order to achieve humility. Humility only comes through the work of the Holy Spirit working the needed changes within you. You must recognize and acknowledge that without Christ you are nothing special. Any success that you have will only occur through the Holy Spirit working within you.

- 6 -

Created in the Image of God

You will never look into the eyes of someone God doesn't love.
(author unknown)

WE are introduced to the fact that mankind was created by God in His image in the first chapter of Genesis. Theologians and Bible scholars have discussed exactly what being created in the image of God means for centuries. There is no question that we have been created in His image. Genesis 1:26-27, *Then God said, "Let us make man in our image, after our likeness. And let them have dominion over the fish of the sea and over the birds of the heavens and over the livestock and over all the earth and over every creeping thing that creeps on the earth." So God created man in his own image, in the image of God he created him; male and female he created them.*

Why are we discussing the Image of God in a Christian leadership book? We hope that you understand and agree that the Image of God in mankind is an important theological issue. The question arises as to what it has to do with leadership. The fact that every person was created in the image of God adds an important aspect to our discussion about Christian leadership being based on following Christ. The idea that we are created in the image of God also adds to vital discussions about love, anger, racism, sexism, and other issues that leaders face. This subject is truly worthy of a full-length book, but we will discuss this concept in a condensed form in this chapter. If we understand that all people are created in the Image of God it will affect how we treat people and lead them. Please be patient as we attempt to find the right words to address this important but complex subject. This discussion does bring up several controversial and uncomfortable subjects that leaders need to approach in a Christlike manner. We will deal with the subject of anger more extensively in Chapter 7. We will discuss the subject of love in greater detail in Chapter 8. Both of those subjects are closely linked to the knowledge that every person is created in the image of God.

The Creation

When we discuss the subject of mankind being created in the Image of God, we must start way back at the beginning. This means starting with Genesis chapter 1 in the Old Testament. This is where we are first introduced to the idea that man was created in the image of God. However, this is not the last place in the Bible that mentions this subject.

We mentioned Genesis 1:26-27 at the start of this chapter. We are all familiar with this initial statement that man was created in the image of God. Genesis 5:1-2 continues with this thought, *This is the book of the generations of Adam. When God created man, he made him in the likeness of God. Male and female he created them, and he blessed them and named them Man when they were created.* God created all men and women in His image. We can state without any doubt that every man and woman is created in the Image of God. Every person on earth, no matter what their race, color, culture, sex, mental ability, character, or religious affiliation was created in the image of God.

The Image of Christ

Paul introduces a different thought about image of God in Romans 8:29, *For those whom he foreknew he also predestined to be conformed to the image of his Son, so that he might be the firstborn among many brothers.* First, we were created in the image of God, and now as believers, we are to be conformed to the image of Christ. Paul states that we are not to be conformed to the world. We are, instead, to renew our minds so that we are made into the image of Christ. In Romans 12:1-3, Paul says, *I appeal to you therefore, brothers, by the mercies of God, to present your bodies as a living sacrifice, holy and acceptable to God, which is your spiritual worship. Do not be conformed to this world, but be transformed by the renewal of your mind, that by testing you may discern what is the will of God, what is good and acceptable and perfect.* John Kilner says it this way, "Ultimately, the image of God is Jesus Christ. People are first created and later renewed according to that image."

2 Corinthians 3:18 continues this discussion, *And we all, with unveiled face, beholding the glory of the Lord, are being transformed into*

the same image from one degree of glory to another. For this comes from the Lord who is the Spirit. While we were created in the image of God, we must be transformed into the image of Christ. In other scriptures, Paul reminds us that Christ is the image of His Father.

This discussion now moves on to some of the issues Christian leaders face that were mentioned above. These issues are ones that all leaders face in the world today, but they cause much conflict in Christian leadership because they have the potential of becoming a spiritual issue. Discussing these issues while keeping in mind that all persons are created in the image of God can help us deal with these issues in a more Christlike manner.

Judgment

Judging others for believing differently than you do is a real problem in Christianity today. One problem with this is that the person being judged perceives that the Christian is condemning them and that those people being condemned cannot see the love and forgiveness of Christ in the judgmental Christian's words and actions. Instead of being drawn toward Christ through the actions and words of the Christian, the judged person is pushed away from Christ's love and forgiveness. They see the condemnation and judgment and it looks more like hatred than love. They are unable to see that Christ is offering them love and forgiveness.

What did Jesus say about judging others? Towards the end of the Sermon on the Mount, He gets pretty straight-forward about judging others. Matthew 7:1-5, *"Judge not, that you be not judged. For with the judgment you pronounce you will be judged, and with the measure you use it will be measured to you. Why do you see the speck that is in your brother's eye, but do not notice the log that is in your own eye? Or how can you say to your brother, 'Let me take the speck out of your eye,' when there is the log in your own eye? You hypocrite, first take the log out of your own eye, and then you will see clearly to take the speck out of your brother's eye."* Jesus speaks pretty plainly here. None of us are perfect. As Paul said in Romans, we have all sinned, everyone of us is guilty. None of us are perfect enough to judge others. Forgiven Christians have many sins in their lives that God has forgiven. Remembering that we have been forgiven, we must approach others in love not condemnation.

Jesus goes on to state it in a different way in Luke 6:36-37, *Be merciful, even as your Father is merciful. "Judge not, and you will not be judged; condemn not, and you will not be condemned; forgive, and you will be forgiven;"* Here Jesus relates that if we judge others, we will be judged for it. In contrast, if we forgive others, we will be forgiven. If you wish Christ to forgive you for your sins, you must forgive others. If you do not wish to be judged by God for your sins, you cannot judge others. Jesus states that God is the Judge. We are not the judge of others. Jesus gave them a parable as an example of what He was saying in Matthew 6:39-42. *He also told them a parable: "Can a blind man lead a blind man? Will they not both fall into a pit? A disciple is not above his teacher, but everyone when he is fully trained will be like his teacher. Why do you see the speck that is in your brother's eye, but do not notice the log that is in your own eye? How can you say to your brother, 'Brother, let me take out the speck that is in your eye,' when you yourself do not see the log that is in your own eye? You hypocrite, first take the log out of your own eye, and then you will see clearly to take out the speck that is in your brother's eye.*

Paul says the same thing in Romans 14:10-13, *Why do you pass judgment on your brother? Or you, why do you despise your brother? For we will all stand before the judgment seat of God; for it is written, "As I live, says the Lord, every knee shall bow to me, and every tongue shall confess to God." So then each of us will give an account of himself to God. Therefore let us not pass judgment on one another any longer, but rather decide never to put a stumbling block or hindrance in the way of a brother.*

We cannot judge others because we all have a huge log in our own eye. We are often unable of seeing this log ourselves. It is so easy to see the faults and sins in others while overlooking our own faults. We are often completely blind to our own faults and sins. Even if we are able to determine that we have a log in our own eye and then remove it, we should be quick to recognize that it is only through the power of Jesus Christ that we have been able to remove that log. If we are thankful for the forgiveness of our own sins, we will no longer be so quick to condemn and judge others. We will be glad to leave the judging to God. After all, God is the judge. We are not the judge. God did not call us to judge people. He called us to love them. Instead of judging them, we will be glad to show them the love and forgiveness that

Christ offers everyone of us. That we are to even love the worst sinner out there without judging them.

As Christians, we are to be followers of Christ. Even though we are sinful people by nature, our goal as a follower of Christ is to be more like Jesus was. He is our example. We are to attempt to be like Him. We are to transform our lives into being Christlike through the power of the Holy Spirit. A good example of how Jesus treated other people is found in Matthew 9.

Matthew 9:9-13, *As Jesus passed on from there, he saw a man called Matthew sitting at the tax booth, and he said to him, "Follow me." And he rose and followed him. And as Jesus reclined at table in the house, behold, many tax collectors and sinners came and were reclining with Jesus and his disciples. And when the Pharisees saw this, they said to his disciples, "Why does your teacher eat with tax collectors and sinners?" But when he heard it, he said, "Those who are well have no need of a physician, but those who are sick. Go and learn what this means: 'I desire mercy, and not sacrifice.' For I came not to call the righteous, but sinners."*

The Pharisees (the religious leaders) were shocked at and offended by Jesus. Not only was He not condemning and judging the sinners, He actually was hanging out with them at the table. He was lounging around with them having friendly discussions. There is no record that Jesus told these sinners that they were condemned and going to hell. He sat down with them and had a nice conversation with them. He showed them love and compassion instead of judgment and condemnation. Does this give us any idea how we are to treat others including those that we might consider sinners?

Sexism

Sexism is a horrible sin against God and women. Men have often treated women in terrible ways throughout history and justified their actions by the Bible. We know that the Bible was written in an patriarchal society and that it was often used by men to excuse their sexism. The Bible does not directly teach against sexism and never mentions that word (sexism). However, the Bible teaches that women are equally loved and honored by God and that both sexes are created in the Image of God. If you are truly following Christ and thereby loving your neighbor as yourself, sexism cannot exist in your life in any form. Sexism is contrary to both the idea that all are created in the image of God and also in the command of Jesus that we are to love our neighbor as ourselves.

Here is Genesis 1:26-28 again. *Then God said, "Let us make man in our image, after our likeness. And let them have dominion over the fish of the sea and over the birds of the heavens and over the livestock and over all the earth and over every creeping thing that creeps on the earth." So God created man in his own image, in the image of God he created him; male and female he created them. And God blessed them. And God said to them, "Be fruitful and multiply and fill the earth and subdue it and have dominion over the fish of the sea and over the birds of the heavens and over every living thing that moves on the earth."* And once again we quote Genesis 5:1-2 as it continues this same thought. *This is the book of the generations of Adam. When God created man, he made him in the likeness of God. Male and female he created them, and he blessed them and named them Man when they were created.*

The point we are making here is that God created both man and woman in His Image. Both men and women were equally created in the image of God. Note a couple of important thoughts in these verses. After God created man and woman, He then blessed both of them, not just the man. Then take notice that God then placed both man and woman in dominion over all creatures on earth. He did not ignore Eve but placed her in the same position and control along with Adam. God loves both of them and treats them equally.

Although the Old Testament records a culture that was patriarchal in nature, there were still women leaders discussed. A close study of the Old Testament in which you pay close attention to the women leaders in the Old Testament would be a good place to start. There are many mentioned. Pay attention to how God used these women to further His plan. Preston Sprinkle (a well-known seminary professor) admits, "I am embarrassed to admit that it was not until three years after I completed my PhD in Bible that I noticed God using a bunch of women to rescue His people from slavery in Egypt. God's choice of female redeemers is a backhanded slap to the patriarchal, male-centered culture He was working within."

Although sometimes Paul's teachings on women in leadership can be controversial, he does recognize that in God's eyes, there is no difference between male and female. Galatians 3:28, *There is neither Jew nor Greek, there is neither slave nor free, there is no male and female, for you are all one in Christ Jesus.* This verse is linked equally to the argument against racism as it is against sexism. Paul makes it clear here that God considers all people the same. Although the Jews were His chosen people, He loves all people, no matter what their race, sex, or sexual orientation are. They are all equal in His eyes. We believers, are all joined together in Christ Jesus. Believers should never be involved in anything racist or sexist. Sexism (and racism) goes against the idea that we are created in His image. It is also a direct violation of Christ's command to us to love our neighbor as ourselves.

If you need proof of this, just study the New Testament carefully and see how Jesus treats and honors women, starting with His mother. Read the New Testament with an eye on Jesus' many interactions with women. He cared for them and treated them with love and respect. This was different from the culture of that time which treated women as property to be used and abused.

Jesus always honors His mother. The closest the Bible records a questionable attitude toward his mother is at the wedding feast where He changed the water into wine in His first recorded miracle. When Mary told Jesus that the wedding party ran out of wine, He was quick to tell her that His time had not come yet. Although He said that to her, He still did as she asked and turned the water into wine. Even as He hung on the cross dying, He looked at John, His beloved apostle, and told him that Mary was now his responsibility to take care of. Mary was one of the several women who traveled with Jesus and His disciples on their journeys. They helped provide for them and care for them. She was there at His crucifixion and also at the tomb to witness that Jesus had risen from the dead.

One of the most telling interactions with women in the Bible was perhaps Mary Magdalene. Luke 8:1-2 introduces her to us, *Soon afterward he went on through cities and villages, proclaiming and bringing the good news of the kingdom of God. And the twelve were with him, and also some women who had been healed of evil spirits and infirmities: Mary, called Magdalene, from whom seven demons had gone out.* Jesus had cast out seven demons from her. By the Jewish customs, Jesus should not have even been around her. After He had cast the demons out of her, she, along with several other women, traveled with Jesus and His disciples. They supported Jesus and the disciples and helped take care of them in their journeys. She was also present at the crucifixion and witnessed it. She was the first one to arrive at the empty tomb on Resurrection Day. Her name is mentioned more times in the New Testament than some of the disciples and she played an important role in the life and ministry of Christ.

There are four other interactions with women that Jesus had that come to mind. It is worth looking at these interactions and how Jesus treated these women. The first one is the Samaritan woman at the well. She was a Samaritan who the Jews refused to talk to or even be around. She has also been married many times and is now living with a man who is not her husband. The story is found in John 4:5-9, *So he came to a town of Samaria called Sychar, near the field that Jacob had given to his son Joseph. Jacob's well was there; so Jesus, wearied as he was from his journey, was sitting beside the well. It was about the sixth hour. A woman from Samaria came to draw water. Jesus said to her, "Give me a drink." (For his disciples had gone away into the city to buy food.) The Samaritan woman said to him, "How is it that you, a Jew, ask for a drink from me, a woman of Samaria?" (For Jews have no dealings with Samaritans.)*

The Jews hated the Samaritans and refused to have anything to do with them, but here Jesus was talking with her and even asking her for water. She was also living in sin with a man who was not her husband. By all normal accounts, Jesus should have stayed far away from her. Instead, He reaches out to her in love and kindness, not with condemnation.

The disciples had been traveling with Jesus for a while. He had been teaching them and mentoring them. He had given them the story of the Good Samaritan in which the Samaritan is the good guy. Still, the disciples were shocked when they returned to Jesus and discovered Him talking to the Samaritan woman. At least the disciples were smart enough that they did not call Jesus out for going against Jewish customs. John 4:27, *Just then his disciples came back. They marveled that he was talking with a woman, but no one said, "What do you seek?" or, "Why are you talking with her?"*

The second woman to consider is the woman with the issue of blood who had spent all her money over the years seeking a resolution to her problem. None of the physicians could help her. She was getting more desperate. Because of the great crowds around Jesus, she could not get His attention in the hope that He would heal her. She struggled through the crowds and reached out and touched His garments. She was immediately healed because of her faith. Luke 8:43-48, *And there was a woman who had had a discharge of blood for twelve years, and though she had spent all her living on physicians, she could not be healed by anyone. She came up behind him and touched the fringe of his garment, and immediately her discharge of blood ceased. And Jesus said, "Who was it that touched me?" When all denied it, Peter said, "Master, the crowds surround you and are pressing in on you!" But Jesus said, "Someone touched me, for I perceive that power has gone out from me." And when the woman saw that she was not hidden, she came trembling, and falling before him declared in the presence of all the people why she had touched him, and how she had been immediately healed. And he said to her, "Daughter, your faith has made you well; go in peace."* He could have gotten angry with her for her sneaky way of obtaining healing, but, instead, He reached out to her with love and compassion.

The third woman we will discuss was the sinful woman (believed by some to be a prostitute) who came to where Jesus was eating and anointed His feet with ointment. She washed His feet with her tears and then dried them with her hair. Some claim that this woman was Mary Magdalene although there is nothing in scripture to confirm this. There is a similar incident mentioned in the book of John that involved Mary, the sister of Martha, and Lazarus at a different meal in a different home.

Luke 7:36-39, *One of the Pharisees asked him to eat with him, and he went into the Pharisee's house and took his place at the table. And behold, a woman of the city, who was a sinner, when she learned that he was reclining at a table in the Pharisee's house, brought an alabaster flask of ointment, and standing behind him at his feet, weeping, she began to wet his feet with her tears and wiped them with the hair of her head and kissed his feet and anointed them with the ointment. Now when the Pharisee who had invited him saw this, he said to himself, "If this man were a prophet, he would have known who and what sort of woman this is who is touching him, for she is a sinner."*

The Pharisee who is hosting the meal is offended by this incident and rebukes Jesus. Jesus then gives the Pharisee man a parable to show that even the worst sinner can be forgiven. Jesus then gently rebukes the Pharisee. Luke 7:44-48, *Then turning toward the woman he said to Simon, "Do you see this woman? I entered your house; you gave me no water for my feet, but she has wet my feet with her tears and wiped them with her hair. You gave me no kiss, but from the time I came in she has not ceased to kiss my feet. You did not anoint my head with oil, but she has anointed my feet with ointment. Therefore I tell you, her sins, which are many, are forgiven-for she loved much. But he who is forgiven little, loves little." And he said to her, "Your sins are forgiven."* Jesus reacts with love, compassion, and forgiveness once again.

The fourth woman was the woman who had been caught in adultery whom the Pharisees brought to Jesus. The Pharisees did not want Jesus to show love and forgiveness to her, but they wanted Him to join them in stoning her like the Law called for. John 8:2-11, *Early in the morning he came again to the temple. All the people came to him, and he sat down and taught them. The scribes and the Pharisees brought a woman who had been caught in adultery, and placing her in the midst they said to him, "Teacher, this woman has been caught in the act of adultery. Now in the Law Moses commanded us to stone such women. So what do you say?" This they said to test him, that they might have some charge to bring against him. Jesus bent down and wrote with his finger on the ground. And as they continued to ask him, he stood up and said to them, "Let him who is without sin among you be the first to throw a stone at her." And once more he bent down and wrote on the ground. But when they heard it, they went away one by one, beginning with the older ones, and Jesus was left alone with the woman standing before him. Jesus stood up and said to her, "Woman, where are they? Has no one condemned you?" She said, "No one, Lord." And Jesus said, "Neither do I condemn you; go, and from now on sin no more."*

The Pharisees came to Jesus with hatred, condemnation, and judgment in their hearts toward the adulteress. To them, there was no room to argue the point. The woman was guilty of breaking the Law and she deserved to be stoned to death. You may be interested to note that they only brought the woman to be stoned. The man committing adultery was apparently to be overlooked. Jesus responded with love and forgiveness here. He gently reminded the Pharisees of their own sins that they deserved to die for. The Pharisees may have been contemplating all of their own sins that they had not been caught doing. It makes you wonder if some of them had been involved in adultery themselves but had been able to get away with it.

The Bible often mentions women whom God has chosen to be leaders in both testaments. God chose these women and used them to lead His people. Each of these women were important enough that their stories were included in the Bible. A few names that come to mind are Ruth, Deborah, Esther, Rahab (the prostitute), Miriam, Lydia, Priscilla, Phoebe, and Mary Magdelene. There are more women leaders than just these few. A study of the women in the Bible and their accomplishments might be a good suggestion for Christian men who have trouble recognizing the importance and worth of women.

The point we are trying to make here is that Jesus treated every one of these women with love, healing, forgiveness, and compassion. The misuse of scripture to browbeat, control, and misuse women is shameful and sinful. Just as Jesus did here on earth, men are to treat women with love, respect, and compassion. Any use of scripture to control or abuse women must be avoided by the church and by every follower of Jesus Christ. The Bible verses such as the ones about submission have often been misused by believers to subjugate women to be under their control.

Racism

This is another important but uncomfortable subject. Historically, white Christians and churches have failed miserably in the matter of racism. This is especially true in their treatment of Blacks. They have followed what their culture and traditions have taught them instead of what the Bible teaches on this subject. Fortunately, in the last few decades, there has been some improvement in this area in the church as well as in the public arena. Racism still has not disappeared from either the world or in the church. It is still a major problem today. It is doubtful that racism will ever be completely eradicated.

Racism against any race, color, language group, or culture is one of the ugliest things that a church or Christian can display. There is no room in the church for any form of racism. Go back to two of our favorite scriptures that Christians love to quote. John 3:16-17, *For God so loved the world, that he gave his only Son, that whoever believes in him should not perish but have eternal life. For God did not send his Son into the world to condemn the world, but in order that the world might be saved through him.*

This is a basic truth in the New Testament. Christianity is based on this truth that God so loved the world that He sent His only Son into the world so that the world might not perish but have eternal life. God loves all the people of the world, not just those of our particular race, color, or national origin. Christ did not die only for our sins but also for the sins of every person in the world, no matter what their skin color, nationality, or what language they speak. Remember what was stated at the beginning of this chapter. All mankind is created in the Image of God. When you hate or show any type of racism toward any person, you are doing it to someone who was created in the Image of God and who is deeply loved by God.

Think back to the story of the Good Samaritan that Jesus told. The Samaritans were considered foreigners, half-breeds, and uncouth people who the Jews were not even allowed to talk to or have anything to do with. Yet, the Samaritan was the only one who had a love and compassion for the injured Jewish traveler. He was the only one to stop and help him. Jesus clearly states that the hated Samaritan was the only one in the parable who loved his neighbor as himself.

Any type of racism is in direct contrast to the command of Jesus to love one's neighbor. Open racism has been reduced in many churches but not all of them. Many megachurches now pride themselves on being multicultural and multiracial churches. This improvement does not show that racism has been completely eliminated in those churches. There has been progress in reducing racism in the church and in society. Much more work is needed in this area. Racism in the church and in the Christian's life is a sin. It is simple, racism goes against both the

Some of the racism of the past may be switching from Blacks toward undocumented foreigners, especially Hispanics. It seems like we humans always seem to have at least one group of people to dislike who do not look quite like us, speak the same language that we do, or they act differently than we do. They may have darker skin than we do and speak with a heavy accent. It is possible that they do not speak the same language that we do at all.

No matter what your stance on the immigration situation looks like, you must understand that those people involved in immigration were created in the image of God and are well-loved by God. God loves them so much that He sent His Son to die on the cross for them. The Christians must love these immigrants. They are not to be maltreated as second-class people because they are important to God. That means that they should be important to us.

When he was asked about the possibility of racism being eradicated, Billy Graham had this to say: "Racism, I've found, is almost universal—but that doesn't make it right. In fact, in God's eyes racism is a serious sin. The reason is because God created every human being, and God made every one of us in His image. Yes, sin has marred and defaced that image, but no matter what our ethnic or racial or cultural background may be, we are all God's creatures, and God has implanted within each of us a soul. The Bible says, 'From one man he made every nation of men' (Acts 17:26). Furthermore, Christ died not just for one race or one ethnic group; He died to save people from every tribe and language and people and nation' (Revelation 5:9). When we come to Christ, we become part of a new family—the family of God. Now we are brothers and sisters with all who share our faith in Christ. Will racism ever be completely eliminated? Perhaps not; racism has its roots in human pride and sin, and these will never be completely erased until Christ comes again. But that shouldn't keep us from reaching out and trying to eliminate the barriers that divide us. Yes, laws have a place—but most of all, our hearts need to be changed, and only God can do that. And He will, as we open our hearts and lives to Christ's transforming love. It is unfortunate that traditionally most evangelicals and fundamentalist Christians have misused and abused scripture to justify their tradition of racism over the years. In centuries past they even misinterpreted the Bible to support their belief that God was okay with them owning and mistreating other people that were created in the image of God and loved by God. After slavery was outlawed in the United States, many of them continued to use scripture to support segregation."

Several writers have presented the idea that racism actually enslaves the racist as much as it does the slave himself. Daniel Henderson states, "It may not be immediately apparent to white people, but racial hatred and enmity enslaves white people as much as physical slavery enslaved Black people. It is a slavery of the soul and conscious." He goes on to say that hatred and bigotry are cruel masters of the soul. Racism denies basic humanity. It reduces slaves to the same level as an animal.

Racism does not only exist in physical slavery. It can appear in may other forms as well. Racism often appears in the current discussions about immigration policies. In the guise of immigration policy this is still a form of racism. Racism, in any form, is still a form of hatred and it is in direct conflict against Christ's command to us to love our neighbor as ourselves. Racism, hatred, and bigotry are all ugly sins against God and all mankind.

Athena Butler has written a small book about white racism. It focuses on the historical and current racism of white evangelicals. It is a real shame that some of the worst racism in our country has been perpetrated by Christians and that this hatred was done in the name of God. This is the same God who teaches love and compassion, not hatred and bigotry. Racism is not only about slavery or Blacks. It takes on may other forms also. Butler states, "It is racism that binds and blinds many white American Evangelicals to the vilification of the Muslims, Latinos, and African-Americans. It is racism that impels many Evangelicals to oppose immigration and turn a blind eye to children in cages at the border. It is racism that fuels Evangelical Islamophobia. It was evangelical acceptance of biblically sanctioned racism that motivated believers to separate and sell families during slavery and march with the Klan. Racist Evangelicals shielded crossburners, protected church burners, and participated in lynchings. Racism is a feature, not a bug, of American Evangelicalism."

It is worth saying again that racism in any form is ugly and it is a sin. It goes directly against the truth that all people are created in the image of God. Loving your neighbor as yourself does not allow you to treat others differently. We are to love them no matter what race, national origin, color of skin, language, or culture they are from. A Christian cannot claim to love God and hate someone who was created in the image of God. There is no way to truly do both at the same time.

A Most Uncomfortable and Controversial Subject

In this chapter, we have discussed racism and sexism. This last section of this chapter approaches another controversial subject in today's world. This subject is probably one of the most controversial issues that the church faces today. You might ask why this book is discussing such a controversial and highly debated subject. The answer is that this is a greatly debated and contested current issue in many churches and Christian organizations. This controversy needs to be handled in a Christlike manner, no matter which side of the issue you stand on. This subject is controversial and there are strong feelings on both sides of the issue. This subject tends to bring a lot of hatred, bitterness, judgment, and condemnation toward those people who take a different viewpoint than they do.

We often quote John 3:16, but we sometimes forget what John 3:17 says, *For God did not send his Son into the world to condemn the world, but in order that the world might be saved through him.* In John 12:46-48, Jesus says, *I have come into the world as light, so that whoever believes in me may not remain in darkness. If anyone hears my words and does not keep them, I do not judge him; for I did not come to judge the world but to save the world. The one who rejects me and does not receive my words has a judge; the word that I have spoken will judge him on the last day.* Jesus verifies that while we will have to answer to the Judge (God) for our sins and actions in the last days, He did not come to earth to judge people. He came to offer light to the lost. Jesus tells us again to not judge others.

The apostle Paul in his writings also reminds us not to judge others. We Christians feel free to condemn and judge others, supposedly, in the name of love. Somehow, this so-called love that they are proclaiming gets lost in the condemnation and judgment. Our judgment and condemnation does not come across as looking much like love at all. Romans 2:1-6, *Therefore you have no excuse, O man, every one of you who judges. For in passing judgment on another you condemn yourself, because you, the judge, practice the very same things. We know that the judgment of God rightly falls on those who practice such things. Do you suppose, O man--you who judge those who practice such things and yet do them yourself--that you will escape the judgment of God? Or do you presume on the riches of his kindness and forbearance and patience, not knowing that God's kindness is meant to lead you to repentance? But because of your hard and impenitent heart you are storing up wrath for yourself on the day of wrath when God's righteous judgment will be revealed.*

Romans 14:10-13, *Why do you pass judgment on your brother? Or you, why do you despise your brother? For we will all stand before the judgment seat of God; for it is written, "As I live, says the Lord, every knee shall bow to me, and every tongue shall confess to God." So then each of us will give an account of himself to God. Therefore let us not pass judgment on one another any longer, but rather decide never to put a stumbling block or hindrance in the way of a brother.* Paul clearly states that God is the judge that everyone of us will have to answer to. Every one of us will have to appear before God to be judged by Him. God never called us to be the judge. That position is reserved for God alone. We usurp His authority when we deign ourselves to be wise enough and holy enough to judge and condemn others.

These verses back up what Jesus told us to do in Luke 6:37, *"Judge not, and you will not be judged; condemn not, and you will not be condemned; forgive, and you will be forgiven;"* Matthew 7:1-2 repeats this while placing a slightly different spin on it. *"Judge not, that you be not judged. For with the judgment you pronounce you will be judged, and with the measure you use it will be measured to you.* In Matthew, Jesus states that when you judge others you will also be judged with the same measurement of judgment that you used toward other people. That makes it sound like the better decision for us to take is to approach others in love and with forgiveness, and compassion.

As you have probably guessed by now, this subject that creates so much hatred and acrimony is the issue of whether homosexuality is a sin and whether or not those who practice it should be welcomed in the church and accepted into leadership roles. As previously stated, this whole issue has created many arguments, fights, splits, and disruptions to Christians and in many churches and denominations. It also causes much acrimony between the gay community and many Evangelicals and Fundamental Christians. It is not a comfortable discussion for many people on both sides of the issue. Their minds are clear on what the Bible says and they think that there is no room for discussion on the subject. Both sides strongly believe that they are right and often refuse to recognize the other side's arguments.

The purpose of this chapter is not to get into a major theological discussion about whether homosexuality is right or wrong. We are not going to tell you whether your church or organization should accept those practicing homosexuality into membership or leadership roles. The role of this book is not to get into a deep theological argument on this subject. That is an issue for another book and is beyond the scope of this one. A good book on this subject is *People to Be Loved: Why Homosexuality is Not Just as Issue* by Preston Sprinkle. He digs deep into what the Bible says about this subject. You may or may not agree with his final thoughts on the subject, but he presents a thorough and in-depth study from the Bible on this issue.

While this book will not directly address the above issue, there is a major related problem that deals with Christian leadership that we need to address. The problem is not whether homosexuality is wrong or right but it is how we Christians are treating those who believe differently than we do on this subject. The way that many Christians and churches treat the gay and transsexual community is not Christlike or loving at all. Remember that we are to treat those who disagree with us with godly love and respect. Many of these people love God just as much as you do and struggle to correctly interpret what the Bible says (just like you do). They may disagree with you but they still must be treated with love. The followers of Christ must find a way to love and respect those who disagree with them.

One problem usually comes from the words and methods that many Christians use to argue against the gay community. The problem is not that they disagree with them, but that they tend to use words and attitudes that produce hatred and hard feelings. The problem is that the words they use often attack the people themselves who are involved in homosexuality. They are not attacking the actions that they consider to be sinful but the people who are involved in those actions. While they claim that they love the person but hate the sin, they turn around and attack the person. They claim that it is love to tell them the truth, but condemnation and judgment are not love.

Genesis 9 brings forth the idea that if a man murders another man, he must pay for this with his own life. Genesis 9:6, *"Whoever sheds the blood of man, by man shall his blood be shed, for God made man in his own image"*. Why must we not kill others? It is because they are also created in the image of God just as we are. We can take this concept a step further. It is because of the idea that all mankind is created in the image of God, that we are to love our neighbor as ourselves. We are not only supposed to love our neighbors as ourselves, but we are even supposed to love our enemies. Remember that our neighbors and even our enemies are all created in the image of God just as we are. Once we understand that all are created in the image of God then we can better understand why things like gossip, theft, murder, and strife with others are so wrong. If we love our neighbor as ourselves, these other things should not be present in our lives at all.

If we understand that God requires us to love others as ourselves because we are all created in the image of God, we can then understand why things like anger, arguments, fighting, and strife are not to be present in the life of a Christian. These things are prevalent in human life because of our sinful natures and selfish desires. We tend to be very sensitive to such things as being called ugly names. People often say terrible things about us in an attempt to feel better about themselves. We are ready to fight if someone calls our mothers an ugly name. We get riled up if they say something bad about our kids.

James had to say something about this subject. In James 3, he discusses the need for believers to tame their tongues. He mentions that the tongue is such a small organ but it wields so much power, both for good and for harm. James 3:9-10 states, *With it we bless our Lord and Father, and with it, we curse people with who are made in the image of God. From the same mouth come blessing and cursing. My brothers, these things ought not to be so.* How simply he states this. These things should not be present in the life of a believer. As James is reminding us, our condemning words can hurt others as much as inflicting physical harm can. Even as you have discussions with those who disagree with you, you must be careful to maintain love, compassion, and respect toward one another.

Daniel Henderson has much to say about how the church has historically treated gay people. He does not approach the question on whether homosexuality is a sin or not here. He rightly considers the hatred and persecution of gay people to be just as much of a sin as racism is. Henderson had this to say, "The intolerance and hostility toward gays that permeates the Evangelical community is not only distasteful but is exactly the opposite of what I read about in the New Testament in the teachings of Jesus. The love of Christ and the inclusiveness of Spirituality makes the continued persecution and exclusion of gay people unacceptable." We Christians are supposed to be following Christ and living and loving others like He did. The church has often failed miserably in doing that in our treatment of gays and other groups. Church members often do not want gays attending their churches even if they are seeking Christ. They would rather the gay person somehow find his or her way to Christ and then clean up their lives before they darken the church door.

We who are followers of Jesus are supposed to be loving others and acting like Jesus did. Read the New Testament again with the thought to see how Jesus approached others, especially the sinners in His time. Other than the Pharisees, you will not see Him approaching people in condemnation or reproach. He even approaches the worst sinners with love, compassion, and forgiveness. He loves them and cares for them. He offers them, including the worst sinners, healing, forgiveness, and eternal life. You see Jesus approaching the worst sinners in love. You can see Him gently offering these sinners a better way of life, not condemnation. He does not attack them or judge them for their sins, no matter how terrible they are. He just offers them love, forgiveness, and eternal life.

If you disagree with someone, you still need to treat them with love and respect. You may disagree with them, but they are still a person created in the image of God and loved by God. You might think that they are completely wrong, but when you attack them as a person for what they believe in, you are treating them with hatred and condemnation, not love. When you state that you love them and then turn around and attack them for what they are, they cannot see the love of God in you at all. All they see is hatred and condemnation. You are not required to agree with them. Not agreeing with them is fine! If you tell them that you love them but hate their sin, and then turn around and treat them like you hate them, then they will never believe you at all. All they will be able to see in you is hatred and judgment. They will not be able to see the love of God in you.

Preston Sprinkle says this about this subject, "The Christian church needs to get past the 'us' (straight people) versus 'them' (gay people) mindset and start cherishing the lives of the beautiful people that experience same-sex attraction. We need to create and cultivate a safe and honest environment where people who experience same-sex attraction don't feel gross or ashamed; where they can talk openly about their struggles in their small group and the room is not filled with cold silence and terrified stares. We allow people to admit their struggle with pride and a weak prayer life. But these are much more hideous - arrogance and a lack of communion with God - than someone's attraction to the same sex. The latter should be easy. But we live in, and have created, a culture where it is terrifying to struggle with same-sex attraction."

Please understand that Sprinkle is a theologian who still understands Scripture to state that homosexuality is a sin. He does not argue against that point. However, he does strongly argue that the Evangelical community has traditionally treated the gay community in an manner that is not Christlike at all. He goes on to state, "Unless you are a Pharisee who thinks you are much better than the rest of the sinners over there, then you should be eager to love and walk with people who are attracted to the same sex." We all know what Jesus thought about the Pharisees and those who thought the same way they did. As followers of Christ, we should be careful to avoid acting or saying anything at all that resembles the Pharisees.

We are supposed to be taking the message of God's love and forgiveness to the world. Why does it become appropriate to approach them in condemnation and judgment? How can they see the love of God at work in you and the freedom and eternal life that Christ offers them in this approach? A better question might be - why would they choose to follow a God whose followers show condemnation and judgment instead of the love of God that offers freedom, love, forgiveness, and eternal life? You may say that it is love to tell them the truth, but it is not love to approach them in judgment and condemnation with an unloving attitude. You are not being asked to change your belief about homosexuality. You are not being asked to change your theology or interpretation of the Bible. You are being asked to reconsider how you approach the subject and remember to act in God's love and grace when dealing with those who disagree with you. The New Testament makes it clear that this is the way that Jesus did it. As a follower of Jesus, you should be careful with how you interact with others who believe differently than you do.

Conclusion

The purpose of this chapter is not to change your mind about what you believe in. The purpose is not to get into a deep theological discussion on what is sin and what is not. The purpose is not to change your interpretation of scripture. The purpose of this chapter is to remind you that everyone on earth is created in the image of God. God loves all mankind, whether they are believers and followers of Christ or not. As followers of Christ, we are to love them and treat them with love and compassion even if we believe that they are in the wrong. Jesus Christ calls His followers to love their neighbor and their enemy. We are to treat them like Christ would treat them, with love and compassion. Remember that throughout the New Testament, both Jesus and Paul repeatedly tell us to love our neighbors while abstaining from judging them. It is time for the Christian leader to study the Bible closely to determine what God thinks about such subjects as racism, sexism, and the way that we treat others who believe differently than we do, look different, talk different, come from a different culture, or have a different skin color. Although we did not discuss this subject, we also need to reconsider how we treat those who attend a different church, denomination, or have a different theology than we do. Jesus calls us to love them all without hesitation or doubt.

- 7 -

Anger

WE include this short discussion about anger is as a separate chapter. Anger is such an important subject for those who follow Jesus Christ. It is even more important for those in Christian leadership. Anger is an uncomfortable subject in some ways as it is present to some extent in every human being on earth. It is an unfortunate result of being human and having selfish desires and wishes. Anger is largely linked to pride and selfishness. Anger often comes from hurt feelings or in reaction to others' anger. As Paul reminds us in Galatians 5:20, anger is one of the fruits or works of the flesh. Christians are supposed to have the Fruit of the Spirit active in their lives, not the fruits of the flesh. Anger is a dangerous and destructive force. It often results in much emotional and spiritual damage to both the angry person and to the victims of their anger.

Although it is beyond the constraints of this book, there should be mention of the medical (physical) consequences of anger. Doctors and researchers have warned us for many years about anger's destructive nature. Anger can contribute to high stress levels, high blood pressure, diabetes, obesity, heart attacks, and other health issues. Excessive stress and anger are not conducive to good health.

Anger is all too often used as a tool of control. Some people have found anger as a way to control other people and regain control when they do not get their way. It can often be used as a response in order to divert other people's anger at them. It can often be a means of denying and deflecting responsibility for their own mistakes or incorrect behavior. It can also be a natural response to strife and difficult situations. This is especially true in organizations when a team member under your leadership is being contrary and argumentative.

The use of anger can be and usually is counterproductive to the person who is angry. Anger, fights, and arguments rarely, if ever, truly settle any disagreements or solve problems. It may initially appear to settle the problem on the surface. One problem with using anger is that it may cause the recipient of one's anger to also become hurt and angry. That person may then simmer in restrained anger for awhile, only for their own anger to explode later on. Using anger to control someone may temporarily work and get past that immediate difficult situation, but it is pretty well guaranteed to resurface later on in some type of conflict.

The Bible has a lot to say about anger, and usually not in a positive way. The King James Version of the Bible mentions anger 234 times. It mentions the word angry 44 times and wrath 198 times. That is a lot of discussion about anger. It is safe to say that we imperfect human beings tend to easily get angry about things. The New Testament is full of verses encouraging us to avoid anger. At the same time, several times it mentions the Wrath of God and the Day of Wrath to come in the future. We are normally driven by pride and have hurt feelings when we are angry. When God is angry, it is a righteous anger. There is a major difference between human anger and God's anger.

Jesus even teaches about anger in the Beatitudes (also called the Sermon on the Mount). The Sermon on the Mount will be discussed in Chapter 11. We tend to consider anger to be a natural part of our lives but Jesus recognizes anger for what it is - sinful, selfish, and destructive behavior. Anger is not only destructive to our physical health but also our spiritual and mental health. Jesus tells us that we will have to answer to God for our anger. Matthew 5: 21 - 22: *You have heard that it was said to those of old, You shall not murder, and whoever murders will be liable to judgment. But I say to you that everyone who is angry with his brother will be liable to judgment; whoever insults his brother will be liable to the council; and whoever says, You fool! will be liable to the hell of fire.*

And speaking of righteous anger, we know that Jesus also got angry a couple of times when here on earth. Do you remember the story about Jesus entering the synagogue? There was a man there with a withered hand. Jesus asked the Pharisees if it was lawful to do good on the Sabbath or to do harm, to save a life or to kill. They refused to answer Him because they were trying to catch Him in healing on the Sabbath so that they could arrest Him. Mark 3:5, *And he looked around at them with anger, grieved at their hardness of heart, and said to the man, "Stretch out your hand."* Jesus was angry at them because, in their hardened hearts, they were more concerned about following man-made rules than using love and compassion to heal the man. It is strange that while Jesus was full of love and compassion for others, the Pharisees, in their self-righteousness, could make Him so angry because of the hardness of their hearts. And then there are the times that Jesus entered the Temple and grew angry at the sellers working inside the Temple and threw them out for defiling the Temple of God.

It is interesting that Paul talks about anger so often in his epistles. There are times in the accounting of Paul's ministry and in his writings that he seems to battle with anger issues himself. Anger is something that all of us must deal with from time to time because of our pride. As Paul did, we must recognize the dangers associated with anger and avoid it as much as possible. We have to understand that anger not only causes harm to ourselves and others, but that it also can also be detrimental to our leadership and ministry.

Ephesians 4:26-32: *Be angry and do not sin; do not let the sun go down on your anger, and give no opportunity to the devil. Let the thief no longer steal, but rather let him labor, doing honest work with his own hands, so that he may have something to share with anyone in need. Let no corrupting talk come out of your mouths, but only such as is good for building up, as fits the occasion, that it may give grace to those who hear. And do not grieve the Holy Spirit of God, by whom you were sealed for the day of redemption. Let all bitterness and wrath and anger and clamor and slander be put away from you, along with all malice. Be kind to one another, tenderhearted, forgiving one another, as God in Christ forgave you.*

Paul is once again warning us not to be angry. He hints at the possibility of having anger without sinning. If we do get angry, we are to release that anger before the sun goes down. The point here is that anger, when it is allowed to brew and linger, causes bitterness, resentment, and harmful stress in our lives. This stress and anger are not only harmful to our emotional and spiritual lives but also to our physical bodies. He tells us that bitterness, wrath, clamor, slander, and malice all grieve the Holy Spirit. Instead of anger, we are to be full of kindness, love, and forgiveness.

Paul is not finished talking about anger. In Colossians 3:8, he says, *But now you must put them all away: anger, wrath, malice, slander, and obscene talk from your mouth.* Here he tells us that we must put these things completely out our lives and avoid them. These are things that should not have any place in our lives. Next Paul tells us that not only are we to stay away from anger, we are not to provoke others to anger. Colossians 3:21: *Fathers, do not provoke your children, lest they become discouraged.* It is translated in the King James Version, *Fathers, provoke not your children to anger, lest they be discouraged.* This is an important verse that seems to be overlooked by many parents. We parents, all too often, unwittingly provoke our children to anger in our attempts to control their attitude or behavior.

In this next scripture, Paul is talking about all of us from the time when we lived in sin before our salvation. We lived our lives fulfilling our passions and desires. He states that we are children of wrath by our own nature. The implication here is that we now walk with Jesus, and are living in the Spirit. We no longer spend our energy and time attempting to fulfill our sinful desires and passions, and yielding to our temptations. Now that we walk in the Spirit, we are to follow the will of the Father. We are no longer to be children of wrath. Ephesians 2:1-3, *And you were dead in the trespasses and sins in which you once walked, following the course of this world, following the prince of the power of the air, the spirit that is now at work in the sons of disobedience— among whom we all once lived in the passions of our flesh, carrying out the desires of the body and the mind, and were by nature children of wrath, like the rest of mankind.*

1 Timothy 2:8, *I desire then that in every place the men should pray, lifting holy hands without anger or quarreling.* Just what is Paul trying to say here? If you place this verse alongside everything else he wrote about anger, you will agree that Paul knew that anger, strife, and quarreling were not conducive to being a child of the Holy God. These things are contrary to the commandments to love God and to love your neighbor. They are even contrary to the command that Jesus gave us to love our enemy. Anger tends to drive itself between us and God.

The Epistle of James is quite different from the other books in the New Testament. James writes from a different direction than Paul does. He does give us a lot of good information about living a godly life as a follower of Jesus and putting our faith into action. He mentions anger in a simple and straightforward way. In these verses, he motivates us to be quick to hear, slow to speak, and slow to anger. He gives us wisdom that we often forget about. It is even more important for the Christian leader to follow these wise words. James 1:19-20, *Know this, my beloved brothers: let every person be quick to hear, slow to speak, slow to anger; for the anger of man does not produce the righteousness of God.*

As mentioned in Chapter 6 of this book, we discuss how the epistle of James has much to say about controlling the tongue. As we know, when anger gets the best of us, it usually shows itself through our words as well as in our actions. James talks about how such a small member of our bodies (the tongue) can take control of us. The tongue is a means of praising others. It is also a means of us showing our love and appreciation toward others. It is a means of communicating information and asking questions. However, when anger becomes involved, our tiny tongue can cause much harm and pain to others. James 3:5-12, *So also the tongue is a small member, yet it boasts of great things. How great a forest is set ablaze by such a small fire! And the tongue is a fire, a world of unrighteousness. The tongue is set among our members, staining the whole body, setting on fire the entire course of life, and set on fire by hell. For every kind of beast and bird, of reptile and sea creature, can be tamed and has been tamed by mankind, but no human being can tame the tongue. It is a restless evil, full of deadly poison. With it we bless our Lord and Father, and with it we curse people who are made in the likeness of God. From the same mouth come blessing and cursing. My brothers, these things ought not to be so. Does a spring pour forth from the same opening both fresh and salt water? Can a fig tree, my brothers, bear olives, or a grapevine produce figs? Neither can a salt pond yield fresh water.* The tongue, especially when it is controlled by anger, can cause much pain and destruction in Christian leadership. Careless words can also cause much damage, even if they were not spoken in anger. Anger does not produce the righteousness of God. It produces unrighteousness.

These next verses are also used in Chapter 10 - The Role of Leadership. The emphasis here though is on the statement that the church elder or leader must not be quick-tempered. Anger can quickly destroy a ministry and reverse any previous good that the leader has accomplished. Titus 1:5-8, *This is why I left you in Crete, so that you might put what remained into order, and appoint elders in every town as I directed you— if anyone is above reproach, the husband of one wife, and his children are believers and not open to the charge of debauchery or insubordination. For an overseer, as*

God's steward, must be above reproach. He must not be arrogant or quick-tempered or a drunkard or violent or greedy for gain, but hospitable, a lover of good, self-controlled, upright, holy, and disciplined. How often do we as a church tend to overlook the problem with having leaders who are quick tempered? The answer unfortunately, is that we tend to overlook this behavior way too much.

Conclusion

It is clear from scripture that the follower of Jesus is to carefully avoid all semblance of anger. The Christian is to be loving, gentle, forgiving, and kind. The Christian leader must immerse himself or herself in the love of Christ and allow that love to flow out to others. Anger and love do not have anything to do with each other and are enemies.

- 8 -

Love in Leadership

DID you know that Jesus gave us a commandment that we are incapable of keeping properly? That is correct, He did. At least none of us are capable of keeping this commandment within ourselves. Jesus told us to love our neighbors as ourselves.

Jesus repeatedly talked about His commandments that He requires His followers to keep. Those two commandments are to love God and to love your neighbor as yourself. He even said that all of the other commandments were wrapped up into these two commandments. Both of these commandments deal with love. Jesus tells His disciples that we are to obey these two commandments. John 14:15, *"If you love me, you will keep my commandments.* Jesus says that if we love Him then we are to obey His commandments. What are His commandments? He mentions these two commandments several times in the New Testament and stresses their importance. Matthew 22:36-40, *"Teacher, which is the great commandment in the Law?" And he said to him, "You shall love the Lord your God with all your heart and with all your soul and with all your mind. This is the great and first commandment. And a second is like it: You shall love your neighbor as yourself. On these two commandments depend all the Law and the Prophets."*

We are not talking about loving leadership itself. We are not talking about loving ourselves. We are talking about the role of love in Christian leadership through loving others. Love is one of the most overlooked aspects of leadership. Christian leadership by definition must include love. Without love, Christian leadership is nothing. Without love, there is nothing Christ-like about that leadership at all. Love is a necessary ingredient of Christian leadership. Unfortunately, this is something that is often overlooked and neglected by many Christian leadership professionals. To start this discussion we must first attempt to define what love is. In today's world, there are many different definitions of love and many misconceptions about what love looks like. Paul gave us one of the greatest descriptions of what biblical love looks like in what we call the Love Chapter. It is the perfect place to start any discussion about love. Paul's description of love in 1 Corinthians 13 will be used as our definition of love. The dictionaries have never come up with a better definition for love than the one Paul gives us.

John Hope Bryant states that "...there are only two basic ways to lead, because there are only two primal forces in the human psyche: love and fear. What you don't love, you fear." According to him, you can only lead through fear or love. There are no other choices. He says, "Being a command-and-control leader who issues orders and overpowers people isn't difficult, and it isn't leadership. It is coercion." He states that tough leaders are not real leaders but they are tyrants and bullies.

The Love Chapter

1 Corinthians 13: *If I speak in the tongues of men and of angels, but have not love, I am a noisy gong or a clanging cymbal. And if I have prophetic powers, and understand all mysteries and all knowledge, and if I have all faith, so as to remove mountains, but have not love, I am nothing. If I give away all I have, and if I deliver up my body to be burned, but have not love, I gain nothing. Love is patient and kind; love does not envy or boast; it is not arrogant or rude. It does not insist on its own way; it is not irritable or resentful; it does not rejoice at wrongdoing, but rejoices with the truth. Love bears all things, believes all things, hopes all things, endures all things. Love never ends. As for prophecies, they will pass away; as for tongues, they will cease; as for knowledge, it will pass away. For we know in part and we prophesy in part, but when the perfect comes, the partial will pass away. When I was a child, I spoke like a child, I thought like a child, I reasoned like a child. When I became a man, I gave up childish ways. For now we see in a mirror dimly, but then face to face. Now I know in part; then I shall know fully, even as I have been fully known. So now faith, hope, and love abide, these three; but the greatest of these is love.*

What does love have to do with leadership? Love is not what we think of as being an attribute of leadership normally. Love defies every secular thought about leadership. It does not agree at all with what the world thinks about leadership. If you read many of the leadership books available, few even mention the idea of love in leadership. Love seems to be anti-leadership to the world. After all, their leadership and organizational goals and even their reasons for existing, differ greatly from that of Christian organizations and leadership. Bryant calls this type of love in leadership to be agape type of love in the Bible. He states, "Love, in the context of love leadership, is not the same type as love for your life partner, love for your children, or even love for a big dish of chocolate ice cream. No, I refer to the agape definition of love found so frequently in the Bible; love meaning unconditional love for your neighbor, a love as powerful as humankind's love for God. It means treating others as you want to be treated." This is the same thing that Jesus said in the Golden Rule in Matthew 7:12, *So whatever you wish that others would do to you, do also to them, for this is the Law and the Prophets.*

As stated before, Christian leadership is a much different entity from secular leadership. It is so different because Christian leadership is based on Christian (Christlike) ideas and methods. This is much different from what the world thinks about leadership. Please note that when we say Christian ideas and methods that this is not defined by any certain church, denomination, or belief system. We are only talking about what can be determined directly from the Bible. Much can be learned from observing what leadership looked like in the New Testament. We can also learn much about what to do and what not to do by observing the Apostles and the leaders in the early church. The Bible does not leave out those leaders' failures or mistakes when mentioning their successes. However, our primary lessons must be learned by watching how Jesus led. He was and is the ultimate Leader.

There is no question or doubt about it. The Christian definition of love is completely different from any definition that the world comes up with. Start by reading Paul's definition in 1 Corinthians 13. We included the text of the whole chapter at the beginning of this section. Reading and understanding this Bible chapter is necessary for understanding just how the Bible defines love. Love does not resemble what the world thinks about love at all.

Paul's words speak for themselves. Carefully reread the love chapter (1 Corinthians 13) and compare Paul's meaning of love to the way you love others. Most of us fail miserably in living up to this standard. If we do not love others in the same way that Paul says, and in the way that Jesus loves others then we are not truly loving others.

There is no argument that this is a difficult task to accomplish. In fact, it is impossible to truly love others in the same way that Christ loves others unless you have the love and Spirit of Christ within you. This type of love only comes through the Holy Spirit dwelling within you. Next, we will look at some scriptures that discuss love in the hope that it will help us understand love better.

Matthew 22:34-40, *But when the Pharisees heard that he had silenced the Sadducees, they gathered together. And one of them, a lawyer, asked him a question to test him. "Teacher, which is the great commandment in the Law?" And he said to him, "You shall love the Lord your God with all your heart and with all your soul and with all your mind. This is the great and first commandment. And a second is like it: You shall love your neighbor as yourself. On these two commandments depend all the Law and the Prophets."*

Numerous times in the New Testament Jesus is quoted teaching that the idea of loving God and loving others are the greatest commandments. The people that heard Jesus teach this struggled with this concept as much as we do. The first commandment was to love God with all of our hearts and minds. The first century Jews had been taught this all of their lives so they could accept that concept. The idea of loving one's neighbor was a complex idea though. This was a new and difficult idea to grasp and put into practice for them.

We now come to one of the most difficult verses in the Bible to follow. It is found in Matthew 5. This idea was foreign to those in the first century people who heard Jesus preach. This idea is still foreign to the way we tend to think today. Jesus not only expects us to love our neighbor as ourselves, but we are to also love our enemies. It is easier to love others when they also love you. It is much harder to love someone when they hate you, call you names, and give you a hard time about things. It is pretty hard to love someone when they are hurting you or someone you care about. We need to be honest here, some people always seem to be mean and ugly. Some people are just difficult people and it seems to be impossible to love them. Unfortunately, some people are unlovable. This makes it difficult for us to remember that they too are created in the image of God and that Jesus Christ loves them so much that He died on the cross for them just as He did for you.

Matthew 5:43-48, *"You have heard that it was said, 'You shall love your neighbor and hate your enemy.' But I say to you, Love your enemies and pray for those who persecute you, so that you may be sons of your Father who is in heaven. For he makes his sun rise on the evil and on the good, and sends rain on the just and on the unjust. For if you love those who love you, what reward do you have? Do not even the tax collectors do the same? And if you greet only your brothers, what more are you doing than others? Do not even the Gentiles do the same? You therefore must be perfect, as your heavenly Father is perfect.*

That last sentence in those verses brings up a question - Is loving God, your neighbor, and your enemy a major part of what makes you perfect? This is something to consider from what Jesus says here in Matthew. Over and over, Jesus taught that we are to love our enemies as well as our neighbors as ourselves. If we are following Jesus, we will have this type of love active in our lives. As John says in his gospel, this love is what sets the believer apart from the world. John 13:34-35, *A new commandment I give to you, that you love one another: just as I have loved you, you also are to love one another. By this all people will know that you are my disciples, if you have love for one another."*

John 15:12-17, *"This is my commandment, that you love one another as I have loved you. Greater love has no one than this, that someone lay down his life for his friends. You are my friends if you do what I command you. No longer do I call you servants, for the servant does not know what his master is doing; but I have called you friends, for all that I have heard from my Father I have made known to you. You did not choose me, but I chose you and appointed you that you should go and bear fruit and that your fruit should abide, so that whatever you ask the Father in my name, he may give it to you. These things I command you, so that you will love one another.*

John covers the subject of love extensively throughout his writings, both in his gospel and in his three epistles. He states repeatedly that the believer is to love his brothers in Christ. The fourth chapter of 1 John is a good example of this. 1 John 4:7-12, *Beloved, let us love one another, for love is from God, and whoever loves has been born of God and knows*

God. Anyone who does not love does not know God, because God is love. In this the love of God was made manifest among us, that God sent his only Son into the world, so that we might live through him. In this is love, not that we have loved God but that he loved us and sent his Son to be the propitiation for our sins. Beloved, if God so loved us, we also ought to love one another. No one has ever seen God; if we love one another, God abides in us and his love is perfected in us. John boldly proclaims that if we do not love others then we are not born of God and we do not know Him. If we do not love others, we do not love God.

The Apostle John repeats this theme throughout his writing, in both the gospel and his epistles. Over and over he reminds believers that they must love their brother. For example, in 1 John 4:19-20, he states, *"We love because he first loved us. If anyone says, 'I love God,' and hates his brother, he is a liar; for he who does not love his brother whom he has seen cannot love God who he has not seen. In addition, this commandment we have from him: whoever loves God must love his brother."* John states right before these verses, *"God is love, and whoever abides in love abides in God, and God abides in him."* 1 John 4:16.

If you want to know what truly makes Christian Leadership different from other types of leadership, the primary answer can be found in the word love. Love truly is what makes Christian leadership so different. The subject of love is a vital part of the subject of the Fruit of the Spirit. The subject of love is important enough to be included here in its own chapter about love in leadership. The subject is touched on briefly in the chapter on the Fruit of the Spirit (Chapter 3).

The Christian leader must show love in his or her leadership. To do otherwise is not Christian leadership at all. It may look like something like leadership, but there is nothing Christian about it. Jonathan Edwards says it this way, "Hence, it is no wonder that Christianity so strangely requires us to love our enemies, even the worst of enemies, as in Matthew 5:44. For love is the very temper and spirit of a Christian: it is the sum of Christianity." We argue that even secular types of leadership could use the idea of love being an important part of leadership. It could change their whole way of doing leadership.

The Apostle Paul defined love for us in 1 Corinthians 13, which most believers call the Love Chapter. Here Paul defines love in a completely different way than the world defines love. The world tends to think of love as being this great sense and feeling that someone has toward another person or thing. This 'love' is often contingent on the other person returning that love. And the person that loves them often only loves the other person for what that other person does for them. In other words, to most people, love must be a two-way street in order for it to be successful and love is all about what you get out of the relationship. It is nice when love is returned and both parties receive what they need from the relationship.

This is not what the Bible defines as love at all. Remember what we said earlier about Christianity being a paradox in many ways? Remember how we said that God's logic and wisdom are different from that of man? Well, this is another way that God is so different from mankind. God first loved us, even before we knew Him and loved Him. As John 3:16 tells us, God so loved us that He sent His only begotten Son to live as a man and then die for us. This is what love truly looks like.

Walk in Love

Ephesians 5:1-2, *Therefore be imitators of God, as beloved children. And walk in love, as Christ loved us and gave himself up for us, a fragrant offering and sacrifice to God.* As followers of Christ, we are to follow Him. We are to use Him as our only example of how to act and live. In this scripture, Paul reminds us that we are to be imitators of God. And how are we supposed to do that? We are to walk in love. We are supposed to love others just as Christ loved us and gave Himself as a sacrifice for us. Everything that He did points toward His love for us. His life here on earth is the perfect example of what love and humility look like. Perhaps the deepest truth is that we are to love others in the same way that Christ loves others and in the way that He loves us.

Galatians 5:13-14, *For you were called to freedom, brothers. Only do not use your freedom as an opportunity for the flesh, but through love serve one another. For the whole law is fulfilled in one word: "You shall love your neighbor as yourself."* Paul is discussing the law and freedom that all believers have, and not just leaders here. Notice what he tells us here. We are to serve others through love. He reiterates what Jesus teaches us that all of the law is summed up in loving our neighbor as ourselves. He gives us an idea of how we can love others just like Christ calls us to do. In verses 16 - 18, he says, "*But I say, walk by the Spirit, and you will not gratify the desires of the flesh. For the desires of the flesh are against the Spirit, and the desires of the Spirit are against the flesh, for these are opposed to each other, to keep you from doing the things you want to do. But if you are led by the Spirit, you are not under the law.*"

Once again we are told to walk in the Spirit. This is an important truth that many Christians overlook. Do you want to love your neighbor? Do you want to lead others in a Christlike manner? Then you must walk in the Spirit. As Paul tells us elsewhere, we must die to ourselves daily. Only through dying to self and walking in the Spirit can we be led by the Spirit and learn to love those around us who are unlovable. That is correct! Somehow, we must love even those who are impossible to be loved.

Do Everything in Love

1 Corinthians 16:14, *Let all that you do be done in love.* Paul is telling the Corinthian church that not only they must love their neighbor as themselves and love their enemies, but that everything they do must be done in love. This means that every decision, every action, and every communication must be done in love. This is a difficult demand for us. However, this type of love is what makes our leadership more like Christian (Christlike) leadership.

Conclusion

This is not a long chapter but it is an important one. Christian leadership must be done in love. It is not an option but it is what God expects from us. We may not be able to tell you exactly what loving others will involve in your particular leadership role but it is vital to your leadership. To omit love in leadership makes it anything but Christlike leadership.

- 9 -

Servant Leadership

SEVERAL years ago, a new understanding about leadership started appearing in some leadership literature. This new aspect was a previously unrecognized leadership characteristic obtained from the Bible. This new understanding of leadership was based on the thought that Christian leadership should involve servant leadership. This idea was first published by Robert K. Greenleaf. Greenleaf did not push this idea as being only reserved for Christian leadership, but he thought that it should be present in all types of leadership. His idea was that every leader is to be a servant leader. Since the leader is a servant, he or she is also a follower.

In 1969, Greenleaf first published a series of articles that introduced the idea that leadership is truly servant-leadership. He came to understand this as a valid concept after many years of studying and teaching leadership in the business world. He states that followers will freely follow those leaders who have been first proven and trusted as servants. He goes on to say, "To the extent that this principle prevails in the future, the only truly viable institutions will be those that are predominately servant-led."

You are encouraged to read one of Greenleaf's books on this subject to discover a more in-depth understanding of servant leadership. He explains how he came to understand the idea of servant leadership. He does not take credit for originating the idea as he developed his theory through the works of several other scholars.

Servant-Leadership in the Bible

After Greenleaf published his book, the idea of servant leadership became a popular idea in Christian circles. Many Christian leaders were quick to accept the thought that true Christian leadership involves servant leadership. Any other type of leadership style was contrary to the leadership that was taught and practiced by Jesus Christ. When one understands the idea behind servant leadership, one can easily see that Jesus both taught and portrayed servant leadership in both His leadership and teachings. Although this can be seen throughout the ministry of Jesus, it can be easiest be seen in the events of the Last Supper. Jesus never used the term 'servant leadership.' We all know the story from John's account of the Last Supper, but it is good to read it again with the thought of servant leadership in mind.

John 13:2-16: *During supper, when the devil had already put it into the heart of Judas Iscariot, Simon's son, to betray him, Jesus, knowing that the Father had given all things into his hands, and that he had come from God and was going back to God, rose from supper. He laid aside his outer garments, and taking a towel, tied it around his waist. Then he poured water into a basin and began to wash the disciples' feet and to wipe them with the towel that was wrapped around him. He came to Simon Peter, who said to him, "Lord, do you wash my feet?" Jesus answered him, "What I am doing you do not understand now, but afterward you will understand." Peter said to him, "You shall never wash my feet." Jesus answered him, "If I do not wash you, you have no share with me." Simon Peter said to him, "Lord, not my feet only but also my hands and my head!" Jesus said to him, "The one who has bathed does not need to wash, except for his feet, but is completely clean. And you are clean, but not every one of you." For he knew who was to betray him; that was why he said, "Not all of you are clean." When he had washed their feet and put on his outer garments and resumed his place, he said to them, "Do you understand what I have done to you? You call me Teacher and Lord, and you are right, for so I am. If I then, your Lord and Teacher, have washed your feet, you also ought to wash one another's feet. For I have given you an example, that you also should do just as I have done to you. Truly, truly, I say to you, a servant is not greater than his master, nor is a messenger greater than the one who sent him.*

In those days it was common, when having visitors, for the host to have a servant wash the feet of the visitors. We know that the roadways of that time were not paved. They consisted of dusty roads and paths. It was impossible for people to travel on foot between towns without get their feet dirty. It was not the job of the host himself to wash the visitors feet. This was a messy and dirty job and the task was reserved for a lowly servant. This was definitely not the job of the Son of God, the leader of those assembled there for the Passover. He was the Messiah, the Son of God. Those men with Him were His disciples. If anything, His disciples should have been washing His feet. After Jesus washed the disciples' feet, He then told them that He expected them to do this act themselves with others. The disciples, as leaders, were to become servants of those they led. They were even to be willing to kneel at their follower's feet and to wash their feet. The Christian leader is to humble themselves before their followers. This is a sign of humility that is rarely seen in today's church world. *As John says, in John 12:26, If anyone serves me, he must follow me; and where I am, there will my servant be also. If anyone serves me, the Father will honor him.*

Have you ever noticed that Paul had a tradition in how he greeted the recipients of his epistles? Several of the other authors of the New Testament epistles also followed this tradition in the opening greetings of their letters. They start their writings by identifying themselves as servants or slaves of Christ. They do not wish to be called the head preacher, evangelist, or missionary. They do not wish to be considered the big boss writing to tell the recipients what they were to do. They wish to be known as the humble servants of Christ.

The following are a few examples of this: Romans 1:1, *Paul, a servant of Christ Jesus, called to be an apostle, set apart for the gospel of God.* Titus 1:1, *Paul, a servant of God and an apostle of Jesus Christ, for the sake of the faith of God's elect and their knowledge of the truth, which accords with godliness.* James 1:1, *James, a servant of God and of the Lord Jesus Christ, To the twelve tribes in the Dispersion: Greetings.* 2 Peter 1:1, *Simeon Peter, a servant and apostle of Jesus Christ, To those who have obtained a faith of equal standing with ours by the righteousness of our God and Savior Jesus Christ.* Jude 1:1, *Jude, a servant of Jesus Christ and brother of James, To those who are called, beloved in God the Father and kept for Jesus Christ.* The Apostle John also calls himself a servant. Revelation 1:1, *The revelation of Jesus Christ, which God gave him to show to his servants the things that must soon take place. He made it known by sending his angel to his servant John.* All of the leaders of the Early Church considered themselves to be servants as well as leaders. As well as being servants of Jesus Christ, they were also the servant leaders of the church.

Again Paul reminds us that he is a servant of Jesus Christ before anything else. Galatians 1:10, *For am I now seeking the approval of man, or of God? Or am I trying to please man? If I were still trying to please man, I would not be a servant of Christ.* Next Paul states that although Jesus is the Son of God, He lowered Himself to be a lowly servant. He had all the power and privileges of being God but was willing to become a man. Philippians 2:5-8, *Have this mind among yourselves, which is yours in Christ Jesus, who, though he was in the form of God, did not count equality with God a thing to be grasped, but made himself nothing, taking the form of a servant, being born in the likeness of men. And being found in human form, he humbled himself by becoming obedient to the point of death, even death on a cross.*

Here is a simple and short reminder of the leadership concept that Jesus tried to teach His disciples. The disciples had a lot of difficulty in grasping this concept. It was so different from everything they had previously observed and been taught about leadership. And to be honest, this concept is still difficult for people to accept and understand in today's world. Mark 9:35, *And he sat down and called the twelve. And he said to them, "If anyone would be first, he must be last of all and servant of all."* To become a leader, one must first of all be last and also a servant. Leadership involves serving others.

Matthew calls Jesus the servant of God in his gospel. He quotes what Isaiah prophesied about Jesus in the Old Testament. Here we have both the New Testament and the Old Testament in agreement that Jesus was called the servant of God. Matthew 12:17-21, *This was to fulfill what was spoken by the prophet Isaiah: "Behold, my servant whom I have chosen, my beloved with whom my soul is well pleased. I will put my Spirit upon him, and he will proclaim justice to the Gentiles. He will not quarrel or cry aloud, nor will anyone hear his voice in the streets; a bruised reed he will not break, and a smoldering wick he will not quench, until he brings justice to victory; and in his name the Gentiles will hope."* Here is the scripture from Isaiah that Matthew quotes. Isaiah 42:1-4, *Behold my servant, whom I uphold, my chosen, in whom my soul delights; I have put my Spirit upon him; he will bring forth justice to the nations. He will not cry aloud or lift up his voice, or make it heard in the street; a bruised reed he will not break, and a faintly burning wick he will not quench; he will faithfully bring forth justice. He will not grow faint or be discouraged till he has established justice in the earth; and the coastlands wait for his law.* Jesus Christ is the ultimate servant leader.

The Old Testament Servant Leaders

We may initially tend to think that the idea of servant leadership began in the New Testament with Jesus. This is not quite true though as throughout the Old Testament we see leaders who are called the servants of God. While they were called the servants of God, there is also an underlying tone of the leader serving those he or she leads.

In the book of Isaiah, God calls three of the Old Testament leaders to be servants of God. Isaiah (Isaiah 20:31), King David (Isaiah 37:35), and Jacob (Isaiah 41:8). Moses was also considered a servant leader. Hebrews 3:5, *Now Moses was faithful in all God's house as a servant, to testify to the things that were to be spoken later.* And again in Revelation 15:3, *And they sing the song of Moses, the servant of God, and the song of the Lamb, saying, "Great and amazing are your deeds, O Lord God the Almighty! Just and true are your ways, O King of the nations!"*

Servant Leader to your Spouse and Children

Here is another area of Christian leadership to consider – that is the concept that being a spouse and/or a parent is also an important form of leadership. This may be something you have never thought about before. This may even cause you to rethink how you react and communicate with your family members. We do not have the time or space to deeply dig into the subject of leadership as a parent or spouse. Those subjects can and do fill many other books that approach the subject in depth. However, since we are discussing the idea that a Christian leader is also a servant leader like Jesus Christ was, then we should definitely consider the idea that Christian spouses and parents should recognize that they are to be servant leaders to their spouses and children.

Spouses

This thought may well be a difficult one to accept for many people. In reality, though, the husband is a servant leader to the wife. The wife is a servant leader to the husband. Both parents are servant leaders to their children. This is so different from what we have been taught over the years. We will include several Bible verses that will help us understand this whole concept better.

Ephesians 5:22-24, *Wives, submit to your own husbands, as to the Lord. For the husband is the head of the wife even as Christ is the head of the church, his body, and is himself its Savior. Now as the church submits to Christ, so also wives should submit in everything to their husbands.*

These verses have often been wrongly used to browbeat wives into meekly submitting to their husband's will and fulfilling his every desire. This form of marriage is contrary to what Jesus taught about loving others and serving them. The key to understanding this form of submission that Paul uses between marriage and the church is the comparison of the relationship between the church and Jesus Christ. When you think about Jesus being the head of the church you think about Christ gently and lovingly leading the church. We do not see Jesus forcing His will on the church or angrily demanding that the church obey His every commandment. Jesus never lorded over His followers. According to this scripture, we are to follow the example of Jesus leading the church in our relationship with our spouse. The husband is to be a servant leader to the wife. He is to love her and to serve her.

Although these verses above speak about the wife submitting to the husband, the important section is about the husband loving the wife just like Christ loves the church. The husband can do this through such activities as cherishing her, listening to her, and valuing and honoring her thoughts, ideas, wants, and desires. This type of spousal leadership has nothing to do with forcing her to bend to his will. It has nothing to do with the husband being the boss and the wife being the compliant and obedient wife. Any marriage in which one spouse lords over the other one is not a healthy or Christ-like relationship.

Next, we come to the part of these verses that some men like to overlook. They love the verses that say that the wife is to submit to the husband's will. They do not want to understand and accept the following verses. Ephesians 5:25-33, *Husbands, love your wives, as Christ loved the church and gave himself up for her, that he might sanctify her, having cleansed her by the washing of water with the word, so that he might present the church to himself in splendor, without spot or wrinkle or any such thing, that she might be holy and without blemish. In the same way, husbands should love their wives as their bodies. He who loves his wife loves himself. For no one ever hated his own flesh, but nourishes and cherishes it, just as Christ does the church, because we are members of his body. "Therefore a man shall leave his father and mother and hold fast to his wife, and the two shall become one flesh." This mystery is profound, and I am saying that it refers to Christ and the church. However, let each one of you love his wife as himself, and let the wife see that she respects her husband.* For some reason, these verses do not seem to be quoted by men as much as the previous verses are quoted and preached on.

Just as Christ loves the church, men are to love their wives. They are to nourish and cherish their wife just as they would their own body. The scripture states that husbands are to love their wives as they love themselves. This is part of that mysterious process that the Bible talks about the husband and wife becoming one. Men are to lovingly lead our wives just as Christ lovingly leads the church. Just as Christ is a servant leader of the church, we are to be servant leaders to our spouses. As we lead, we also serve. And yes, this often involves doing things that we would rather not do.

Spouses are leaders to each other. Maybe this would be good place to remember what Jesus said about leaders being servants. Matthew 20:25-28, *But Jesus called them to him and said, "You know that the rulers of the Gentiles lord it over them, and their great ones exercise authority over them. It shall not be so among you. But whoever would be great among you must be your servant, and whoever would be first among you must be your slave, even as the Son of Man came not to be served but to serve, and to give his life as a ransom for many."*

Accepting that the husband is a leader to the wife and the wife is a leader to the husband, there are two ideas to get from these verses. The first thought is that the leader must be servant to those people that he or she leads. Jesus even mentions that they must be considered a slave to them. The second thought comes from what Jesus says about the way that the Gentile leaders lead. They lead by lording over those they lead and exercising authority over them. There is a strong indication here that Jesus believes that this way of leading must be avoided by the follower of Christ. If Jesus is teaching that the Christian leader must not lead in this manner, it sounds reasonable that the Christian husband and wife must also avoid leading each other through lording over the other one, using intimidation, or exercising authority over the other one. Jesus says here that the husband and wife are servants to each other and that they must use Christ's example through serving each other.

1 Peter 3:7, *Likewise, husbands, live with your wives in an understanding way, showing honor to the woman as the weaker vessel, since they are heirs with you of the grace of life, so that your prayers may not be hindered.* Colossians 3:19, *Husbands, love your wives and do not be harsh with them.* These two verses emphasize the danger with the above statements about one spouse lording over the other one. They contain important rules for a healthy Christian marriage. Husbands must learn to live with their wives in an understanding way and they are not to be harsh with them. This is contrary to the idea that the husband is to be master and the wife is to bow down to the husband's every wish and desire.

In his first epistle to the Corinthians, Paul throws in a slightly different curve on the concept of submission. 1 Corinthians 7:3-5, *The husband should give to his wife her conjugal rights, and likewise the wife to her husband. For the wife does not have authority over her own body, but the husband does. Likewise, the husband does not have authority over his own body, but the wife does. Do not deprive one another, except perhaps by agreement for a limited time, that you may devote yourselves to prayer; but then come together again, so that Satan may not tempt you because of your lack of self-control.* Paul is saying that there must be some form of mutual submission for both spouses toward the other one. The husband is be servant of the wife and the wife is to be servant of the husband.

Parents and Children

Now we come to the idea of a parent being a servant leader to the children. There are several ways of looking at this concept. Being a parent involves so many areas of serving. When the children are little, we must provide everything for them. We serve them by feeding them, dressing them, cleaning them, and caring for every need. We serve them by teaching them and mentoring them to grow up to be good, productive, and loving adults. We serve them by training them and teaching them right from wrong. We also serve them by making sure they get a good education and learn about God.

As we have seen in other verses, Colossians 3:20-21 states, *Children, obey your parents in everything, for this pleases the Lord. Fathers, do not embitter your children, or they will become discouraged.* God expects us to teach our children to obey us just as we are to obey our heavenly Father. Verse 21 goes on to tell the parents that we are not to embitter them so that they become discouraged. Parenting is not an easy task and all of us fail at times in our attempts to do our best. Ephesians 6:4 adds to the command to fathers to be careful about how they treat and raise their children. *Fathers, do not provoke your children to anger, but bring them up in the discipline and instruction of the Lord.* Children do need discipline, correction, and training, but parents need to find a way to do this in a manner that is Christlike.

The purpose of this book is not to tell you how to raise your children. It is not meant to tell you what you must do or not do to be a parent. This short section is just meant to introduce you to the idea that as a spouse you are also a servant leader to your spouse. As a parent, you are also a servant leader to your children. This may mean that you change your way of dealing with your spouse and children so that you relate to them in a more Christlike manner.

Conclusion

As taught and practiced by Jesus, Christian leadership is servant leadership. There is no Christian leadership without servant leadership. The disciples of Jesus had trouble grasping this concept at first. It was so contrary to their previous ideas about leadership. Jesus taught them that leadership was different from what the world thought it was, but it was not until He demonstrated servant leadership to them that they began to understand it better. Even after hearing Him teach on the subject for three years, it was not until the Last Supper that they finally began to understand what Christian (and servant) leadership was.

- 10 -

Role of a Leader

Note: This book attempts to be gender-neutral as much as possible. A Christian leader can be either male or female. This book does not get into the argument of whether women can or should be pastors or leaders in the church.
That discussion is
beyond the purpose and scope of this book.
****

IT can be difficult to define the exact role of a leader in general terms. The role of a leader may often change according to the type of organization and its needs and goals. The leader of a religious nonprofit organization may share many aspects with the leader of a local church but face many different challenges at the same time. Since change is inevitable, circumstances may cause an organization to reorganize or change directions. This may cause the role of the leader to either change his or her methods and efforts at times. If the leader does not change, they may be in danger of failing or possibly even being replaced by a new leader. For this chapter, we will concentrate on general roles in Christian leadership as defined by the Bible. While these characteristics and roles are general, they are the biblical requirement for good ministry or Christian organization leadership. Most of these roles are directed toward leadership in a local church since Christian nonprofit organizations did not exist as such in the early days of the church.

When we start talking about leadership in the Bible, it is important to include Paul's first epistle to Timothy. As we know Paul thought of Timothy as his spiritual son and was mentoring him to be a minister and a leader. It is natural that Paul covers much material on what a Christian leader should look like and how he or she should minister and lead.

The Role of an Elder (Overseer)

1 Timothy 3 is a good example of this. Paul first starts by describing the characteristics necessary to be an overseer or elder. 1 Timothy 3:1-7: *The saying is trustworthy: If anyone aspires to the office of overseer, he desires a noble task. Therefore an overseer must be above reproach, the husband of one wife, sober-minded, self-controlled, respectable, hospitable, able to teach, not a drunkard, not violent but gentle, not quarrelsome, not a lover of money. He must manage his household well, with all dignity keeping his children submissive, for if someone does not know how to manage his household, how will he care for God's church? He must not be a recent convert, or he may become puffed up with conceit and fall into the condemnation of the devil. Moreover, he must be well thought of by outsiders, so that he may not fall into disgrace, into a snare of the devil.*

These are some pretty well defined characteristics and qualifications that are necessary for leading in the church. Where are all of the leadership requirements and characteristics that modern leadership experts and teachers tell us are necessary for good leadership? Do not look too hard, as those things are not in the Bible at all. As stated before, good Christian leadership qualifications and expectations are quite different from those in modern secular leadership. They have different goals, needs, expectations, and requirements.

Above Reproach

The overseer must be above approach. This is the first necessary qualification listed. This is one of the most important characteristics listed. The leader must have integrity. He or she has to have enough integrity that others do not question their decisions or motives. The Christian leader must be well respected in both the church and the community. He or she must be dependable and honest. Others may disagree with your theology and teachings but your integrity must be apparent to everyone. This means that the overseer has to have proven himself or herself over time.

Husband of One Wife

There are two major controversies in the church about this part of the verse. The first controversy is that men are the only gender allowed to be a pastor. As noted above, that is an argument and discussion for others to debate and decide on. The second controversy is whether Paul is saying that people who have been divorced and remarried cannot hold the office of overseer. Many denominations and churches teach that people who are divorced and remarried are allowed to hold this office while others hold to a different standard on this issue. It is not this book's place to make these decisions for churches or denominations about whether or not women pastors should be allowed in their church. The same holds true about pastors who have been divorced and remarried.

Interpreting this verse implicitly to mean that the leader must be a man and that he must be married to just one wife brings up another question here. Does this also mean that the leader must be married and cannot be single? Some churches and denominations seem to believe this is true. It is difficult to believe that Paul meant that to be the case since this rule would have prevented both Jesus and Paul himself from holding any leadership roles in the church. Neither one of them were married. Paul stated in 1 Corinthians 7:8 that he was not married. Two of the greatest leaders in the New Testament were not married. The purpose of this paragraph is not to stir up conflict or arguments on theology, but to warn the reader to be careful on how they interpret certain scriptures in order to create strict rules that may not agree with the original meaning that the author meant them to have.

Sober-minded

The overseer is to be serious (sober) minded. Does this mean that pastors are not allowed to have fun, laugh, or make jokes? Surely, this is not what Paul was talking about here. Overall, the overseer is to be serious-minded though. This is especially true about spiritual matters.

Self-Controlled

Being self-controlled is a rare thing in today's world. Today's mindset has become focused on each individual doing what feels right to him or herself. There used to be a popular saying that said, "If it feels good, just do it!" The post-modern philosophy of truth and reality is focused on what you think it is. It is a selfish ideology. This philosophy even tells you that truth is not an absolute, it is whatever each person thinks it is. This philosophy leads to people focusing on themselves and their own personal desires. Self-control and self-discipline are often not expected of anyone other than athletes. Here, in Paul's writings, we learn that self-control is expected for the Christian leader.

Respectable

An elder must be respected by others. Ministers and other Christian leaders must first be respected by the local church members. A leader that has no respect from his or her followers cannot be successful. This is seen so many times in the secular world, as well as in the church world, when someone is selected for a leadership role for all of the wrong reasons. The leader may have no leadership skills and quickly loses the respect of the followers. This makes for a hostile workspace for everyone involved and usually ends in failure. This situation is even worse when it occurs in a church.

A church leader who does not have the respect of the people will soon lose those people. Sometimes, though, there is an exception to the people leaving the church. In this case, an older member of the church may take an attitude that they were there before the leader was and they will still be there long after the problem leader leaves. These members refuse to leave because of the poor leadership. They wait it out knowing that sooner or later the leader will leave and be replaced. This is not a healthy situation at all.

An elder should also be respectable to the outside world. An elder that has no respect from others will not be able to work with other ministers and will not be able to draw people from the outside world into the church. He or she will be unable to do any successful ministry within the neighborhood or community. Respect is a must for any successful leader.

Hospitable

Church leaders must be hospitable. Hospitality is largely a forgotten aspect of Christianity. What does this even mean to a Christian? A couple of points come to mind. We know that in the Old Testament, the Israelites were to show hospitality to strangers and visitors. The second thought that comes to mind is the relationship between hospitality and the command that Jesus gave us that we are to love our neighbor (and our enemy) as ourselves. It is impossible to separate hospitality from loving others. A major part of loving others would involve showing them hospitality. Each person and church must define what hospitality looks like but keep in mind that we are to love others as ourselves. A local church is not a private social club reserved for the members of the church alone. The church must be hospitable and reaching out to others in the community.

Able to Teach

An elder must be able to teach and mentor others. He is tasked with teaching the gospel message to others. Most pastors seem able to preach the Gospel relatively well. Of course, some are better communicators and orators than others. The Holy Spirit can, and sometimes He does, use a message from a poorly preached sermon. But, everyone of us would much rather hear a sermon preached in a well-communicated manner.

Not a Drunkard

This requirement should be true for any type of Christian leadership. Excessive alcohol usage can damage the reputation of an elder and definitely can affect their ability to teach or preach effectively. Alcohol can also affect the elder's relationships with their family members and others. This book will not discuss the argument on whether Christians should drink alcohol or whether Jesus turned the water into wine or grape juice at the wedding feast. That discussion often brings much acrimony and fighting between Christians. However, if one does choose to drink alcoholic beverages, moderation has to be a key element, and drunkenness is to be avoided at all costs.

Gentle - Not Violent

Elders are to be gentle and not violent. This requirement should be understood without the need to say it. Violence has absolutely no place in the ministry. See Chapter 7 for the discussion about anger in leadership. This includes verbal violence as well as physical violence. An example of this happened a number of years ago where a member stood up in a church business meeting and questioned the pastor about a decision the pastor had made. The pastor angrily and publicly berated the member for daring to question his decision. This member who had been publicly called down in such a manner soon left the church to never return. Many other members eventually left this church because of the pastor's temper and controlling ways.

As opposed to violence, Paul now includes gentleness as a requirement for leadership. After reading many leadership books, we have not found any of them that mention gentleness as a good characteristic of leadership. To be honest, gentleness is not something one normally thinks about when considering leadership. But in 1 Timothy, Paul includes gentleness as being important for a Christian leader. Secular leadership often does not include anything approaching gentleness. Consider this thought, Christian leadership is that type of leadership that is done by a follower of Jesus Christ who has the Holy Spirit dwelling inside. Remember also that gentleness is one of the Fruit of the Spirit. Galatians 5:22, *But the fruit of the Spirit is love, joy, peace, patience, kindness, goodness, faithfulness, gentleness, self-control; against such things, there is no law.* It stands to reason then that gentleness should always be a factor in Christian leadership no matter what the other leadership books and classes tell you.

Not Quarrelsome

The next requirement goes along with gentleness. The elder is not to be quarrelsome. You may have met pastors who are quarrelsome. They love to shout their particular theology and argue with anyone who disagrees with them. This especially seems to be true in Christian groups on social media. Anyone who disagrees with them is considered a heretic. To state it simply, quarrelsomeness is in direct contrast to being Christlike. Arguing and fighting with others has nothing to do with loving others. Arguments are never gentle and they are not very loving in nature.

Not a Lover of Money

The elder is not to be a lover of money. This requirement has seemingly been overlooked by some of the megachurch pastors as well as some televangelists in today's world. An emphasis on riches does not advance the gospel message and it does not look much like the example that Jesus Christ gave us. We all agree that living in the world and doing ministry does take a certain amount of money to operate. Without any money, the ministry will quickly fold. But, so many people have fallen into the trap that success is linked to money. The faulty idea is that a successful ministry should bring riches. Ministers do need to earn a living wage to support themselves and their families. At some point, money often takes over as the prime motivation and goal of ministry. Fortunately, obtaining riches is not a major problem for the average pastor in the United States as the average church tends to be small. Even then, the love of money may still afflict the pastor of a lower-paying church. It often causes some pastors to drop out of the ministry to seek more money, or at least a living wage, in order to support their family.

Manage Household Well

The elder is expected to manage his or her household well. We have to remember that Paul wrote this in an male dominated culture. In those days the husband tended to rule the household with an iron fist. The wife and the children were considered to be property of the husband/father. In today's culture, wives and even their children live in a much different world with more rights and freedom.

It is unknown exactly to what level this requirement should be expected. Should a pastor be fired because their son gets on drugs or their unmarried daughter becomes pregnant out of wedlock? These are tough questions that occasionally happen in real life just like it does in the lives of church members. Should the pastor or leader be held accountable for situations in their family that are often beyond their control? Should a pastor or church leader lose his or her position because of these or other problems occur in their family? This is a decision that each church must make in that situation. Love, understanding, compassion, and forgiveness will go a lot further than judgment and condemnation.

Not a Recent Convert

The elder or leader should not be a recent convert. This requirement seems to be reasonable. This is not a desire to discourage or prevent new converts from going into the ministry. They should be encouraged to seek these roles if God calls them into ministry. There are good reasons to require all believers (including new believers) to prove themselves over time and to receive education, training, and mentoring before being allowed into positions of leadership in the church.

Well Thought of by Outsiders

This requirement goes along with the comments in the previous section above about respectability. The pastor or other minister should be well thought of by those outside the church. He or she has to have respect from the members of the church. Even if the pastor is respected within the church, without the respect of those outside the church, his or her success in reaching the community will be limited. The success of their ministry and service to the community will largely depend on how well the minister is respected within the community.

Qualifications for Deacons

After the above description of the requirements for an elder, Paul goes on next to describe the requirements to be a deacon. These requirements are a little different than those of an elder but similar. The deacon is an important leader in the local church. Although this church leadership position was not one that Christ called for, the early disciples agreed that the deacon played an important role in helping the pastor lead the local church. The position of deacon was designed to free up many of the duties of the pastor so that the pastor could devote more of his or her time to prayer and studying God's word instead of spending so much time in the business of the church.

The First Martyr

Acts chapter 5 tells the story about how the early church decided to select certain men to be deacons. Although the idea of having deacons in the church was not something pushed by Jesus, it was a wise idea in order to solve some of the problems that the pastors of the early church faced. The idea of having deacons taking care of much of the daily business and ministry of the church still makes sense in today's churches. Having deacons allows the pastor to better spend his or her time in prayer and teaching the Word.

Stephen is not the only deacon named in the New Testament. He may be the most impressive deacon in the record of the early church. Acts 6:5 says, *And what they said pleased the whole gathering, and they chose Stephen, a man full of faith and of the Holy Spirit, and Philip, and Prochorus, and Nicanor, and Timon, and Parmenas, and Nicolaus, a proselyte of Antioch.* Notice that the descriptions of Stephen do not mention how great he is. They do not mention what a great leader or teacher he is. It never mentions how charismatic and personable he is. It never lists his leadership attributes and skills, but it does mention his spiritual attributes and characteristics. Acts simply tells us that he was full of faith and the Holy Spirit. Those two things are his primary qualifications for being selected to be a deacon. Then in verse 8 it continues, *And Stephen, full of grace and power, was doing great wonders and signs among the people.* Here we add two more characteristics of Stephen. He was full of grace and power. Both of those things are due to him being full of the Holy Spirit. There is still nothing listed about any leadership qualifications. All of his mentioned leadership attributes come directly from being full of the Holy Spirit.

The story continues with Stephen teaching the Word and doing many wonders and signs. This made the Jews angry and they came against him and began arguing with him. Acts 6:10 explains what happens when he answers their arguments, *But they could not withstand the wisdom and the Spirit with which he was speaking.* What a powerful statement about Stephen. There is no mention of the power and eloquence of his words. There is no mention of his intelligence, education, and mastery of language. There is only mention of the wisdom and the Spirit in which he was speaking with. The power of the Holy Spirit operating within him confounded those who heard him speak.

The high priest and other religious leaders could not find the right words to dispute the wisdom and power of the Holy Spirit speaking through Stephen. They were so angry at him that Acts 7:54-55 says, *Now when they heard these things they were enraged, and they ground their teeth at him. But he, full of the Holy Spirit, gazed into heaven and saw the glory of God, and Jesus standing at the right hand of God.* Even in facing death, the only mention about Stephen is that he was full of the Holy Spirit. He was so full of the Holy Spirit that he looked into heaven and saw the glory of God.

Although Stephen had a short time of ministry as a deacon, he had a great impact on the early church and the community. In some ways he was one of the greatest leaders mentioned in the New Testament. Yet the Bible never mentions any leadership characteristics or attributes that made him great. The only attributes mentioned about him were that he was full of faith, grace, and the Holy Spirit. He is the epitome of what a Christian leader should look like. This suggests that we should change our expectations for leaders, ministers, and deacons in the church. Our new expectations should look more like Stephen - full of the Holy Spirit, grace, and faith. That is truly what the successful Christian leader looks like even though it cost Stephen his life through being stoned.

Here is one more quick observation about Stephen. He is so full of the Holy Spirit that even in death he remains Christlike. Acts 7:59-60, *And as they were stoning Stephen, he called out, "Lord Jesus, receive my spirit." And falling to his knees he cried out with a loud voice, "Lord, do not hold this sin against them." And when he had said this, he fell asleep.* Do you see the parallel to Jesus there? Just as Jesus did on the cross, he willingly gave up his life and he requested that God not hold the sin of murdering him against those participating in his stoning. Could we leaders today be like Stephen was? Could we be so full of the Holy Spirit and grace that we would willing to give up our lives and ask the Father not to hold them responsible for this sin?

The Deacon's Spouse

1 Timothy 3:9-13, *Deacons likewise must be dignified, not double-tongued, not addicted to much wine, and not greedy for dishonest gain. They must hold the mystery of the faith with a clear conscience. And let them also be tested first; then let them serve as deacons if they prove themselves blameless. Their wives likewise must be dignified, not slanderers, but sober-minded, faithful in all things. Let deacons each be the husband of one wife, managing their children and their households well. Those who serve well as deacons gain a good standing for themselves and also great confidence in the faith that is in Christ Jesus.*

These verses bring up a completely unexpected aspect about Christian leadership. That different aspect is that the leader's spouse plays an important role in the person selected for these positions. The spouses's personality, character, and bearing can either help make or break the chances for the leader's success in Christian leadership. The leader's spouse and their character must be considered in even choosing the elder or deacon. Has God called you into the ministry or to be a deacon? This suggests that you must choose your spouse carefully. It is rare in the secular world for your spouse to play a part in whether or not you get a certain position. This is just another way in which Christian leadership is quite different from other types of leadership.

Some of the characteristics of the spouse of a Christian leader according to Paul:

* Not Double-tongued
* Not Addicted to Much Wine
* Not Greedy
* Must Hold to Doctrine
* Must Be Tested
* Wife Must be Dignified
* Wife Not Slanderer
* Wife Faithful in All Things
* Wife Sober-Minded
* One Wife
* Manage Children and Household

The Financial Side of Leadership

We will briefly discuss the financial side of Christian leadership. Finances can play an important part in leadership, but that is not the purpose of this book. Paul mentions finances here in his letter to Timothy as he understood that there is a real danger from desiring financial gain. Here he is warning Timothy to be aware of this danger and not allow greed for money to creep into his life or ministry. We have all seen the harm that comes from the desire for wealth in ministry - especially relating to some preachers and televangelists who prey on the poor. 1 Timothy 6:6-10: *But godliness with contentment is great gain, for we brought nothing into the world, and we cannot take anything out of the world. But if we have food and clothing, with these we will be content. But those who desire to be rich fall into temptation, into a snare, into many senseless and harmful desires that plunge people into ruin and destruction. For the love of money is the root of all kinds of evil. It is through this craving that some have wandered away from the faith and pierced themselves with many pangs.*

Immediately after the above statements to Timothy, Paul sums up what the Christian leader is supposed to look like. 1 Timothy 6:11 says, *But as for you, O man of God, flee these things. Pursue righteousness, godliness, faith, love, steadfastness, gentleness.* What is it exactly that Paul is urging Timothy to flee? He is telling the Christian leader to flee from the love of money and the desire to be rich. In today's world, we tend to associate success with riches and wealth. This is true even in the ministry. God has much different ideas about what success consists of. The Christian is to flee and to run away from such things. So what are we to pursue in the place of wealth and riches? Paul answers this question in just a few words. We are to seek righteousness, godliness, faith, love, steadfastness, and gentleness. Do you mean to tell me that things like gentleness is more important in leadership than financial gain and riches? Are you saying that love is more important than worldly gains? The answer is yes, that is exactly what the Bible states. Christian leaders' priorities must line up with what God expects from us, not what other people expect from us. These things that Paul is urging us to pursue look just like the Fruit of the Spirit. This is another way of saying this is that the Christian leader will be producing the Fruit of the Spirit. This is another indication that displaying the Fruit of the Spirit in the leader's life is a vital characteristic and attribute of the successful Christian leader.

Titus

Paul writes to Titus about leadership in his epistle to him. Much of what he writes to Titus mirrors what he wrote in his letters to Timothy. Titus 1 is directed toward those people who were chosen to be leaders in their local churches. Chapter 2 deals with some situations that were occurring, but the included verses are about the older men and women in the church teaching and mentoring the younger members. Chapter 3 seems to be mostly aimed toward all believers but it definitely holds true for Christian leaders since they must, first of all, be believers in Jesus Christ.

Titus Chapter 1

This is why I left you in Crete, so that you might put what remained into order, and appoint elders in every town as I directed you— if anyone is above reproach, the husband of one wife, and his children are believers and not open to the charge of debauchery or insubordination. An overseer, as God's steward, must be above reproach. He must not be arrogant or quick-

tempered or a drunkard or violent or greedy for gain, but hospitable, a lover of good, self-controlled, upright, holy, and disciplined. He must hold firm to the trustworthy word as taught, so that he may be able to give instruction in sound doctrine and also to rebuke those who contradict it.

Titus Chapter 2

But as for you, teach what accords with sound doctrine. Older men are to be sober-minded, dignified, self-controlled, sound in faith, in love, and in steadfastness. Older women likewise are to be reverent in behavior, not slanderers or slaves to much wine. They are to teach what is good, and so train the young women to love their husbands and children, to be self-controlled, pure, working at home, kind, and submissive to their own husbands, that the word of God may not be reviled.

Titus Chapter 3

Remind them to be submissive to rulers and authorities, to be obedient, to be ready for every good work, to speak evil of no one, to avoid quarreling, to be gentle, and to show perfect courtesy toward all people. For we ourselves were once foolish, disobedient, led astray, slaves to various passions and pleasures, passing our days in malice and envy, hated by others and hating one another. But when the goodness and loving kindness of God our Savior appeared, he saved us, not because of works done by us in righteousness, but according to his own mercy, by the washing of regeneration and renewal of the Holy Spirit, whom he poured out on us richly through Jesus Christ our Savior, so that being justified by his grace we might become heirs according to the hope of eternal life. The saying is trustworthy, and I want you to insist on these things, so that those who have believed in God may be careful to devote themselves to good works. These things are excellent and profitable for people. But avoid foolish controversies, genealogies, dissensions, and quarrels about the law, for they are unprofitable and worthless. As for a person who stirs up division, after warning him once and then twice, have nothing more to do with him, knowing that such a person is warped and sinful; he is self-condemned.

Even in Christian leadership, we tend to admire and select those who are tall, white, male, good-looking, charismatic, good orators, and have the right education. We tend to overlook the requirements listed in the New Testament for church leadership. We are aware that Paul wrote about these things but tend to overlook them when selecting our church leaders. After all, some people just look and sound like what we think a pastor is supposed to look and sound like. Many others are qualified according to the Bible but may not look, act, or talk like the image that we have in our minds of a pastor. The leadership characteristics that Paul mentions point to a follower of Christ who is filled and walking in the Holy Spirit. The leadership attributes of the New Testament have nothing to do with being good-looking, smart, well educated, or a dynamic speaker.

Romans 12

You may be asking yourself how Romans 12 got stuck in the middle of a discussion on leadership. Romans 12 plays an important part in our theology of Christian leadership. Remember that the Book of Romans was written to the believers in Rome. Also remember that a Christian leader must be first a follower of Jesus Christ. The whole chapter (Romans 12) is included here in order to be read again. It has so many thoughts that are vital to being a successful Christian leader. So here it is without any commentary. Please read this chapter slowly and carefully. Then think about what this text is expecting from you as a Christian leader. As you read this, you will notice that Paul has a lot to say about leadership and ministry in this chapter.

Romans 12: *I appeal to you therefore, brothers, by the mercies of God, to present your bodies as a living sacrifice, holy and acceptable to God, which is your spiritual worship. Do not be conformed to this world, but be transformed by the renewal of your mind, that by testing you may discern what is the will of God, what is good and acceptable and perfect. For by the grace given to me, I say to everyone among you not to think of himself more highly than he ought to think, but to think with sober judgment, each according to the measure of faith that God has assigned. For as in one body we have many members, and the members do not all have the same function, so we, though many, are one body in Christ, and individually members one of another. Having gifts that differ according to the grace given to us, let us use them: if prophecy, in proportion to our faith; if service, in our serving; the one who teaches, in his teaching; the one who exhorts, in his exhortation; the one who contributes, in generosity; the one who leads, with zeal; the one who does acts of mercy, with cheerfulness. Let love be genuine. Abhor what is evil; hold fast to what is good. Love one another with brotherly affection. Outdo one another in showing honor. Do not be slothful in zeal, be fervent in spirit, serve the Lord. Rejoice in hope, be patient in tribulation, be constant in prayer. Contribute to the needs of the saints and seek to show hospitality. Bless those who persecute you; bless and do not curse them. Rejoice with those who rejoice, weep with those who weep. Live in harmony with one another. Do not be haughty, but associate with the lowly. Never be wise in your own sight. Repay no one evil for evil, but give thought to do what is honorable in the sight of all. If possible, so far as it depends on you, live peaceably with all. Beloved, never avenge yourselves, but leave it to the wrath of God, for it is written, "Vengeance is mine, I will repay, says the Lord." To the contrary, "if your enemy is hungry, feed him; if he is thirsty, give him something to drink; for by so doing you will heap burning coals on his head." Do not be overcome by evil, but overcome evil with good.*

1 Peter 4

Although the first epistle of Peter is not directed toward leaders specifically, his letter does contain a few things of interest for leaders. 1 Peter 4:7-11, *The end of all things is at hand; therefore be self-controlled and sober-minded for the sake of your prayers. Above all, keep loving one another earnestly, since love covers a multitude of sins. Show hospitality to one another without grumbling. As each has received a gift, use it to serve one another, as good stewards of God's varied grace: whoever speaks, as one who speaks oracles of God; whoever serves, as one who serves by the strength that God supplies--in order that in everything God may be glorified through Jesus Christ. To him belong glory and dominion forever and ever. Amen.* Here Peter is reminding the believer that he or she should maintain self-control and to be sober-minded. Once again the emphasis is placed on loving one another, in other words to love your neighbor as yourself. This agape type of love even covers a multitude of sins according to Peter. Hospitality comes about through loving your neighbor and in turn is a method of loving your neighbor as yourself.

Peter, like Paul, reminds the believer that he or she has been given at least one spiritual gift from God. Along with this gift comes the responsibility of the believer to be a good steward of that gift and to use it for the glory of God and His Kingdom. Some people are given the gift of teaching and the teacher must be careful to teach the truth. All of us have been called to serve, and we are all to serve others just as if we were doing that service to Christ. Peter reminds us that we serve through the strength that God gives us. We do not serve in our own strength or wisdom. We depend on those things from God.

Some of the Scariest Verses in the Bible

Sometimes Jesus taught things that confused or angered His listeners. Some of these things that He taught still confuse or anger believers and nonbelievers today. These next words, that Jesus spoke, may even be called by some as the scariest verses in the Bible. These verses are directed toward all believers, not just toward leaders in specific. However, this means that leaders should be holding these truths dear to their hearts and also be teaching these to others. Do not overlook these things as they are important. This is not included to tell you what you need to do as a Christian leader, but is provided in order to help you understand that you may need to consider adjusting some areas in your life, leadership, and ministry to include what Jesus mentions here.

Here are the scariest Bible verses. Matthew 7:21-25, Jesus says, *"Not everyone who says to me, 'Lord, Lord,' will enter the kingdom of heaven, but the one who does the will of my Father who is in heaven. On that day many will say to me, 'Lord, Lord, did we not prophesy in your name, and cast out demons in your name, and do many mighty works in your name?' And then will I declare to them, 'I never knew you; depart from me, you workers of lawlessness.'*

These verses can be confusing because, on the surface, they seem to be stating that a believer (and a leader) can believe in Christ and think that they are getting their eternal reward in heaven. Some of these people that Jesus mentions here were preachers and teachers. They went about and won lost souls to the kingdom of heaven. They even did miracles and cast out demons in the name of Jesus. Surely these people should be accepted into the kingdom of heaven at Judgment Day. Jesus states that at the Judgment Day, these people will be called workers of iniquity and that they will not be able to enter the kingdom of heaven. This is confusing and scary. What does it mean?

Jesus later explains in a little more detail about this subject in Matthew 25. These verses are a little long but they are vital to understanding the message that Jesus is trying to teach here.

Matthew 25:31-46: *"When the Son of Man comes in his glory, and all the angels with him, then he will sit on his glorious throne. Before him will be gathered all the nations, and he will separate people one from another as a shepherd separates the sheep from the goats. And he will place the sheep on his right, but the goats on the left. Then the King will say to those on his right, 'Come, you who are blessed by my Father, inherit the kingdom prepared for you from the foundation of the world. For I was hungry and you gave me food, I was thirsty and you gave me drink, I was a stranger and you welcomed me, I was naked and you clothed me, I was sick and you visited me, I was in prison and you came to me.' Then the righteous will answer him, saying, 'Lord, when did we see you hungry and feed you, or thirsty and give you drink? And when did we see you a stranger and welcome you, or naked and clothe you? And when did we see you sick or in prison and visit you?' And the King will answer them, 'Truly, I say to you, as you did it to one of the least of these my brothers, you did it to me.' "Then he will say to those on his left, 'Depart from me, you cursed, into the eternal fire prepared for the devil and his angels. For I was hungry and you gave me no food, I was thirsty and you gave me no drink, I was a stranger and you did not welcome me, naked and you did not clothe me, sick and in prison and you did not visit me.' Then they also will answer, saying, 'Lord, when did we see you hungry or thirsty or a stranger or naked or sick or in prison, and did not minister to you?' Then he will answer them, saying, 'Truly, I say to you, as you did not do it to one of the least of these, you did not do it to me.' And these will go away into eternal punishment, but the righteous into eternal life."*

Please note here that Jesus did not mention anything about choosing those who went to the right church. He did not mention anything about praying the sinner's prayer. He does not even mention that the sheep were those who had believed on Christ and called upon His name. He does not mention anything about obeying the Ten Commandments. He does not mention anything about being baptized in water. He does not mention that the believer must have the right theology. He does not mention that these believers worshipped the correct way. The purpose of including these verses is not to challenge any of your current theology, but to remind you not to minimize your efforts in loving your neighbor as yourself. It is good to care for others spiritual needs, but Jesus expects us to also care about their other needs.

This brings to mind the message that John the Baptist preached to the crowds in the wilderness. He was telling the people that repentance must be accompanied by producing fruit. Without this fruit, repentance was meaningless. If God has forgiven you then you must produce fruit in love. What is this fruit that John the Baptist was talking about? Luke 3:8-11 tells us, *Bear fruits in keeping with repentance. And do not begin to say to yourselves, 'We have Abraham as our father.' For I tell you, God is able from these stones to raise up children for Abraham. Even now the axe is laid to the root of the trees. Every tree therefore that does not bear good fruit is cut down and thrown into the fire." And the crowds asked him, "What then shall we do?" And he answered them, "Whoever has two tunics is to share with him who has none, and whoever has food is to do likewise."* Even before Jesus preached his message about this subject in Matthew, John the Baptist was preaching a similar message that believers must love their neighbor as themselves. One part of loving your neighbor is to share what God has provided for you with those who are in need. Jesus took this message one step further and stated that if you do not do this, the final judgment will not be a happy occasion for you.

Jesus even encouraged people to be generous with those in need when they host a dinner. Luke 14:12-14, *He said also to the man who had invited him, "When you give a dinner or a banquet, do not invite your friends or your brothers or your relatives or rich neighbors, lest they also invite you in return and you be repaid. But when you give a feast, invite the poor, the crippled, the lame, the blind, and you will be blessed, because they cannot repay you. For you will be repaid at the resurrection of the just."*

One more Bible verse to add to this subject is from James. James has a habit of encouraging believers to put their faith and their love for their neighbors into action. In James 1:27, he states, *Religion that is pure and undefiled before God, the Father, is this: to visit orphans and widows in their affliction, and to keep oneself unstained from the world.* Remember that this is directed toward all believers. It is the leader's place to first practice this and to teach those under their ministry to also practice this 'pure religion.'

The purpose of this section is not to condemn any of us in this matter but to remind us the heart of Jesus toward those in need. Unfortunately, this is an area in which many of us fall short. As a follower of Jesus Christ and as a Christian leader we all need to be more generous. A major part of following Christ involves loving your neighbor as yourself. If you love your neighbor as yourself, you will find food for them when you see them hungry. If you love your neighbor as yourself, you will find clothing for them when they are naked. If you love your neighbor as yourself, you will help them find shelter when they have no home. If you love your neighbor as yourself, you will do your best to help those in need. That is what Jesus tells us that we must do. As always, the Christian leader must set the example to others in doing this. In your efforts to love your neighbor, do not forget about the orphans, widows, and prisoners. Love your neighbor as yourself.

Peter

When you start discussing Christian leadership from a biblical standpoint, you usually start with what Jesus says about leadership. Then you move on to what Paul and the other disciples had to say about Christian leadership. Most Christian leaders take much of their leadership theology from the teachings of Paul. Jesus and Paul were not the only two people to join into the discussion on Christian leadership. There is a surprise entry into the discussion. Peter does not write as much about leadership as Paul did but he did direct part of his first epistle toward the leaders. He gives the leaders some great advice. Many of these directions for leaders sound like what both Jesus taught about leadership and the attributes of a Christian leader that Paul wrote.

1 Peter 5:1-11: *So I exhort the elders among you, as a fellow elder and a witness of the sufferings of Christ, as well as a partaker in the glory that is going to be revealed: shepherd the flock of God that is among you, exercising oversight, not under compulsion, but willingly, as God would have you; not for shameful gain, but eagerly; not domineering over those in your charge, but being examples to the flock. And when the chief Shepherd appears, you will receive the unfading crown of glory. Likewise, you who are younger, be subject to the elders. Clothe yourselves, all of you, with humility toward one another, for "God opposes the proud but gives grace to the humble." Humble yourselves, therefore, under the mighty hand of God so that at the proper time he may exalt you, casting all your anxieties on him, because he cares for you. Be sober-minded; be watchful. Your adversary the devil prowls around like a roaring lion, seeking someone to devour. Resist him, firm in your faith, knowing that the same kinds of suffering are being experienced by your brotherhood throughout the world. And after you have suffered a little while, the God of all grace, who has called you to his eternal glory in Christ, will himself restore, confirm, strengthen, and establish you. To him be the dominion forever and ever. Amen.*

The first sentence in these verses tell us that we are to shepherd the flock in our care. In John 10:11 and 14, Jesus calls Himself the Good Shepherd. *I am the good shepherd. I know my own and my own know me.* In Hebrews 13:20, the author calls Jesus the Great Shepherd. *Now may the God of peace who brought again from the dead our Lord Jesus, the great shepherd of the sheep, by the blood of the eternal covenant.* Just as Jesus was the Great Shepherd, we are to shepherd those that God has placed under our leadership. We are to exhibit oversight over them in a Christlike manner. We are not to be domineering over them. We are to instead, be an example to them. We lead in love and by example, not by demanding and definitely not by expecting blind obedience. If you do this, you will gain a crown of glory when the Great Shepherd arrives. Jesus shows us how we are to shepherd those within our care.

We are to exercise oversight, not under compulsion, but willingly as Christ did with His followers. He wants us to shepherd those within our flock in the same manner that He does. We are to be examples to the flock. This means that we must practice what we teach or preach.

Leaders must lead by example. Even many secular leadership teachers will tell you that leading by example is important. The flock who sees you teach one thing and live a different way will sooner or later leave the flock. Peter says that we are not to lead for shameful gain. Just as Jesus stated back in Matthew, we are not to be domineering over those we lead, but we are to be an example to them.

Clothe yourself in humility for God opposes the proud, but gives grace to the humble. We are to recognize that everything we are and everything we accomplish is because of Christ. We are not only to strive towards humility, but we are to completely immerse ourselves in it. Everything we do or say should portray humility. Displays of pride and ego have no place in the Christian leader's life and leadership.

Peter says to humble your self under the hand of God. God himself will exalt the successful leader. There is no reason for the leader to exalt him self or her self. Any success that we have accomplished is not because of our own doing but through allowing God to work through us. It is through the Holy Spirit working within us and through us. Peter also throws in here that the leader has nothing to be worried about. He says that we are to cast all of our anxieties upon God for He cares for us. We know that there are many concerns, trials, and tribulations in leadership. There are a lot of responsibilities that need to be taken care of in leadership. Peter states that there is no need for us to be anxious about these things. We are to give God all of our anxiety.

The next three warnings tie together. Be sober-minded, be watchful, and resist the devil. Why do we have to do all of these things? It is necessary because the devil roams around like a roaring lion seeking someone to devour or destroy. The Christian leader is always a target for Satan. He would love to destroy the leader and will do so in any manner that he can. Peter links resisting the devil with suffering. He says that we should gladly endure this suffering as believers around the world also suffer the same sufferings and God promises to "restore, confirm, strengthen, and establish you."

Conclusion

This chapter has covered a large number of areas in which Christian leaders are to fit into. Some of these things are characteristics that the leader is to display even before being selected into leadership. Other areas are those that the leader should be doing as a follower of Jesus Christ. Here a few more verses that leaders should keep in mind as they lead others. These verses were actually written for all followers of Christ, not just the leaders. As we have seen in this chapter Paul, and the other leaders of the early church understood that leadership is all about followership.

Paul gave Timothy a quick little reminder that he is to practice what he preaches. This is a good reminder to all of us that we are to watch what we say, along with our attitudes, and our actions. 1 Timothy 4:12, *Let no one despise you for your youth, but set the believers an example in speech, in conduct, in love, in faith, in purity.*

James 1:26, *If anyone thinks he is religious and does not bridle his tongue but deceives his heart, this person's religion is worthless.* This is a difficult task for all of us but it is so important for the Christian leader.

In the epistle to the Hebrews, the author lists a number of things that the believer should always keep in mind. They are even more important for the Christian leader as he or she follows Christ. These are offered without comment as the verses speak for themselves. Hebrews 13:1-6, *Let brotherly love continue. Do not neglect to show hospitality to strangers, for thereby some have entertained angels unawares. Remember those who are in prison, as though in prison with them, and those who are mistreated, since you also are in the body. Let marriage be held in honor among all, and let the marriage bed be undefiled, for God will judge the sexually immoral and adulterous. Keep your life free from love of money, and be content with what you have, for he has said, "I will never leave you nor forsake you." So we can confidently say, "The Lord is my helper; I will not fear; what can man do to me?"*

- 11 -

The Beatitudes
(The Sermon on the Mount)

IF a Christian leader is someone who not only leads others but is also a follower of Christ, then we must link the teachings of Jesus to Christian leadership. In Matthew 5 and 6, Jesus taught the crowds of people what has been commonly called The Beatitudes (or the Sermon on the Mount). We have previously discussed the many paradoxes that exist in Christian leadership and Christianity itself. The Beatitudes are chock full of even more paradoxes that are involved in following Christ. We should at least need to look at the beatitudes and consider how they affect leadership.

After reading these two chapters in Matthew and hearing many sermons about the Sermon on the Mount, how do we still get much of what Jesus said so wrong? Remember what Isaiah 55 told us? God's ways and thoughts are not ours. His way is so different from men's. His thinking is different from man's thinking. Then why are we surprised that Christian leadership is so different from world's idea of leadership? Why do we think that we try to copy the leadership ways of the world? Why do we tend to ignore so much of what Jesus taught when it comes to leadership? We take the things from Jesus' teaching that we like and ignore those that are uncomfortable. We love it that God loved us so much that He sent His Son to die for us and offer us love and forgiveness that we do not deserve. Then we want to ignore those teachings from Christ that are so different, and maybe uncomfortable, from what the world teaches.

Most of the Beatitudes are in contrast to anything approaching what the world considers to be good leadership. However, as a Christian leader, you should at least consider all of the teachings of Jesus Christ and consider how those teachings affect your leadership styles and actions. If your leadership style does not look anything like the way Jesus led, then you may be a leader without truly being a Christian leader.

Matthew 5:2-12:

And he opened his mouth and taught them, saying:

Blessed are the poor in spirit, for theirs is the kingdom of heaven.
Blessed are those who mourn, for they shall be comforted.
Blessed are the meek, for they shall inherit the earth.
Blessed are those who hunger and thirst for righteousness, for they
    shall be satisfied.
Blessed are the merciful, for they shall receive mercy.
Blessed are the pure in heart, for they shall see God.
Blessed are the peacemakers, for they shall be called sons of God.
Blessed are those who are persecuted for righteousness sake, for theirs
    is the kingdom of heaven.
Blessed are you when others revile you and persecute you and
    utter all kinds of evil against you falsely on my account. Rejoice
    and be glad, for your reward is great in heaven, for so they
    persecuted the prophets who were before you.

Here Jesus is teaching on who is blessed by God.

Until this time, the expectation was that the people who were blessed by God were those who had obtained many riches, land, livestock, wives, and children. Those were considered to be the people who had been blessed by God. All too often, we also follow that line of thinking today. Most of us do not claim to believe in the prosperity gospel but we often look in envy at those ministers and evangelists who have attracted large numbers of people and who have been blessed by financial success. But now, Jesus is teaching a different expectation! He is denying the traditional measures of success. He is saying that it is not the rich and powerful who have been blessed by God. He is calling for a completely different way of thinking for His followers. The listeners at the Sermon on the Mount must have been conflicted to hear something so different from their traditional ways of thinking. Most churches today teach some about the Sermon on the Mount but few seem to put into practice what Jesus taught there.

What does all of these things mean for the Christian leader? Way too often leadership brings along with it a certain amount of power and pride. Leaders tend to look at their successes as being through their personal efforts and greatness. Pride is a natural occurrence for many leaders. They have worked hard to achieve their goals and they are proud of their successes. Pride is a normal human response to success.

While pride is a common thing in human nature, there are major problems with having pride. Pride is in conflict with following Jesus Christ. Nothing that we have in life is ours except through the grace of God. Any attributes and abilities we posses have come only from God. There is nothing Christlike in prideful boasting or in leading others in an overbearing way. Pride may be a form of idolatry as it takes the credit for success instead of giving the proper credit to God. Humility is what Christ expects from us.

Blessed are the poor in spirit, for theirs is the kingdom of heaven.

The meaning of this verse can be puzzling. What does it mean? There seems to be several interpretations on what Jesus meant in this verse. Surely He does not want us to be poor in Spirit. He wants us to be rich in His Spirit, not poor. We must be poor in spirit in recognizing that we depend on the Holy Spirit for our spirituality and success. There is nothing that we have done through our own efforts to earn ay success. We are poor in spirit because we humbly acknowledge that every success that we have is due to God working within us.

Blessed are those who mourn, for they shall be comforted.

The Father promised the gift of the Holy Spirit (the Comforter). The work that the Holy Spirit does in our lives is amazing when you think about it. He teaches us, encourages us, leads us and He comforts us.

Blessed are the meek, for they shall inherit the earth.

Meekness is not an attribute that is normally assigned to leadership. Most people would consider it to be the least desired attribute that a leader could have. Leaders are supposed to be strong, and are expected to be aggressive leaders. Merriam-Webster defines *meek as:*

1: enduring injury with patience and without resentment: Mild;

2: deficient in spirit and courage: Submissive;

3: not violent or strong: Moderate.

This sure sounds like meekness is closely related to humility although they are different words. Merriam-Webster defines *humble:*

1: not proud or haughty: not arrogant or assertive;

2: reflecting, expressing, or offering in a spirit of deference or submission;

3: ranking low in a hierarchy or scale: Insignificant, Unpretentious.

Just like humility, meekness, at first glance, has little or nothing to do with leadership. But remember that Jesus said that Christian leadership is different from that of the world. His ways, wisdom, thoughts, and methods of doing things seem like foolishness to the world. His ways and His methods of doing things are direct paradoxes to those of the world.

This brings to mind a few Bible verses. 1 Corinthians 1:20a: *Has not God made foolish the wisdom of the world?* 1 Corinthians 1:25: *For the foolishness of God is wiser than men, and the weakness of God is stronger than men.* 1 Corinthians 3:18-19: *Let no one deceive himself. If anyone among you thinks that he is wise in this age, let him become a fool that he may become wise. For the wisdom of this world is folly with God. For it is written, "He catches the wise in their craftiness," and again, "The Lord knows the thoughts of the wise, that they are futile.* And once again, Isaiah 55:8-9: *For my thoughts are not your thoughts, neither are your ways my ways, declares the LORD. For as the heavens are higher than the earth, so are my ways higher than your ways and my thoughts than your thoughts.*

Those verses explain how God's thoughts, His ways, and His wisdom are completely different from that of man. From these verses, we can then understand a little more how God expects His followers who are also leaders to be meek. It is still hard for us to reconcile the idea of meekness with leadership. How did Jesus expect us to be leaders and meek at the same time? Leadership and meekness seem to be in conflict with each other. We know that He expects us to be humble, as we talk about in Chapter 5. We can see that although meekness and humility are not the same thing, they work hand-in-hand together. Jesus expects us to be both humble and meek.

So, what does meekness look like? Jesus does not explain in detail what He expects from His followers in meekness but He does give us a hint. Matthew 20:25:-28: *But Jesus called them to him and said, "You know that the rulers of the Gentiles lord it over them, and their great ones exercise authority over them. It shall not be so among you. But whoever would be great among you must be your servant, and whoever would be first among you must be your slave, even as the Son of Man came not to be served but to serve, and to give his life as a ransom for many."* The story is repeated in Mark 10:42-45.

The background for this story is that the two sons of Zebedee, John and James, approached Jesus and asked to be rewarded for being two of His top disciples by having Jesus place one of them on each side of Him in His coming kingdom. They felt like they were the two top leaders in Jesus' group of disciples and that they then deserved special rights and privileges. They wished to be the top leaders under Jesus when He became the king. It sounds like they wanted to rule over the other disciples. They felt like they deserved these positions and they wanted them. Of course, the other disciples were furious. They may have even been jealous of James and John's closeness to Jesus.

Jesus saw through their pride and desire for power and fame. Jesus shot down their request for special benefits and power. In the first place, it was the right of His Father to select who sat on the right and left sides of the throne of Jesus. His second point was that James and John still did not understand or have the heart of Jesus. His followers were not to be like the worldly leaders were. The worldly model was for the leader to lord over their followers. The Christian leader was to follow a different model. The Christian leader has to be a servant to those he or she leads. If he or she wanted to be great, he or she must be a servant. To be the greatest one must be a slave to others. Even Jesus said that He did not come to be served, but He came to serve others. Mark 10:31 adds, *But many who are first will be last, and the last first.* That sounds like a good example of both humility and meekness.

Blessed are those who hunger and thirst for righteousness, for they shall be satisfied.

Jesus says that they will be satisfied! That is an amazing thought! Satisfaction is a rare occurrence in today's world. Nobody seems to be satisfied about anything today. Everyone seems to be seeking self-indulgence and self-satisfaction. Most are seeking for material riches, and blessings instead of seeking righteousness. True satisfaction does not come through the material things.

Blessed are the merciful, for they shall receive mercy.

Mercy. What does mercy have to do with leadership? Sometimes leaders must make tough and often painful decisions. Leadership can be painful and difficult. How does mercy interplay with those awkward situations? Leadership in the world usually displays little if any mercy. It can be difficult to display mercy in awkward situations involving disputes or discipline. Exactly what mercy looks like will depend on the situation, organizational policies, and the leadership style. Mercy may or may not be an option in some organizations that have strict guidelines. However, according to Jesus, mercy should always be considered for Christian leaders. Jesus indicates that for a person to receive mercy, they must also show mercy to others.

Merrian-Webster has some definitions for mercy, including a few that directly connect with the type of mercy Jesus was talking about. 1: compassion or forbearance (shown especially to an offender or one subject to one's power); 2: a blessing that is an act of divine favor or compassion; 3: compassionate treatment of those in distress.

It is impossible to predict just how much mercy should be shown in every situation that a leader is involved in. The issue is that the idea of mercy raises the question if there may be times when mercy would mean that there are no consequences for poor actions or behavior. Discipline may have to be executed while still showing some mercy. Mercy is closely intertwined with love and forgiveness. You cannot have one without the other. Even if discipline is required, remember that love and forgiveness must also be shown at the same time. The apostle Paul taught about church discipline in his writings. He taught that church discipline must always be done in love and with the goal of the offender obtaining grace and forgiveness and hopefully returning to the church. Discipline is never to be done in anger or as retribution.

Blessed are the pure in heart, for they shall see God.

What does purity in heart mean? We know that we are all imperfect beings here on earth. Earlier Jesus encouraged us to seek and hunger after righteousness. A pure heart involves us loving God and loving our neighbors as ourselves. Although we are imperfect, purity in heart comes through loving God and others.

Blessed are the peacemakers, for they shall be called sons of God.

We live in an age of much strife and conflict. Wars are constantly being waged or threatened around the world. Arguments and fights are common between people and even between the different divisions of Christians. Bitterness, hatred, and strife seem to be the way of the world. The Way of Jesus is heavily involved with peace and love. Those who are the sons and daughters of God will seek a path of peace and bring peace to others.

Blessed are those who are persecuted for righteousness sake, for theirs is the kingdom of heaven.

Jesus made it plain to His followers that they would be persecuted for their faith in the future. We in the West have been fortunate in avoiding much of this persecution in the past while believers in many parts of the world suffer much for their faith. There may be coming a time in the future when all believers will have to face lots of persecution even here in the western world.

Blessed are you when others revile you and persecute you and utter all kinds of evil against you falsely on my account. Rejoice and be glad, for your reward is great in heaven, for so they persecuted the prophets who were before you.

Even good leadership often brings hatred and persecution. This is especially true for Christian leadership and ministry. Unfortunately, these problems and persecutions sometimes may come from within, as well as outside, the church or organization. There is probably no way to get around this problem. Leadership is often difficult and sometimes awkward and uncomfortable decisions may have to be made that will offend some people. You cannot please everyone all of the time, even in the church. Some people will never be pleased no matter what the situation is. These types of people always seem to like to complain and stir up trouble for others. Ministry and leadership in such times of strife can become almost impossible to accomplish.

This internal conflict can and sometimes does result in the removal of the pastor or leader. Many churches have long-time members who love to control the church. Those members are the unofficial leaders of the church and they desire to control everything. They want everything to be just the way they like it to be. If the pastor leads the church into a different direction, they will quickly stir up trouble for the pastor. Jesus is talking about outsiders reviling the believer and causing trouble. Unfortunately, sometimes the persecution also comes from within the local church.

Anger

Matthew 5:21-26, *"You have heard that it was said to those of old, 'You shall not murder; and whoever murders will be liable to judgment.' But I say to you that everyone who is angry with his brother will be liable to judgment; whoever insults his brother will be liable to the council; and whoever says, 'You fool!' will be liable to the hell of fire. So if you are offering your gift at the altar and there remember that your brother has something against you, leave your gift there before the altar and go. First be reconciled to your brother, and then come and offer your gift. Come to terms quickly with your accuser while you are going with him to court, lest your accuser hand you over to the judge, and the judge to the guard, and you be put in prison. Truly, I say to you, you will never get out until you have paid the last penny.*

We know that a leader must not murder his or her followers. It is contrary to good leadership practices to kill off your followers. Of course, many kings and emperors in the past did not get that message. So murder is definitely out for the Christian leader. But Jesus goes on to state that even anger is a major problem for the believer. Jesus even warns about the danger of judgment for being angry. He also reveals that there is a danger of hell for calling someone else a fool.

Anger is a tough subject to discuss. Anger is a natural human emotional response to complicated situations. As we all know, some people just love to make you angry. Some people seem to enjoy and live for making others angry. They thrive on constant conflict and anger. Others may not mean to make you angry on purpose but in their blind selfishness, immaturity, or stubbornness, they can do or say things that can make you very angry.

Here Jesus states that anger makes you liable to judgment. He even mentions the threat of hellfire. So, anger is a real danger to all believers. Human nature tells us that if someone disrespects you or hurts your feelings it is alright to get angry at them. But somehow, Jesus does not think that anger is consistent with loving your neighbor and your enemy as yourself. Imagine that! Anger and love cannot both dwell together in the believer's life. They are in direct conflict with each other.

The Christian leader must love those who are following him or her. And somehow, he or she must not allow anger to exist in their life. Anger is inconsistent with being a follower of Christ. No one claims that this is an easy task, especially when you are in leadership. A leader must deal with many people who have different personality types and temperaments. Some people will refuse to complete the tasks assigned to them. Others will complete the tasks but do it with a difficult attitude. Some people love to argue with others constantly. These types of people love stirring up trouble. Anger is a natural human response, but Jesus says that if you follow Him, you must fill your life with love and avoid anger.

Oaths

Matthew 5:33-37, *"Again you have heard that it was said to those of old, 'You shall not swear falsely, but shall perform to the Lord what you have sworn.' But I say to you, Do not take an oath at all, either by heaven, for it is the throne of God, or by the earth, for it is his footstool, or by Jerusalem, for it is the city of the great King. And do not take an oath by your head, for you cannot make one hair white or black. Let what you say be simply 'Yes' or 'No'; anything more than this comes from evil.* This is a subject that we usually do not hear being taught or preached about in today's world. Jesus wants our reputation to be such that we always tell the truth and others take our communications to be the truth without swearing an oath.

Retaliation

Matthew 5:38-42, *"You have heard that it was said, 'An eye for an eye and a tooth for a tooth.' But I say to you, Do not resist the one who is evil. But if anyone slaps you on the right cheek, turn to him the other also. And if anyone would sue you and take your tunic, let him have your cloak as well. And if anyone forces you to go one mile, go with him two miles. Give to the one who begs from you, and do not refuse the one who would borrow from you.*

Retaliation is closely related to anger. It is difficult to have one without the other one. As we saw above, Jesus wanted His followers to love others. Loving others involves mercy and forgiveness but it does not include anger or retaliation. It is natural to believe that Christians will never retaliate against anyone. It is so hard to forgive others when they talk badly about you, physically harm you, disrespect you, or disagree with you. As we mentioned above, some people love to stir up strife. They seem to thrive on arguments, conflict, and retaliation. Jesus says that not only are we to not get angry, but also that we cannot retaliate in any way. This is tough when you are a leader and the problems come from those people who are following you. Retaliation is in direct conflict with the type of love and forgiveness that Jesus taught and lived.

Love Your Enemies

Matthew 5:43-48, *"You have heard that it was said 'You shall love your neighbor and hate your enemy.' But I say to you, Love your enemies and pray for those who persecute you, so that you may be sons of your Father who is in heaven. For he makes his sun rise on the evil and on the good, and sends rain on the just and on the unjust. For if you love those who love you, what reward do you have? Do not even the tax collectors do the same? And if you greet only your brothers, what more are you doing than others? Do not even the Gentiles do the same? You therefore must be perfect, as your heavenly Father is perfect.*

Over and over we hear the first two commandments that Jesus taught: We are to love God and love our neighbor as ourselves. In some ways the first commandment is relatively easy for us. God, the Creator sent His only begotten Son to live and die for us. He provided us with a means to obtain forgiveness for our many sins. God loved us first and showed His love toward us when we did not deserve that love. The second commandment is a little tougher than the first one, but with God's love and help we can manage to love our neighbor, at least part of the time. your neighbor may or may not have shown you love first. Loving your neighbor as yourself is not an easy task in some situations.

Now Jesus is telling us here to do something completely different. Not only are we to love God and our neighbor as ourselves, but we must also love our enemy. If loving your neighbor is difficult, how is loving your enemy even remotely possible? Jesus says that we have to love those who hurt us with actions and words. We must love those who put us in danger. We must love those who steal from us. We must even love those who wish to harm us because of our beliefs.

A good example of loving your enemy occurred when Jesus was on the cross. Remember how He prayed to His Father to forgive those who whipped Him, slapped Him, stripped His clothing off, spit on Him, and then hung Him on the cross. He forgave them and asked God the Father to also forgive them for this great crime. Loving your enemy is not an easy task but the follower of Jesus Christ who is filled with His love must do it. The command that we must love our enemies includes the Christian leader. The leader must learn how to love their enemies. If you love your enemy, is he truly still your enemy?

Forgiveness

Matthew 6:14-15, *For if you forgive others their trespasses, your heavenly Father will also forgive you, but if you do not forgive others their trespasses, neither will your Father forgive your trespasses.*

Forgiveness is included here because Jesus included it in His sermon. Forgiveness is a powerful word. With forgiveness comes much love and healing. It is closely linked to love and the lack of anger and retaliation. Jesus expects us to forgive others. Remember this important concept! Forgiveness may seem like an impossible task in leadership, but it is important. Often leadership involves difficult decisions as well as situations resolving conflicts. Forgiveness does not always mean avoiding a difficult or painful decision or situation. Even in those cases, love and forgiveness must find their way into the situation, even when discipline or correction is found to be necessary.

One of the best examples of forgiveness in the New Testament occurred while Jesus was at the Temple teaching. This story is found in John 8. The Pharisees came to listen to Jesus there. They brought in a woman who had been caught in adultery. The Law clearly stated that the death penalty by stoning was the penalty for adultery. Note that the

Pharisees wanted to stone the woman to death while allowing the man involved to go free.

John 8:2-11, *Early in the morning he came again to the temple. All the people came to him, and he sat down and taught them. The scribes and the Pharisees brought a woman who had been caught in adultery, and placing her in the midst they said to him, "Teacher, this woman has been caught in the act of adultery. Now in the Law Moses commanded us to stone such women. So what do you say?" This they said to test him, that they might have some charge to bring against him. Jesus bent down and wrote with his finger on the ground. And as they continued to ask him, he stood up and said to them, "Let him who is without sin among you be the first to throw a stone at her." And once more he bent down and wrote on the ground. But when they heard it, they went away one by one, beginning with the older ones, and Jesus was left alone with the woman standing before him. Jesus stood up and said to her, "Woman, where are they? Has no one condemned you?" She said, "No one, Lord." And Jesus said, "Neither do I condemn you; go, and from now on sin no more."* How slow we are to forgive others while Jesus was quick to forgive us our sins.

What Do You Treasure?

Mathew 6:19-21, *"Do not lay up for yourselves treasures on earth, where moth and rust destroy and where thieves break in and steal, but lay up for yourselves treasures in heaven, where neither moth nor rust destroys and where thieves do not break in and steal. For where your treasure is, there your heart will be also.*

What do you treasure? This will be one of the primary differences between secular leadership and Christian leadership. What are your values, ethics, and goals in leadership and in life? In a Christian ministry or organization, the need for money to operate is often an issue, but it should never become the prime goal or value. We recognize that all organizations need a certain amount of money to operate and in order to achieve their goals. However, money should never be the prime goal of a Christian ministry or organization. Do not forget the true reason for your organization's existence. Make sure that you are laying up treasures in the right place. This is not only an important thing for individual

Christians to do, but also for ministries and Christian organizations. We have all seen churches, ministries, and nonprofit organizations get off-track when they see the flood of money coming in. Money often becomes the goal instead of the means to achieve their goals.

Matthew 6:24, *"No one can serve two masters, for either he will hate the one and love the other, or he will be devoted to the one and despise the other. You cannot serve God and money.* This verse, of course, goes right along with the previous section on laying up your treasures in the right place. Being blessed by God may at times involve some financial rewards but usually being blessed by God has a different meaning. Money is important to ministries and organizations but you must not get off-track and make money the most important goal. Jesus makes it clear that you cannot serve money and God. It does not get any simpler than that.

Anxiety and Worry

Matthew 6:25-34, *"Therefore I tell you, do not be anxious about your life, what you will eat or what you will drink, nor about your body, what you will put on. Is not life more than food, and the body more than clothing? Look at the birds of the air: they neither sow nor reap nor gather into barns, and yet your heavenly Father feeds them. Are you not of more value than they? And which of you by being anxious can add a single hour to his span of life? And why are you anxious about clothing? Consider the lilies of the field, how they grow: they neither toil nor spin, yet I tell you, even Solomon in all his glory was not arrayed like one of these. But if God so clothes the grass of the field, which today is alive and tomorrow is thrown into the oven, will he not much more clothe you, O you of little faith? Therefore do not be anxious, saying, 'What shall we eat?' or 'What shall we drink?' or 'What shall we wear?' For the Gentiles seek after all these things, and your heavenly Father knows that you need them all. But seek first the kingdom of God and his righteousness, and all these things will be added to you. "Therefore do not be anxious about tomorrow, for tomorrow will be anxious for itself. Sufficient for the day is its trouble.*

Anxiety. Worry. Fretting. Stress. The world is full of these things, but Jesus told us that we are not to be anxious. We know that the medical world agrees with Jesus that anxiety is a major threat to our health. We do not need to be worried about anything. God promised that He will provide for us. Doctors have proven that stress is a major contributor to health issues and death in today's world. Stress causes anxiety, high blood pressure, obesity, and often leads to heart problems and diabetes. All of these health issues can lead to an early death as well as a stress-filled life.

Do not be anxious about tomorrow. We are to take things one day at a time. God promised to provide all our needs for us. This provision from God may or not involve exactly what we think we need or as much as we desire, but God will take care of us. We may not ever have riches or an abundance. In contrast to what some televangelists would have you believe, God never promised us that we would be prosperous. The key phrase here is that we are to seek first the kingdom of God. God will provide the way for everything that we need, not necessarily, what we want.

Conclusion

Anxiety is caused by the lack of faith that God will keep His promises to us. Anxiety comes from not believing that God is in control of the situation and the desire to control of our situation.

- 12 -

Follow Me

WE now come to the subject that is the basic premise for this entire book, the idea that we have mentioned several times throughout this book. That premise is that Christian leaders must be followers of Jesus Christ. It all starts with that truth. What does it mean to become a follower of Jesus Christ? In some ways that is a loaded question. Theologians and believers often disagree about what they think that following Christ means and involves. They argue about what being a follower of Christ looks like. Many people take a more legalistic viewpoint than others and they list many rules and guidelines that you must follow if you are a follower of Christ. If you don't agree with their interpretation and follow their set of guidelines and rules, then they say that you must not be a true follower of Christ. Other groups list a very different set of rules for the follower to use as a guideline for following Christ. Which one of them is correct?

When you study the life of Christ, you will not find a set of rules to follow. Instead of a list of rules and guidelines to follow, the follower of Christ must use the teachings and the life of Christ as an example and guideline. We are to follow His example. He told us that if we love Him that we are to obey His commandments. Repeatedly throughout the gospels, He taught what those commandments were. Those commandments are that we are to first love God and then we are to love our neighbor as ourselves. These two commandments are the only rules and commandments that He gave us for following Him.

By extension, these two commandments are the basic guidelines for Christian leadership. Everything revolves around these commandments. Jesus even told us that these two commandments cover all of the other commandments and rules. Any guidelines, commandments, or rules that do not mesh with these two commandments are worthless. These two commandments are the guidelines for following Christ. Everything we do and say should reflect our love for God and our love for our neighbor. Since we are to use Christ as our example in following Him, we should look at how He lived His life and did His ministry and use that as our guideline. When we consider Christ's examples that we have recorded in the gospels, we can see certain characteristics in His life and ministry are apparent. These characteristics that appear throughout His life include: loving one's neighbor, compassion, forgiveness, meekness, humility, loving one's enemies, and patience.

When Jesus called His disciples to become His disciples, there is a reoccurring theme. He would walk up to His chosen person and tell them, "Follow me." Can you imagine in today's world a random person walking up to another person on the street in the city and simply saying to them, "Follow me"? That is exactly what Jesus did when He chose His disciples. He simply told them to follow Him. Jesus had been creating such a stir throughout the area that the future disciples had to have known who Jesus was and what He had been teaching. Simon (Peter), his brother Andrew, James, and his brother John were all at work. They were on their boats on the lake mending their nets. They immediately put down their nets and left the boats to follow Jesus. Matthew was also at work. He was sitting at the tax table collecting the taxes. Jesus told him the same thing, "Follow me." Matthew immediately rose from his table and left his lucrative job of collecting taxes and fleecing the people in order to follow Christ.

Matthew 4:18-22: *While walking by the Sea of Galilee, he saw two brothers, Simon (who is called Peter) and Andrew his brother, casting a net into the sea, for they were fishermen. And he said to them, "Follow me, and I will make you fishers of men." Immediately they left their nets and followed him. And going on from there he saw two other brothers, James the son of Zebedee, and John his brother, in the boat with Zebedee their father, mending their nets, and he called them. Immediately they left the boat and their father and followed him.*

Follow me! Repeatedly Jesus gave this same request. He used this not only to select His disciples but also He used this simple request to others who heard His teachings and followed Him from place to place. John 12:26: *If anyone serves me, he must follow me; and where I am, there will my servant be also. If anyone serves me, the Father will honor him.* If we are to follow Christ, we must have some type of understanding of what following Christ means. As stated above, following Christ has nothing to do with obeying a set of man-made rules and regulations. Following Christ is more about copying Christ's love for His Father and for other people.

Although following Christ does not involve a specific list of rules and guidelines to follow, this does not mean that holiness is not involved. After all, the Bible proclaims that we are to be holy. So holiness is involved with following Christ. Holiness has nothing to do with following a set of rules proclaimed by a man, church, or denomination. When you follow Christ's commandments to love God and then to love your neighbor as yourself, holiness will be present in your life. Jesus indicates that loving God and loving your neighbor as yourself is what holiness consists of.

The role of the leader as a leader is important, but the role of the leader as a follower is of more importance. As noted above, the most important role of the Christian leader is to be a follower of Jesus Christ. This role involves the leader continually moving toward becoming the image of Christ. It is important to remember that this work is a continual movement. We never fully arrive to that point in this life. Jimmy Clinton says it this way, "God does not stop working on character after moving someone into leadership. This development does not focus on testing to enter ministry, but on the relationship with God." Developing one's character through ever drawing yourself into a closer relationship with Christ is more important than any leadership qualities or traits. According to Geiger and Peck, "When we look at the leaders God has formed throughout the ages, we see over and over again that the Lord cares for their response to His holiness more than how many responsibilities they steward." The Blackabys say this about God's leaders in the Bible, "Their phenomenal success as spiritual leaders was not based on their superior oratorical abilities or their organizational genius. Rather, their amazing success as spiritual leaders can be traced to their consummate submission to Christ."

While much effort has traditionally been applied to the study of leadership, there has been little effort in studying or teaching followership. W. Goodwin states in his doctoral dissertation, "Previously, the study of leadership was addressed through the eyes of the leader or focused on the accomplishments of a great man. Followership has always existed but passively so in the study of leadership." With so much emphasis on the importance of leadership, the significance of followership has been largely ignored. Howell states, "Being a follower has a negative connotation because it is usually used to refer to someone who must be constantly told what to do."

While there are plenty of resources and help for those who wish to learn how to become the best leader they can be, there is little literature available for those who want to become better followers or leaders who are also followers. Mills says it this way, "Unfortunately, there is not much help available for those in our churches who want to learn to follow, and if we want to be fruitful in ministry, learning how to follow is far more important than learning how to lead." Slowly, leadership experts and scholars are coming around to recognize the importance of followership in the subject of leadership. Hurwitz and Hurwitz say, "However, in real life, followership is mostly under-acknowledged, underrated, and underdeveloped. It's more than the elephant in the room: it's the invisible elephant in the room." It is now time for that invisible elephant to come out from hiding.

The primary role of the leader as a follower then becomes that of walking and living in the Spirit in order to draw ever closer to Christ. Through this process, the Fruit of the Spirit will become evident in the leader's life. Developing a character that has the image of Christ is not something that people can do in their own power. This can only occur through the process of the Holy Spirit working within the leader. However, this is not some magic potion that the leader drinks to magically have the Fruit of the Spirit suddenly working within their life. The Apostle Peter also had much to say about the leader's character development. Stephen Smith tells us, "Peter tells us to make every effort. Character doesn't just happen. We participate in our transformation. We choose to sit on the wheel of the divine potter and be pinched here and pressed there." We allow the Holy Spirit to shape and develop our hearts and character.

This character development is the primary role of the leader as a follower. Aubrey Malphurs explains, "I call this character development soul work because it has to do with our innermost being. To be successful, a leader must develop his or her character." This character development or spiritual formation must be the primary goal of the follower. Paul Petit agrees, "As a leader, spiritual formation should be the primary focus of life. It is essential to effective function in a leadership capacity."

David Platt wrote a book called *Follow Me.* In this book, he gives his ideas on what following Christ means. One of his primary themes in the book follows what Paul taught about dying to oneself daily. Most of his book does not contain material directly pertaining to the subject of this book, but he does offer this outtake on following Christ, "As we turn to Jesus, he transforms us. As we die to ourselves, we live in him. He gives us a new heart. - cleansed of sin and filled with his Spirit. He gives us a new mind - an entirely new way of thinking. He gives us new desires - entirely new senses of longing. And he gives us a new will - an entirely new way of living."

The following verses are a little long but they are important for an introduction to the subject of following Jesus. The role of this book is not to get into a long theological discussion about what following Christ means and involves. Many other authors have published their thoughts on this subject. Here are an introduction and some suggestions about following Christ.

John 15:1-11

"I am the true vine, and my Father is the vinedresser. Every branch in me that does not bear fruit he takes away, and every branch that does bear fruit he prunes, that it may bear more fruit. Already you are clean because of the word that I have spoken to you. Abide in me, and I in you. As the branch cannot bear fruit by itself, unless it abides in the vine, neither can you, unless you abide in me. I am the vine; you are the branches. Whoever abides in me and I in him, he it is that bears much fruit, for apart from me you can do nothing. If anyone does not abide in me he is thrown away like a branch and withers; and the branches are gathered, thrown into the fire, and burned. If you abide in me, and my words abide in you, ask whatever you wish, and it will be done for you. By this my Father is glorified, that you bear much fruit and so prove to be my disciples. As the Father has loved me, so have I loved you. Abide in my love. If you keep my commandments,

you will abide in my love, just as I have kept my Father's commandments and abide in his love. These things I have spoken to you, that my joy may be in you, and that your joy may be full.
Some keywords and phrases in these verses:
* Producing fruit
* Abiding in Christ
* Abiding in Christ's Love
* Obeying His Commandments

Do you want to follow Christ? Jesus gives you a big hint of how to do that right here. He wants us to follow Him through abiding in Christ and allowing Him to abide in us. Then He goes on to tell us that we are to abide in Christ's love and to obey His commandments (to love God and to love our neighbor as ourselves).

As Jesus said in Matthew 22:37-40 when asked what the greatest commandment was, *He said to him, "You shall love the Lord your God with all your heart and with all your soul and with all your mind. This is the great and first commandment. And a second is like it: You shall love your neighbor as yourself. On these two commandments depend all the Law and the Prophets."* Several times throughout the New Testament Jesus quotes these two commandments as being the basis that all believers are to live by.

It is safe to state that there are a few things that believers can do to follow Christ. First of all, they must abide in Christ and allow Him to abide in them. They must follow the commandments of Christ, that is to love God with all of their heart, soul, and mind and they must love their neighbor as themselves.

How does someone abide in Christ and allow Him to abide in them? The apostle Paul gives us a thought or two about this. Galatians 5:16-18: *But I say, walk by the Spirit, and you will not gratify the desires of the flesh. For the desires of the flesh are against the Spirit, and the desires of the Spirit are against the flesh, for these are opposed to each other, to keep you from doing the things you want to do. But if you are led by the Spirit, you are not under the law.* Paul continues that discussion later in that same chapter in verses 24 and 25, *And those who belong to Christ Jesus have crucified the flesh with its passions and desires. If we live by the Spirit, let us also keep in step with the Spirit.* Here he talks about crucifying the flesh. Ephesians 5:19-20, *And do not get drunk with wine, for that is debauchery, but be filled with the Spirit, addressing one another in psalms and hymns and spiritual songs, singing and making melody to the Lord with your heart,* Here again Paul is emphasizing the importance of believers being filled with the Holy Spirit.

Paul explains what he means by dying to self a little better in Galatians 2:20, *I have been crucified with Christ. It is no longer I who live, but Christ who lives in me. And the life I now live in the flesh I live by faith in the Son of God, who loved me and gave himself for me.* As Paul mentions we believers have much freedom, but not all things are expedient or good for us. We are not to follow a bunch of legalistic rules and man-made regulations. We are to rather make sure that all of our words and actions are done in love. If we truly love God and love our neighbor as ourselves, we are doing well in following Christ.

The apostle John also tells us that we are to abide in Christ. 1 John 2:27-28, *But the anointing which ye have received of him abideth in you, and ye need not that any man teach you: but as the same anointing teacheth you of all things, and is truth, and is no lie, and even as it hath taught you, ye shall abide in him. And now, little children, abide in him; that, when he shall appear, we may have confidence, and not be ashamed before him at his coming.* If Christ abides within us, we are to abide in Him. He tells us that in order to be unashamed when Christ returns we are to abide in Him.

John 15:12-17

"This is my commandment, that you love one another as I have loved you. Greater love has no one than this, that someone lay down his life for his friends. You are my friends if you do what I command you. No longer do I call you servants, for the servant does not know what his master is doing; but I have called you friends, for all that I have heard from my Father I have made known to you. You did not choose me, but I chose you and appointed you that you should go and bear fruit and that your fruit should abide, so that whatever you ask the Father in my name, he may give it to you. These things I command you, so that you will love one another.

Some keywords and phrases that stick out in these few verses:

* Servant
* Friend
* Love
* Bear fruit

1 John 2:3-6

The love apostle has more to say about following Christ in his first epistle. 1 John 2:3-6, *And hereby we do know that we know him, if we keep his commandments. He that saith, I know him, and keepeth not his commandments, is a liar, and the truth is not in him. But whoso keepeth his word, in him verily is the love of God perfected: hereby know we that we are in him. He that saith he abideth in him ought himself also so to walk, even as he walked.* As we know that Christ abides within us, we are to also abide in Him. If we abide in Him, we will attempt to live and walk as Christ did. This is what following Christ and abiding in Him is all about - living and walking like Christ did.

Jesus Christ, the Leader - Jesus Christ, the Follower

We now are introducing a slightly different subject about following Christ. This is a subject that you may not have ever thought about. We know that we, as believers, must follow Jesus Christ. That makes Jesus our leader and the Head of the church. In our thoughts of Jesus as the ultimate leader, we often miss something. What we often overlook in our reading and studying the Bible is that Jesus was not only our leader, but that He was also a follower. We will cover several Bible verses in which Jesus explains that He is a servant. He also proclaims that everything He says and does is authorized by God the Father. Everything He does is the will of the Father. He is the follower of His Father.

Christian leadership studies normally present Jesus as the greatest leader in history. They will proclaim that Christian leaders are to lead as Jesus taught and to follow His example. Most Christians will proclaim that Jesus was the greatest leader to ever live. We cannot argue with that statement. We fully agree that Jesus was and is the greatest leader to ever live on Earth. In many ways, Jesus who was the as the greatest leader, was also a follower. One might also state that Jesus was the greatest follower. He was the best example for us to follow as we learn better how to both follow and lead. This sounds like another contradiction to the way that we normally think about Jesus, but Jesus Himself made it clear that He was a follower.

The question arises though about what Jesus said concerning Himself. Did He ever call Himself a follower? If so, whom did He follow? At least that last question is easy to answer because Jesus made it clear that He followed His Father and that He did the Father's will. The Gospel of John relates many verses in which Jesus made statements that support the concept that Jesus was a follower. These verses about Jesus will also support the idea that the Christian leader is first a follower before becoming a leader. If Jesus was a follower, then surely it is even more important for us, as Christian leaders, to be followers.

Old Testament Prophesies About Jesus

It may surprise some of you to learn that even in the Old Testament, some of the prophecies about the coming of Jesus proclaim that He is the servant of the Father. We often read and teach these same prophesies to help prove that Jesus is the promised Messiah. We often do not pay attention to the inclusion of the term *servant.* Zechariah 3:8, *Hear now, O Joshua the high priest, you and your friends who sit before you, for they are men who are a sign: behold, I will bring my servant the Branch.* Do you see that? God called the coming Jesus as the Messiah to be His servant. The same subject appears in other prophecies that we often use in teaching and discussing the prophecies about Jesus.

Isaiah 49:3-7

He said to me, "You are my servant, Israel, in whom I will display my splendor." But I said, "I have labored in vain; I have spent my strength for nothing at all. Yet what is due me is in the LORD's hand, and my reward is with my God." And now the LORD says— he who formed me in the womb to be his servant to bring Jacob back to him and gather Israel to himself, for I am honored in the eyes of the LORD and my God has been my strength - he says: "It is too small a thing for you to be my servant to restore the tribes of Jacob and bring back those of Israel I have kept. I will also make you a light for the Gentiles, that my salvation may reach to the ends of the earth." This is what the LORD says - the Redeemer and Holy One of Israel— to him who was despised and abhorred by the nation, to the servant of rulers: "Kings will see you and stand up, princes will see and bow down, because of the LORD, who is faithful, the Holy One of Israel, who has chosen you."

Who expected God, the Father, to call His only Son to be His servant? And once again in Isaiah 42:1-4: *Behold my servant, whom I uphold, my chosen, in whom my soul delights; I have put my Spirit upon him; he will bring forth justice to the nations. He will not cry aloud or lift up his voice, or make it heard in the street; a bruised reed he will not break, and a faintly burning wick he will not quench; he will faithfully bring forth justice. He will not grow faint or be discouraged till he has established justice in the earth; and the coastlands wait for his law.*

These prophets are writing in these verses about the coming of the Messiah, who is Jesus Christ. God is proclaiming that He will send His servant, Jesus to be the Messiah. Also, please notice that these prophesies did not call Jesus 'a' servant or 'the' servant. In all of these prophesies God calls Jesus 'His' servant. These scriptures describe Jesus too well for them to be talking about anyone else except Jesus.

Jesus, as a Follower

We will now move back to the New Testament. Paul and others of the New Testament authors often made clear that they identified themselves as servants (or slaves) of Jesus Christ. We now have to consider that the One (Jesus) who we are servants of is also a servant of God the Father. This is an important concept but one that is often overlooked in our thinking about Jesus Christ being the Head of the church and the perfect leader. After all, He is the Leader that we believers are supposed to be following.

Remember the story about the mother of the sons of Zebedee (John and James) came to Jesus and asked that her sons be allowed to sit on the right and left hand sides of Jesus when He came into His reign? Jesus made it clear that she and her sons did not fully realize what they were requesting. Matthew 20:26-28 gives the answer that Jesus gave her. *It shall not be so among you. But whoever would be great among you must be your servant, and whoever would be first among you must be your slave, even as the Son of Man came not to be served but to serve, and to give his life as a ransom for many."* Even after following Jesus and being part of His inner circle, the disciples still did not understand the primary theology behind Christian leadership, the followership concepts that Jesus taught and practiced. The Christian leader must be a servant. His disciples knew that Jesus was the promised Messiah. Jesus probably startled them here by stating that He (the Messiah) did not come to be served but that He came to serve others. Jesus came to earth in human form to be a servant. We usually do not consider servants as being leaders but Jesus taught us that the leader must be a servant.

Mark puts a similar but slightly different spin in his relating of the incident in the above paragraph. Mark 10:42-25, *And Jesus called them to him and said to them, "You know that those who are considered rulers of the Gentiles lord it over them, and their great ones exercise authority over them. But it shall not be so among you. But whoever would be great among you must be your servant, and whoever would be first among you must be slave of all. For even the Son of Man came not to be served but to serve, and to give his life as a ransom for many."* Here Jesus mentions how the leaders of the Gentiles lord over their followers while the leaders who are followers of Jesus are not to do that. He makes it clear that the Christian leader is to be a servant. Not only is the leader a servant, but Jesus states that the leader who wishes to be first must be a slave to all. Now, that is a difficult concept for us to consider. The leader must become a slave to all, just as Jesus, the ultimate leader, came to serve others.

Luke tells the story differently. The basic truth is the same but he covers the incident from a different angle. Luke 22:24-27, *A dispute also arose among them, as to which of them was to be regarded as the greatest. And he said to them, "The kings of the Gentiles exercise lordship over them, and those in authority over them are called benefactors. But not so with you. Rather, let the greatest among you become as the youngest, and the leader as one who serves. For who is the greater, one who reclines at table or one who serves? Is it not the one who reclines at table? But I am among you as the one who serves.*

The Characteristics of Jesus

There are some things about Jesus that we tend not to think about often. He came in human form as the Son of God. He had all power over illness, demons, the weather, plant life, and even death. He had the power to do many miracles. He healed the sick, cast out demons, raised the dead, and calmed the storm. He turned the water into wine and fed thousands of people with just a few loaves of bread and a few fish. We think of Jesus as having all power to do anything that He wanted to do.

There is another side to Jesus that we should not overlook. We tend to overlook this because of our understanding that Jesus is the Son of God. He is eternal. He is all-powerful. He is God. We tend to overlook the fact that while Jesus was the Son of God, while He lived on earth He still needed much strength and guidance from the Father. Throughout His ministry, He spent much time in prayer. Notice how many times in the New Testament that Jesus withdrew Himself to the Wilderness in solitude. He often spent time in the Wilderness alone talking with God. Numerous times He depended on angels to minister to Him. He heavily depended on the Holy Spirit within Him. Jesus understood the need for rest, solitude, fasting, and prayer.

Remember the story in Mark 6 where Jesus sent the twelve disciples out to teach and minister throughout the land two-by-two. They came back tired and hungry. The crowds were demanding and did not give the disciples time to even eat, much less to rest. Mark 6:30-32, *The apostles returned to Jesus and told him all that they had done and taught. And he said to them, "Come away by yourselves to a desolate place and rest a while." For many were coming and going, and they had no leisure even to eat. And they went away in the boat to a desolate place by themselves.* As we know from the New Testament, Jesus was a firm believer in getting away in solitude, resting, and restoring one's strength in the Holy Spirit.

We forget that even Jesus often needed to get away from the crowds and ministry. He often needed times of solitude away from even His disciples. He greatly depended on the Holy Spirit to minister to His spirit. Here Jesus was trying to teach His disciples that they needed the same things. Teaching and leading can never be successful in one's own knowledge and strength. It takes the working of the Holy Spirit within.

Matthew 14 tells a story that we often overlook one important part of. The story starts with Jesus receiving word that John the Baptist had been beheaded. Upset and sad about this news, Jesus immediately sought out solitude. Matthew 14:13 states, *Now when Jesus heard this, he withdrew from there in a boat to a desolate place by himself. But when the crowds heard it, they followed him on foot from the towns.* Now comes the part that we usually hear taught and preached about. The crowds followed Him and would not leave Him alone. Even in the midst of His sorrow about the death of John the Baptist, Jesus had compassion on the crowds and did the miracle of feeding the massive crowd with a few fish and loaves of bread. The miracle of feeding the people with so little food gets all of the attention. We forget the part of Jesus dealing with grief and needing a time of solitude.

With the many people crowding Jesus the question arises, "What about the grieving Jesus?" He still needs the time alone to grieve and to commune with His Father. In His busy ministry and now in His grief, He needs time to recharge His batteries, so to speak. He needs time in solitude without the crowds demanding His constant teaching and miracles. Matthew 14:22-23, *Immediately he made the disciples get into the boat and go before him to the other side, while he dismissed the crowds. And after he had dismissed the crowds, he went up to the mountain by himself to pray. When evening came, he was there alone.* After doing the miracle of feeding the crowds, Jesus sent the crowds away. It is worth noting that before He sent the crowds away, He sent His disciples away. He still needed His time of solitude and prayer without the presence of either the crowds or His disciples.

The Holy Spirit

Jesus depended on the power and leading of the Holy Spirit. Several places in the New Testament clearly state that Jesus was full of the Holy Spirit. The primary point here is that although Jesus was the Son of God, with all the benefits and rights that entails, He still needed and operated through the power and the leading of the Holy Spirit. If Jesus depended so heavily on the Holy Spirit operating daily in His life, how can we lowly mortals depend on leading in our own power, knowledge, and wisdom? The answer is that we cannot and must not. The Christian leader has to walk in the Spirit daily. This is imperative. He or she must depend on the Holy Spirit in order to be a successful leader in God's eyes.

The involvement of the Holy Spirit in the life of Jesus started even before He was born. An angel appeared to Mary and spoke to her about the Holy Spirit. Luke 1:35 states, *And the angel answered her, "The Holy Spirit will come upon you, and the power of the Most High will overshadow you; therefore the child to be born will be called holy—the Son of God.* Is it any surprise that Jesus is full of the Holy Spirit? The Holy Spirit is involved in His conception. As John the Baptist proclaims in Luke 3:16, *John answered them all, saying, "I baptize you with water, but he who is mightier than I is coming, the strap of whose sandals I am not worthy to untie. He will baptize you with the Holy Spirit and fire.* In like manner to Isaiah's prophesying about Jesus, John the Baptist prophesied about Jesus both being filled with and baptizing others in the Holy Spirit.

The next time that the Holy Spirit is mentioned in conjunction with Jesus is when John the Baptist baptizes Him in the river. The Holy Spirit descends on Jesus in the form of a dove and God audibly speaks His approval of His Son. Luke 3:21-22 gives us the story. *Now when all the people were baptized, and when Jesus also had been baptized and was praying, the heavens were opened, and the Holy Spirit descended on him in bodily form, like a dove; and a voice came from heaven, "You are my beloved Son, with you I am well pleased."* Luke 4:1, *And Jesus, full of the Holy Spirit, returned from the Jordan and was led by the Spirit in the wilderness for forty days, being tempted by the devil.* Luke states that Jesus was full of the Holy Spirit. Note here that Jesus was then led into the wilderness by the Holy Spirit. Even though He was the Son of God, He still needed the Holy Spirit. This does not disprove in any way His divinity. Acts 10:36-38 describes it this way, *As for the word that he sent to Israel, preaching the good news of peace through Jesus Christ (he is Lord of all), you yourselves know what happened throughout all Judea, beginning from Galilee after the baptism that John proclaimed: how God anointed Jesus of Nazareth with the Holy Spirit and with power. He went about doing good and healing all who were oppressed by the devil, for God was with him.*

After His water baptism, Jesus disappears into the wilderness where He is subjected to forty days of temptations by Satan. At the end of this period, the angels came and ministered to Him. Then Luke 4:14-15 says, *And Jesus returned in the power of the Spirit to Galilee, and a report about him went out through all the surrounding country. And he taught in their synagogues, being glorified by all.* The key phrase here is that Jesus returned in the power of the Holy Spirit. This is immediately after spending forty days and nights in the wilderness while being tempted by Satan. He was very tired and hungry. Jesus heavily depended on the power of the Holy Spirit.

Luke 4:16-19, *And he came to Nazareth, where he had been brought up. And as was his custom, he went to the synagogue on the Sabbath day, and he stood up to read. And the scroll of the prophet Isaiah was given to him. He unrolled the scroll and found the place where it was written, "The Spirit of the Lord is upon me because he has anointed me to proclaim good news to the poor. He has sent me to proclaim liberty to the captives and recovering of sight to the blind, to set at liberty those who are oppressed, to proclaim the year of the Lord's favor."* Here Jesus is reading what the prophet Isaiah had prophesied about the Messiah. The key phrases here are that the Holy Spirit is upon Jesus and anointed Him to preach just like Isaiah prophesied.

When the Pharisees accuse Jesus of casting out demons through the power of Beelzebub, Jesus answers them in Matthew 12:28, *But if it is by the Spirit of God that I cast out demons, then the kingdom of God has come upon you.* He knew that they could not accept that He was the Messiah and that He was doing miracles through the power of the Holy Spirit within Him.

Hebrews 9:13-14, *For if the blood of goats and bulls, and the sprinkling of defiled persons with the ashes of a heifer, sanctify for the purification of the flesh, how much more will the blood of Christ, who through the eternal Spirit offered himself without blemish to God, purify our conscience from dead works to serve the living God.* The author of Hebrews is claiming that Jesus offered Himself as a sacrifice through the Holy Spirit. Without the Holy Spirit in Christ's life, there would have not been the crucifixion and resurrection. There definitely would not have been the cleansing power of His blood without the Holy Spirit working in this event.

Paul agrees with the above statement in his epistle to the Romans. Romans 1:4 states, *And was declared to be the Son of God in power according to the Spirit of holiness by his resurrection from the dead, Jesus Christ our Lord.* Christ's resurrection, once again, is declared to be through the work and power of the Holy Spirit. It is amazing how often we overlook that fact when we are talking about the crucifixion and resurrection. It seems that this is an important part of the story. Without the Holy Spirit, none of this would have taken place. And again in Romans 8:11, *If the Spirit of him who raised Jesus from the dead dwells in you, he who raised Christ Jesus from the dead will also give life to your mortal bodies through his Spirit who dwells in you.*

Prayer

Luke 5:15-16, *But now, even more, the report about him went abroad, and great crowds gathered to hear him and to be healed of their infirmities. But he would withdraw to desolate places and pray.* Jesus often felt the need to withdraw and pray alone. He was ministered to by angels and He was full of the Holy Spirit. And yet, He still needs to withdraw from the crowds and His disciples to spend much time in prayer.

When it came time for Jesus to choose His disciples, He first withdrew Himself and spent all night in prayer before calling His disciples. Luke 6:12-13. *In these days he went out to the mountain to pray, and all night he continued in prayer to God. And when the day came, he called his disciples and chose from them twelve, whom he named apostles.*

Often, Jesus would withdraw to a desolate place to spend much time in prayer in solitude. He would even leave the disciples behind to spend this time alone. In Mark 1 the disciples had to go look for Him. Everyone was looking for Jesus but He needed His time in solitude and prayer. Mark 1:35-37, *And rising very early in the morning, while it was still dark, he departed and went out to a desolate place, and there he prayed. And Simon and those who were with him searched for him, and they found him and said to him, "Everyone is looking for you."* It sounds like the disciples were finally beginning to catch on to Jesus' habits. They figured out that He needed lots of time in prayer and solitude. They had to go out and search for Him. They may not have understood why the Son of God needed this time in solitude and prayer, but they got used to it.

Jesus did not rely on His own power for anything, even though He was the Son of God. He spent much time daily in prayer and communicating with His Father. If even Jesus needed the Father and the Holy Spirit in His life every day, it shows us that we need to be following Him and depending on Him for everything. We cannot lead successfully within our own power, knowledge, abilities, and strength. We just cannot do it - it is impossible to do so. One reason God designed leadership this way is that pride must not be a part of Christian leadership. If we were able to lead without the Holy Spirit working within us then we would have reason to be proud of ourselves. We have to acknowledge that everything we do is through the power of the Holy Spirit operating within our lives.

Even in the Garden of Gethsemane on the night Jesus was arrested, it was apparent that He was unable to get through that horrible night without prayer and the ministry of angels. Luke 22:39-41, *And he came out and went, as was his custom, to the Mount of Olives, and the disciples followed him. And when he came to the place, he said to them, "Pray that you may not enter into temptation." And he withdrew from them about a stone's throw and knelt down and prayed.* Did you notice that one little phrase there? It was His custom to go to the Garden of Gethsemane and pray. While He spent much time in the wilderness, He also often went to the garden alone to pray.

Angels

In Matthew 4, we read the account of Jesus spending forty days and nights of fasting and temptations in the Wilderness. After Satan left Him there, verse 11 says, *Then the devil left him, and behold, angels came and were ministering to him.* The Bible does not give much detail on what this ministering consisted of, but obviously, Jesus needed their ministry to Him. After forty days of fasting and temptations, He had to be extremely hungry and weak.

Next, we move on to the events that took place in the Garden of Gethsemane in Luke 22. Jesus knew what was going to take place later that night. He was agonizing about the pain and suffering that He was going to incur. He spent much time in prayer to His Father about this. He asked the Father if things could somehow be done differently. Jesus then told His Father that He would do the Father's will, not His own will. Luke 22:43-44 then records, *And there appeared to him an angel from heaven, strengthening him. And being in agony he prayed more earnestly; and his sweat became like great drops of blood falling down to the ground.* Even with an angel ministering to Him and strengthening Him, He still was in agony and prayed harder. He needed this ministry and strengthening from the angel. The Bible does not tell us exactly what this ministry from the angel consists of.

There were angels present at several other events during the life of Christ. It started with His birth, as told in Luke 2, where the birth of the Messiah was announced to the shepherds out in the field. A mighty band of angels was praising God in His proclamation of the birth of Christ to the shepherds. The story of His resurrection in Matthew 28 also involved an angel. Matthew 28:2-4, *And behold, there was a great earthquake, for an angel of the Lord descended from heaven and came and rolled back the stone and sat on it. His appearance was like lightning, and his clothing white as snow. And for fear of him the guards trembled and became like dead men.* There was a great earthquake and an angel shows up to roll the stone away. It is unknown why God chose an angel to roll the stone away when the earthquake that occurred could have just as easily rolled it away.

Acts 1:9-11 tells the story of the ascension of Jesus. *And when he had said these things, as they were looking on, he was lifted up, and a cloud took him out of their sight. And while they were gazing into heaven as he went, behold, two men stood by them in white robes, and said, "Men of Galilee, why do you stand looking into heaven? This Jesus, who was taken up from you into heaven, will come in the same way as you saw him go into heaven."*

Even the Second Coming of Christ will involve angels. Matthew 24:30-31, *Then will appear in heaven the sign of the Son of Man, and then all the tribes of the earth will mourn, and they will see the Son of Man coming on the clouds of heaven with power and great glory. And he will send out his angels with a loud trumpet call, and they will gather his elect from the four winds, from one end of heaven to the other.*

This involvement of angels begins before the birth of Jesus. The angels were involved with The Son of God being born, all throughout His life and during His death and resurrection. Angels appeared to both Mary and Joseph to announce the upcoming birth of Jesus. An angel later appeared to Joseph to warn him to flee to Egypt when King Herod was seeking to kill Jesus as a child. And then an angel appeared to Joseph in Egypt when it was time for the family to return to Israel.

We usually think of angels as being the messengers of God, which they often are. We know that Jesus, as the Son of God, is higher than the angels. While He was on earth though, He needed and relied upon the angels to minister to Him and strengthen Him. Even Jesus Christ needed the power of the Holy Spirit and heavily depended on the assistance from the angels.

Will

Here is another aspect of leadership and followership that needs to be discussed. This aspect is the matter of one's will, doing what you want to do versus doing the will of God the Father. We all have wants, desires, and will. One of the greatest battles between parents and their children is over will. By the same token, we all battle the fight between doing our own will and doing the will of the Father. We all want to do what we want to do. We all have our own plans, desires, and motives. One of leadership's greatest challenges is how to motivate followers to do the work that needs to be done when the follower does not want to do it. A good follower will do the will of the leader so that the task is done or the goal is met, no matter how they personally feel about doing it. Did you realize that Jesus had His own will just like we do? Well, He did. Although He desired to do the will of the Father, He still had to consider His own will in contrast to that of the Father. Even though He was God, He was still human and had His own desires and will.

Matthew 26:39 says, *And going a little farther he fell on his face and prayed, saying, "My Father, if it be possible, let this cup pass from me; nevertheless, not as I will, but as you will."* He knew what the near future held for Him. He also knew what the will of His Father was. He knew the suffering and death that He was about to face and everything else that He would have to go through. He knew the pain, the abuse, and the painful death that He was facing. He also knew the reason why He had to go through all of this suffering. In the end, though, He was a follower of God and bowed His will to the will of the Father.

Now we come to the story about the Samaritan woman at the well. Jesus had sent His disciples into the city to obtain food. Jesus met the woman at the well while His disciples were away. The woman left the well right after the disciples returned with the food from the city. The disciples were amazed that Jesus would be talking with the Samaritan woman. No religious Jew would be caught talking to a Samaritan woman. John 4:31-34, *Meanwhile the disciples were urging him, saying, "Rabbi, eat." But he said to them, "I have food to eat that you do not know about." So the disciples said to one another, "Has anyone brought him something to eat?" Jesus said to them, "My food is to do the will of him who sent me and to accomplish his work."* The disciples knew that Jesus was hungry for He had sent them into the city to buy bread. When they bring the food back to Jesus and ask Him to eat, He is more interested in doing the will of the Father than He is in eating food even though He is hungry. He is fed through doing the will of the Father.

As the Apostle Paul reminds us in Philippians 2:5-8, *Have this mind among yourselves, which is yours in Christ Jesus, who, though he was in the form of God, did not count equality with God a thing to be grasped, but emptied himself, by taking the form of a servant, being born in the likeness of men. And being found in human form, he humbled himself by becoming obedient to the point of death, even death on a cross.* There are two key phrases here. The first is that Jesus, even though He is the Son of God, became a servant. The second key phrase here is that He was obedient. His own will told Him to do something else, but instead He obeyed the Father's will, even though it led Him down the path toward His suffering and death.

The gospel of John emphasizes that Jesus followed His Father and did the will of the Father. We are going to include a number of these verses here as Jesus says these things about will in answering different situations. He brings out different aspects about following the Father and doing the will of the Father over what Jesus Himself desires. Through these discussions about will, we can see both the divinity of His being as well as His humanity. Although we get a glimpse of His humanity here, His divine nature wins out in doing the will of the Father. This is also an example of how we are to act when our will and desires are so strong but we need to be doing the will of the Father. Jesus did the will of the Father, in Matthew 7:21, *"Not everyone who says to me, 'Lord, Lord,' will enter the kingdom of heaven, but the one who does the will of my Father who is in heaven."* In the same manner, we must follow in the footsteps of Jesus in doing the will of the Father.

John 5:19, *So Jesus said to them, "Truly, truly, I say to you, the Son can do nothing of his own accord, but only what he sees the Father doing. For whatever the Father does, that the Son does likewise."* Jesus is the only Son of God. John 5:18 states that the Jews were wanting to kill Jesus because when He claimed to be the Son of God, He was also proclaiming Himself to be equal to God the Father. Jesus states in John 5:30, *"I can do nothing on my own. As I hear, I judge, and my judgment is just, because I seek not my own will but the will of him who sent me."* In John 5:36-37, Jesus says, *But the testimony that I have is greater than that of John. For the works that the Father has given me to accomplish, the very works that I am doing, bear witness about me that the Father has sent me. And the Father who sent me has himself borne witness about me. His voice you have never heard, his form you have never seen.*

These verses above bring up another important point. Jesus states that He can do nothing at all on His own. Everything He does is for the

Father and because it is the will of the Father. If Jesus made it clear that He was not able to do anything without the Father, how can we today claim that any of our accomplishments were done through our own power, abilities, and wisdom?

John 6:38-40, *For I have come down from heaven, not to do my own will but the will of him who sent me. And this is the will of him who sent me, that I should lose nothing of all that he has given me, but raise it up on the last day. For this is the will of my Father, that everyone who looks on the Son and believes in him should have eternal life, and I will raise him up on the last day."* Our eternal life is possible because Jesus was willing to do the will of the Father. If Jesus had not followed through on doing the will of the Father, our salvation and eternal life would not be possible.

John 8:28-29, *So Jesus said to them, "When you have lifted up the Son of Man, then you will know that I am he, and that I do nothing on my own authority, but speak just as the Father taught me. And he who sent me is with me. He has not left me alone, for I always do the things that are pleasing to him."* There are at least four points here about doing the will of the Father. The first point is that Jesus does everything that He does through the authority of the Father. Not only is He doing the Father's will but He is doing everything under the authority of the Father. The second point is that everything that Jesus says and teaches was taught to Him by the Father. The third point is that the Father is with Jesus. Although they are separated by Jesus coming in human form and living on earth, the Father is still with Him. The Father has not left Jesus alone. The fourth point is that because Jesus is doing the will of the Father everything that He does is pleasing to the Father. In verse 42, Jesus continues, Jesus said to them, *"If God were your Father, you would love me, for I came from God and I am here. I came not of my own accord, but he sent me."*

In John 12:49-50, Jesus again mentions His authority from the Father. *For I have not spoken on my own authority, but the Father who sent me has himself given me a commandment—what to say and what to speak. And I know that his commandment is eternal life. What I say, therefore, I say as the Father has told me."* Again Jesus has proclaimed that everything He says and does is through the authority of the Father. Everything He has spoken was given to Him by the Father. Once again in John 14:10-11, Jesus states His authority. *Do you not believe that I am in the Father and the Father is in me? The words that I say to you I do not speak on my own authority, but the Father who dwells in me does his works. Believe me that I am in the Father and the Father is in me, or else believe on account of the works themselves.* The Father dwells within the Son and the Son dwells within the Father. Jesus does not speak in His own authority but in the authority given to Him by the Father.

John 10:18-19, *For this reason the Father loves me, because I lay down my life that I may take it up again. No one takes it from me, but I lay it down of my own accord. I have authority to lay it down, and I have authority to take it up again. This charge I have received from my Father."* There was no power on earth that could have prevented Jesus from doing the will of the Father. Jesus had the power and the authority to prevent His crucifixion. As He said in Matthew 26:53-43, *"Do you think that I cannot appeal to my Father, and he will at once send me more than twelve legions of angels? But how then should the Scriptures be fulfilled, that it must be so?"*

In John 15, Jesus spoke to His disciples about bearing fruit, keeping His commandments, and loving others. In John 15:9-10 He states, *As the Father has loved me, so have I loved you. Abide in my love. If you keep my commandments, you will abide in my love, just as I have kept my Father's commandments and abide in his love."* These two simple verses have a lot of meaning in them. Once again Jesus makes it clear that He kept His Father's commandments. He told the disciples that He loves them as the Father loves Him. Then He goes on to tell the disciples that they are to abide in the love of Christ and they are to obey His commandments. If you keep His commandments to love God and to love your neighbor as yourself you will abide in His love.

The commandments to love God and love your neighbor as yourself are intertwined with abiding in the love of Christ. Without abiding in His love it is impossible to love your neighbor as yourself. It is even more impossible to love your enemy, like Jesus taught us to do, unless you are following Christ and abiding in His love. The other side of the coin might be that if you do not love your neighbor as yourself and do not love your enemy, you are not truly abiding in His love and you are not following Him.

Follow Me

What did Jesus tell people who believed in Him, besides telling them to be baptized in water and to obey His commandments, especially the commandments to love God and to love your neighbor as yourself? You probably have guessed where we are going with this, Jesus told His disciples to follow Him. Over and over He told people, "Follow me!" If you believe in Him, follow Him. If you want eternal life, follow Him. Believers are to be followers of Christ.

Jesus was not only a leader, but also a follower (a servant). He was a follower of God, His Father. So when it comes down to the bottom line, we are to follow Jesus Christ just as He follows the Father. He is our example of the way we are to do this. Jesus had His own will and battled having to do what the Father planned for Him. He was in such agony in the Garden of Gethsemane that His sweat was like blood. When it comes to the time to make a decision to do something that we do not want to do, we must be like Jesus was in Luke 22:42-43, *And he withdrew from them about a stone's throw, and knelt down and prayed, saying, "Father, if you are willing, remove this cup from me. Nevertheless, not my will, but yours, be done."*

The Holy Spirit in Following

As we saw above, Jesus lived in the Spirit and His words and works were authorized by the Father and done through the Holy Spirit. We have also seen that the resurrection of Christ was through the power of the Holy Spirit. Is it any wonder that Paul wrote often that we are to live and walk in the Spirit? The Christian leader must be full of the Holy Spirit and walk daily in the Spirit.

Romans 8:5-10, *For those who live according to the flesh set their minds on the things of the flesh, but those who live according to the Spirit set their minds on the things of the Spirit. For to set the mind on the flesh is death, but to set the mind on the Spirit is life and peace. For the mind that is set on the flesh is hostile to God, for it does not submit to God's law; indeed, it cannot. Those who are in the flesh cannot please God. You, however, are not in the flesh but in the Spirit, if the Spirit of God dwells in you. Anyone who does not have the Spirit of Christ does not belong to him. But if Christ is in you, although the body is dead because of sin, the Spirit is life because of righteousness.*

The indwelling and the power of the Holy Spirit is a necessary ingredient for following Christ. Just as Jesus needed the presence and the power of the Holy Spirit in His life, we also need the Holy Spirit dwelling and operating within our lives. We are incapable of following Christ without the Holy Spirit abiding within us.

The Fruit of the Spirit

Chapter 3 is devoted to the subject of the Fruit of the Spirit. It is a worthy subject all by itself in discussing Christian leadership. It is so intertwined with the subject of following Christ and living in the Spirit that it is mentioned again here. The Fruit of the Spirit should be the primary attribute of every believer and follower of Christ. If the Fruit of the Spirit is not evident in a believer's life, one may wonder if they are truly a believer and if they are truly following Christ.

Galatians 5:16-26, *But I say, walk by the Spirit, and you will not gratify the desires of the flesh. For the desires of the flesh are against the Spirit, and the desires of the Spirit are against the flesh, for these are opposed to each other, to keep you from doing the things you want to do. But if you are led by the Spirit, you are not under the law. Now the works of the flesh are evident: sexual immorality, impurity, sensuality, idolatry, sorcery, enmity, strife, jealousy, fits of anger, rivalries, dissensions, divisions, envy, drunkenness, orgies, and things like these. I warn you, as I warned you before, that those who do such things will not inherit the kingdom of God. But the fruit of the Spirit is love, joy, peace, patience, kindness, goodness, faithfulness, gentleness, self-control; against such things there is no law. And those who belong to Christ Jesus have crucified the flesh with its passions and desires. If we live by the Spirit, let us also keep in step with the Spirit. Let us not become conceited, provoking one another, envying one another.*

The first subject here is that the Christian leader must avoid the desires of the flesh. These desires or fruit of the flesh that Paul mentions here are normal for the nonbeliever but they are counterproductive in the life of the believer. It is even more important for Christian leaders as they set an example for those they are leading. Needless to say that these actions of the flesh are in direct conflict with leading in the way that Christ did. Paul does go so far as to state that those who do these things will not inherit the Kingdom of God. The fruit of the flesh comes from yielding to our fleshly desires in an attempt to satisfy our inner desires and egos.

The opposite of the fruit (or works) of the flesh is the Fruit of the Spirit. It is easy to see that the Fruit of the Spirit is closely tied to loving God and loving our neighbor as ourselves. We can see that if we have the Fruit of the Spirit active in our lives, we can then lead the same way that Jesus did. And leading like Christ did should be the main goal of a Christian leader. If we lead in a contrary manner, then there is nothing Christian at all about our leadership.

So, how do we obtain the Fruit of the Spirit in our lives in place of the fruit of the flesh? Paul answers this question here with three steps.

Led by the Spirit

The first step that Paul mentions is that the believer must be led by the Spirit. Remember that we discussed that even Jesus was led and ministered to by the Holy Spirit. We must allow the Holy Spirit access to our inner selves and allow Him to lead us. Jesus promised that the Holy Spirit would be our comforter and our helper. Jesus did not leave us alone in the world when He returned to the Father. He sent the Holy Spirit to dwell within us and to lead and guide us.

Here are three scriptures where Jesus promised the disciples that He would send the Holy Spirit to lead and help them. He knew that He was returning to the Father and that His followers would need the Holy Spirit to teach them, lead them, comfort them, and empower them. John 14:15-17, *"If you love me, you will keep my commandments. And I will ask the Father, and he will give you another Helper, to be with you forever, even the Spirit of truth, whom the world cannot receive, because it neither sees him nor knows him. You know him, for he dwells with you and will be in you."* John 14:26 says, *But the Helper, the Holy Spirit, whom the Father will send in my name, he will teach you all things and bring to your remembrance all that I have said to you.* John 16:13, *When the Spirit of truth comes, he will guide you into all the truth, for he will not speak on his authority, but whatever he hears he will speak, and he will declare to you the things that are to come.*

Die Daily

The second step that Paul mentions is that the believer must crucify the flesh along with its passions and desires. Crucifying the flesh is obviously not related to physical death. To die daily involves crucifying one's selfish desires and ego. Paul proclaims that he dies daily in 1 Corinthians 15:13, *I protest, brothers, by my pride in you, which I have in Christ Jesus our Lord, I die every day!* While Jesus never explicitly told us to die daily, Paul mentions several variations on that theme in his writings.

Romans 8:13, *For if you live according to the flesh you will die, but if by the Spirit you put to death the deeds of the body, you will live.* Once again, Paul is writing about walking and living in the Spirit. He seems to be directly linking this to putting to death the deeds and desires of the flesh. We must live according to the Spirit and not according to the flesh. And the way we do this is to put to death our fleshly deeds. He even mentions that putting to death the deeds of the flesh is accomplished through the Holy Spirit. A few verses before this he talks about the Mosaic law and how mankind was incapable of living up to that law. We now have the Holy Spirit to lead us. We must live and walk according to the Holy Spirit. To do that, we must put our fleshly desires and actions to death. Romans 8:3-6, *For God has done what the law, weakened by the flesh, could not do. By sending his own Son in the likeness of sinful flesh and for sin, he condemned sin in the flesh, in order that the righteous requirement of the law might be fulfilled in us, who walk not according to the flesh but according to the Spirit. For those who live according to the flesh set their minds on the things of the flesh, but those who live according to the Spirit set their minds on the things of the Spirit. For to set the mind on the flesh is death, but to set the mind on the Spirit is life and peace.* To have your mind set on the flesh brings death, but to live in the Spirit brings life and peace.

Paul also uses similar wording in his epistle to Colossians. Colossians 3:1-5, *If then you have been raised with Christ, seek the things that are above, where Christ is, seated at the right hand of God. Set your minds on things that are above, not on things that are on earth. For you have died, and your life is hidden with Christ in God. When Christ who is your life appears, then you also will appear with him in glory. Put to death therefore what is earthly in you.* He then goes on to list several items, like idolatry, that lead to death. We are to set our minds on the things above, not on the things of earth. Although we live here on earth in our fleshly bodies, our minds, and thoughts must be on spiritual things. Paul says that we are to put to death anything earthy within us.

How do we die to self? Paul hints at this in Galatians 2:20, *I have been crucified with Christ. It is no longer I who live, but Christ who lives in me. And the life I now live in the flesh I live by faith in the Son of God, who loved me and gave himself for me."* We must crucify ourselves with Christ. In other places, Paul talks about us sharing in the death of Christ.

Jesus says that His followers must die daily. He just uses different words than Paul does, but the same meaning comes through His words. Luke 9:23-25, *And he said to all, "If anyone would come after me, let him deny himself and take up his cross daily and follow me. For whoever would save his life will lose it, but whoever loses his life for my sake will save it. For what does it profit a man if he gains the whole world and loses or forfeits himself?* Here we have another paradox. If you wish to save your life, will lose it. If you lose your life for His sake, you will save it in the end. Jesus states that we must deny ourselves. Putting to death anything fleshy within us in not an easy or painless task.

In Galatians 5, Paul talks about the Fruit of the Spirit. This has to be one of the most important and obvious characteristics of the life of a believer who is walking in the Spirit. Galatians 5:16-17 states, *But I say, walk by the Spirit, and you will not gratify the desires of the flesh. For the desires of the flesh are against the Spirit, and the desires of the Spirit are against the flesh, for these are opposed to each other, to keep you from doing the things you want to do.* The desires of the flesh are in constant battle against the desires of the Spirit. Everyone of us wage this battle within ourselves between the fruit of the flesh and the Fruit of the Spirit. Paul has warned us several times that those desires of the flesh lead us to death and destruction. Following the desires of the Spirit, in contrast, leads to life and peace. And how do we follow the desires of the Spirit over the desires of our flesh? Paul says it this way in Galatians 5:24, And those who belong to Christ Jesus have crucified the flesh with its passions and desires. Paul once again reminds us that we are to crucify the flesh along with its passions and desires.

Living in the Spirit

What does living in the Spirit and staying in step with Him look like? Paul gives us a hint at that in both Galatians 5 with his message about the Fruit of the Spirit and also in Colossians 3:12-17, *Put on then, as God's chosen ones, holy and beloved, compassionate hearts, kindness, humility, meekness, and patience, bearing with one another and, if one has a complaint against another, forgiving each other; as the Lord has forgiven you, so you also must forgive. And above all these put on love, which binds everything together in perfect harmony. And let the peace of Christ rule in your hearts, to which indeed you were called in one body. And be thankful. Let the word of Christ dwell in you richly, teaching and admonishing one another in all wisdom, singing psalms and hymns and spiritual songs, with thankfulness in your hearts to God. And whatever you do, in word or deed, do everything in the name of the Lord Jesus, giving thanks to God the Father through him.* Walking and living in the Spirit, along with dying to self daily, results in the Fruit of the Spirit being evident in the believer's life. This is the method of following Christ.

Conclusion

We believers are to follow Jesus. Even as Jesus followed God the Father, and was subservient to Him, we are to follow Christ. Christ did the will of the Father. We are, in turn, to follow Christ and do His will. We see that the ways we do that involve living and walking in the Spirit and crucifying our fleshly desires and passions. If we do this, our lives will have the Fruit of the Spirit evident in our lives. In turn, we will have life and peace in place of the death that we all truly deserve. If you want to know what a true follower of Christ looks like, look for the person who has the Fruit of the Spirit active in their life. This person will be different from others around them. This is because that person is following Christ and walking and living in the Holy Spirit.

Conclusion

AS stated in the Introduction section of this book, the purpose of this book is not to list rules or tasks that will lead you to be a better Christian leader. This book did not give you skills or personality styles for you to develop. It did not list habits or theories for you to follow to become a great leader. There is not a magic formula that can transform you into the perfect leader.

The purpose of this book is to help you understand the difference between Christian leadership and other types of leadership. Its purpose is to help you to change your way of thinking about Christian leadership. This book will hopefully help you to develop a better theology of Christian leadership. That leadership theology will be directly linked to the idea that leadership is more about followership than it is about leadership. The true characteristic of Christian leadership is that the Christian leader is a follower of Christ. Christian leadership is all about followership, in other words, following Jesus Christ. Preston Sprinkle puts a different spin on this, "God doesn't help those who help themselves. God creates righteousness like the stars - out of thin air."

This book does not contain any magical steps for you to follow in order to transform into the perfect leader. It does not contain lists of skills, theories, habits, or characteristics for you to follow and develop in your own life. It remains different from most other leadership books in this way. This book will assist you in developing a solid biblical theology of Christian leadership to use as a foundation for becoming a successful Christian leader. Upon that theological foundation you can then develop your leadership skills and methods. Those leadership skills and methods must be developed upon biblical principles.

If you desire to become a successful Christian leader, you must follow Christ. The successful Christian leader will have the Fruit of the Spirit obvious in his or her life. The Christian leader will lead in love. The love that they have for others will be evident. The Christian leader will be walking and living in the Spirit daily. These things are what make a Christian leader successful, not gaining great attendance or financial success. God looks at the success of leadership quite differently than people do. The Christian leader is a follower!

References

Introduction

Chan, Francis, (2011). *Erasing Hell.*

Hamlin, Allen, Jr., (2016). *Embracing Followership: How to Thrive in a Leader-Centric Culture.*

Chapter 1

Sprinkle, Preston, (2014). *Charis: God's Scandalous Grace For Us.*

Chapter 2

Barton, Ruth Haley, (2008). *Strengthening the Soul of Your Leadership: Seeking God in the Crucible of Ministry.*

Blackaby, Henry and Richard, (2001). *Spiritual Leadership, Moving People on to God's Agenda.*

Blomberg, Craig L., (2006). *From Pentecost to Patmos: An Introduction to Acts Through Revelation.*

Boers, Arthur, (2015). *Servants and Fools.*

Bowling, John C., (2000). *Grace-full Leadership, Understanding the Heart of a Christian Leader.*

Bruce, F.F., (1977). *Paul: Apostle of the Heart Set Free.*

Clinton, Jimmy, (2013). *The Making of a Leader: Recognizing the Lessons and Stages of Leadership.*

Fry, Louis W., (December 2003). Toward a Theory of Spiritual Leadership. *The Leadership Quarterly,* Volume 14, Number 6.

Geiger, Eric and Peck, Kevin, (2016). *Designed to Lead, The Church and Leadership Development.*

Gibson, Ann, (Spring 2012). Walking in the Light. *The Journal of Applied Christian Leadership.* Volume 5, Number 1.

Greenleaf, Robert K., (2002). *Servant Leadership: A Journey into the Nature of Legitimate Power and Greatness. 25th Anniversary Edition.*

Hamlin, Allen, Jr., (2016). *Embracing Followership: How to Thrive in a Leader-Centric Culture.*

Hanna, Martin Frederick, (Summer 2006). What is Christian About Christian Leadership. *The Journal of Applied Christian Leadership,* Volume 1, Number 1.

Hansen, G. Walter, (1994). *Galatians. The IVP New Testament Commentary Series.*

Huizing, Russell L., (2011). Bringing Christ to the Table of Leadership: Moving Towards a Theology of Leadership. *The Journal of Applied Christian Leadership.* Volume 5, Number 2.

Kellerman, Barbara, (2008). *Followership: How Followers are Creating Change and Changing Leaders.*

Krishnakumar, Sukumarakurup, et al, (2005). The Good and the Bad of Spiritual Leadership. *Journal of Management, Spirituality & Religion,* Volume 12, Number 1.

Malphurs, Aubrey, (2003). *Being Leaders: The Nature of Authentic Christian Leadership.*

Schreiner, Thomas R.; Arnold, Clinton E., (2010). *Galatians: Zondervan Exegetical Commentary of the New Testament.*

Smith, Stephen W., (2015). *Inside Job: Doing the Work Within the Work.*

Stott, John R., (1984). *The Message of Galatians: Bible Speaks Today Series.*

Strobel, Kyle C., (2013). *Formed for the Glory of God.*

Weatherhead, Leslie, (1990). *The Transforming Friendship.*

Wright, Christopher J.H., (2017). *Cultivating the Fruit of the Spirit.*

Chapter 4

Spong, John Shelby, (1991). *Rescuing the Bible From Fundamentalism.*

Sprinkle, Preston, (2014). *Charis: God's Scandalous Grace For Us.*

Weatherhead, Leslie D., (1990). *The Transforming Friendship: A Book About Jesus and Ourselves.*

Chapter 5

Murray, Andrew, (1895). *Humility.*

Chapter 6

Butler, Anthea, (2021). *White Evangelical Racism: The Politics of Morality in America.*

Graham, Billy; Answers; (July 27, 2005). *https://billygraham.org/answer/do-you-think-our-nation-will-ever-completely-overcome-its-racism/*

Henderson, Daniel, (2022). *Confessions of a Recovering Evangelical: Overcoming Fear and Certainty to Find Faith Through Doubt and Questioning.*

Kilner, John F., (2015). *Dignity and Destiny: Humanity in the Image of God.*

Sprinkle, Preston, (2014). *Charis: God's Scandalous Grace For Us.*

Sprinkle, Preston. (2015). *People to Be Loved, Why Homosexuality is Not Just an Issue.*

Chapter 8

Bryant, John Hope, (2009). *Love Leadership: the New Way to Lead in Fear-Based World.*

Edwards, Jonathan, (2012). *Charity and Its Fruits: Living in the Light of God's Love.*

Chapter 9

Greenleaf, Robert K., (2002). *Servant Leadership: A Journey into the Nature of Legitimate Power and Greatness. 25th Anniversary Edition.*

Chapter 12

Blackaby, Henry and Richard, (2001). *Spiritual Leadership, Moving People on to God's Agenda.*

Clinton, Jimmy, (2013). *The Making of a Leader: Recognizing the Lessons and Stages of Leadership.*

Goodwin, W. (2012). *Taxonomy for Followership Rooted in the Study of Leadership. (Doctoral Dissertation).*

Geiger, Eric and Peck, Kevin, (2016). *Designed to Lead, The Church and Leadership Development.*

Howell, Don, (2003). *Servants of the Servant: A Biblical Theology of Leadership.*

Hurwitz, Marc and Hurwitz, Samantha, (2015). *Leadership Is Half the Story.*

Malphurs, Aubrey, (2003). *Being Leaders: The Nature of Authentic Christian Leadership.*

Mills, Bill, (2010). *Keys to Effective Leadership: Developing Your Followership Skills.*

Petit, Paul, (2008). *Foundations of Spiritual Formation: A Community Approach to Becoming Like Christ.*

Platt, David, (2013). *Follow Me: A Call to Die, A Call to Live.*

Smith, Stephen W., (2015). *Inside Job: Doing the Work Within the Work.*

Conclusion

Sprinkle, Preston, (2014). *Charis: God's Scandalous Grace For Us*

Bible Quotations

All quoted Bible verses are from the English Standard Version (ESV) unless otherwise noted.

Thank you for reading our book.
We hope that it has been a help to you in forming
your own theology of Christian Leadership.

The Author

Pocataligo

Pocataligo Books

Danielsville Georgia

www.ingramcontent.com/pod-product-compliance
Lightning Source LLC
Chambersburg PA
CBHW072343090426
42741CB00012B/2901

* 9 7 9 8 9 9 0 5 7 4 9 0 8 *